D1265715

WORLD RUBBER AND ITS REGULATION

A Publication of the

FOOD RESEARCH INSTITUTE

Established at Stanford University, California, in 1921, jointly by Carnegie Corporation of New York and the Trustees of Leland Stanford Junior University, for research in the production, distribution, and consumption of food

STAFF

Commodity Policy Studies

No. 6. *World Rubber and Its Regulation*, by K. E. KNORR, October 1945

No. 5. *Tin under Control*, by K. E. KNORR, January 1945

No. 4. *Tea under International Regulation*, by V. D. WICKIZER, April 1944

No. 3. *Petroleum and American Foreign Policy*, by HERBERT FEIS, March 1944

No. 2. *The World Coffee Economy, with Special Reference to Control Schemes*, by V. D. WICKIZER, August 1943

No. 1. *International Agreements on Conservation of Marine Resources*, by JOZO TOMASEVICH, March 1943

A complete list of publications of the Food Research Institute will be furnished on request.

WORLD RUBBER

AND ITS

REGULATION

By

K. E. KNORR

STANFORD UNIVERSITY PRESS

Stanford University, California

STANFORD UNIVERSITY PRESS
STANFORD UNIVERSITY, CALIFORNIA
OXFORD UNIVERSITY PRESS
LONDON: HUMPHREY MILFORD

———

THE BAKER AND TAYLOR COMPANY
55 FIFTH AVENUE, NEW YORK

HENRY M. SNYDER & CO.
440 FOURTH AVENUE, NEW YORK

PREFACE

The world rubber economy is in a period of upheaval and transition. The Japanese occupation of the rubber-producing plantation countries of southeastern Asia and the advent of large synthetic-rubber industries in the United States are greatly affecting world rubber production, consumption, and trade. It is useful to analyze the presumable effects of these developments and the adjustments necessitated by them. The main focus of this book, however, is on controls—especially on international control arrangements.

Advocacy of international commodity agreements is rampant in some quarters where the displacement of free-market by controlled conditions is welcomed as part and parcel of a brave new world of ubiquitous planning. To others, the very mention of the words "planning" and "control" is anathema.

The present author is committed in neither direction. Raw-commodity control schemes are not in fact primarily born of certain philosophical predispositions or predilections. Their origin lies in the desire of special-interest groups, notably producers and investors, to increase their income or prevent its decline in a world of changing patterns of production, consumption, and trade. Once these groups manage to secure government support, the stage is set for attempts at regulation—with controls restricted in area and purpose often breeding others of wider scope and more ambitious objectives.

Whether or not any particular control arrangement is considered desirable depends upon the standards of judgment applied. To lay down such standards is perhaps not the business of the economist as economist. But it is his proper province to analyze the major consequences of proposed and applied control measures, and in evaluating their net effect he can take certain fundamental standards as given.

Following are the basic standards recognized in this study. In economic as well as political affairs, the general public interest must dominate over the conflicting interests of any special group. In the economic sphere, the chief interests of the general

v

public are general elevation of consumption levels and prevention of their temporary decline as a result of violent business
fluctuations. The raising of consumption levels requires optimum utilization of the low-cost, more efficient units, constant
encouragement of improvements in efficiency, and the extension
to consumers of the fruits of augmented efficiency. The prevention of transitory declines in consumption levels requires the
moderation of booms and depressions. To maximize the public
good, conflict between measures taken in pursuit of these two
basic objectives must be kept at a minimum.

These principles are basic to the appraisal of international
commodity agreements. Producers of raw materials have had
several genuine grievances in the past. One of these grievances,
for example, resulted from the recurrence of violent price gyrations. As far as these are generated by extreme cyclical fluctuations in consumption, the interests of producers and the general
public are one, and general remedies must be applied which
attack the evil at its source. As far as severe price fluctuations
are the consequence of unresponsiveness of supply to price
changes, direct and specific remedies may be desirable and
feasible. Yet it is essential that the regulatory devices employed
do not materially violate the requirements of an expansive and
adaptable world economy. In the past, indeed, violent price
fluctuations were frequently the result of previous interference
with the free market.

The emergence and persistence of surplus output capacity
resulting in excess supplies and depressed prices have fostered
another grievance of many industries producing raw materials.
Conditions of free competition often promised selective disinvestment only after a long period of attrition spelling acute
distress for all producers and for those producing countries
whose prosperity depended heavily on the industry in question.
The demand for redress by control appears economically justified provided devices can be found that are not only acceptable
to producers and producing countries, but are also compatible
with the general public stake in an expansive world economy.

During the interwar period, commodity control devices have
ordinarily been of the restrictive type and restriction of production, exports, or imports ordinarily meant the straitjacketing of

the forces operating toward increasing efficiency of production. They offered no prospect of augmenting world real income in the long run. In this respect, indeed, they were regressive rather than progressive. Exercising monopoly power, they pursued a beggar-my-neighbor protectionism. Especially when confronted with redundant and inefficient output capacity, they aimed at protecting the value of these investments rather than at accelerating the requisite adjustments.

Yet the record of the past should not be interpreted as prejudging the case for any type of planning and control. Where genuine grievances can be relieved by expedients that do not restrict the forces of economic progress, there is a legitimate case for the exercise of purposive direction over production and/or trade. The real problem lies not so much in the inadequacy of the planner's analytical tools and institutional ingenuity as it does in the complex of pressure-group politics. Vested interests constantly endeavor to gain government support or tolerance for schemes beneficial to themselves but harmful to the general good. Because they are well organized, their endeavors too often come to fruition, especially when the social damage of uneconomic practices seems to be heavily concentrated in foreign countries. How to overcome these impediments to intelligent planning is a political problem, to the solution of which the economist cannot make more than an incidental contribution. But so long as the problem defies satisfactory solution, the case for control remains weak even where the absence of control is accompanied by certain evils.

World Rubber and Its Regulation is a product of a research program on international commodity agreements conducted by the Food Research Institute. This focus on policy required the Institute to look beyond food products for pertinent examples of commodity control. The present study is the sixth in a series that has previously dealt with marine resources, coffee, petroleum, tea, and tin, while the projected international wheat agreement was discussed in the Institute's *Wheat Studies*.

The author is indebted to a great many experts for generously extending criticism and advice. Of those in industry, trade, and government I wish to name two whose help was outstanding: R. G. Seaman, Technical Editor of the *India Rubber World* in New York, and E. G. Holt, Director of the Commercial Research Division of the Rubber Development Corporation and formerly Chief of the Rubber Division of the Department of Commerce. Among my colleagues at the Food Research Institute, I owe most to J. S. Davis, from whose studies of the general problems of international commodity agreements I have greatly profited. He, as well as M. K. Bennett, Karl Brandt, V. D. Wickizer, and V. P. Timoshenko, read the manuscript, and all made valuable comments.

Among the other staff members I wish to thank P. Stanley King for the many ways in which he contributed to the final shape of the manuscript—he drew the map and the charts and did much to make the book more readable than it would have been without his criticisms; Rosamond H. Peirce for her invaluable help with statistical problems; and Dorothy Adams, who prepared the manuscript for press.

Grateful acknowledgment is made to the Rockefeller Foundation for a grant of funds that made possible the preparation and publication of this work. It may be superfluous to add that the Foundation is in no way responsible for the treatment or even for the choice of the subject. Final responsibility for the book rests with the author himself.

K. E. Knorr

August 1945

CONTENTS

ix

WORLD RUBBER AND ITS REGULATION

CHAPTER I

INTRODUCTION

Rubber is one of the New World's outstanding material contributions to mankind. Observing its use by American Indians, the Spanish explorers regarded it as one of the exotic curiosities of the newly discovered continent. Two hundred years elapsed before European scientists began to study this remarkable substance. Useful applications were gradually discovered in the form of erasers and waterproof clothing and boots. Yet, even during the first two-thirds of the last century, rubber was still a material of decidedly minor significance. Only the swift advance of machine technology in the present century provided setting and stimulus for rubber's spectacular commodity career.

THE IMPORTANCE OF RUBBER

In the 1920's and 1930's the production and marketing of natural rubber furnished a source of livelihood to several million natives in southeastern Asia and to tens of thousands of European and Asiatic investors, company directors, business and production managers, brokers, agents, merchants, and workers. Rubber exports were of outstanding importance to the entire economy of some of the major producing countries. In 1937, for example, rubber represented 54, 31, and 23 per cent of the total value of exports from British Malaya, the Netherlands Indies, and Ceylon respectively. To countries from whose currency area rubber was exported, these shipments constituted invaluable sources of foreign purchasing power.

In all industrially advanced countries rubber has become one of the most essential materials in peace and war. It is hardly an exaggeration to say that it ranks with iron and steel, coal, and petroleum. Amazingly versatile, it enters into factory and household, farm and transportation facilities, peacetime goods and implements of war. There is scarcely a modern electrical and automotive device in which rubber does not serve vital functions. To it the entire automobile industry owes its extraordinary development. There are about 300 rubber parts in an ordinary passenger automobile and more than 400 in a two-engine airplane. A single American rubber-goods manufacturer, before World War II, turned out about 32,000 different rubber products, counting all sizes, colors, and styles.[1]

Because of the extreme industrialization, far-flung transportation systems, and large per capita income of the United States, rubber is more important here than in any other country. In value, crude rubber was the leading commodity imported into this country before the war. In 1939 about 500,000 tons—half of all the rubber shipped from producing countries—entered United States ports.[2] These imports were valued at over 178 million dollars and provided the chief raw material for a rubber-manufacturing industry which in the same year produced goods valued at 902 million dollars. Obvious as the importance of rubber was to the observant mind, it took the experience of an extreme rubber shortage during World War II to bring it home to the general public.

RUBBER PROBLEMS

In August 1944 representatives of the governments of the United States, the United Kingdom, and the Netherlands met in London to discuss common problems arising from the production, manufacture, and use of rubber. One of the decisions of this conference was that the three governments would participate in a series of similar discussions on wartime and postwar rubber problems.[3] The postwar world will, indeed, be confronted with rubber problems of imposing complexity. Some will be inherited from the prewar past, others will reflect changes wrought by the war itself, and still others will make their appearance in the future.

Before World War II, the crude-rubber industry was encumbered with large surplus output facilities which, under condi-

[1] B. F. Goodrich Company, *A Wonder Book of Rubber* (Akron, 1942).

[2] Rubber Manufacturers Association, Inc., *Crude Rubber* (New York, May 10, 1943), p. 3.

[3] *Bulletin* (U.S. State Dept.), Sept. 24, 1944, XI, 328.

tions of free competition, tended to result in excess supplies and severely depressed prices. Moreover, owing to the peculiar nature of the demand for and the supply of rubber, prices exhibited abrupt and violent fluctuations. Both phenomena caused intense suffering to the producing industry. In 1934, the major rubber-producing countries concluded a scheme of tight export regulation for the express purpose of coping with these problems. Control succeeded in raising rubber prices, but did not remove redundant production capacity nor steady prices appreciably. Some consuming countries, especially the United States, asserted that—at times, at least—rubber prices were maintained at an excessively high level.

If these rubber problems of the past—surplus output facilities and extreme price fluctuations—reappear after the war, they will do so in a substantially different setting. Cut off from the major rubber-growing areas of southeastern Asia, the United States built a huge synthetic-rubber industry, while wartime Europe also became largely dependent on the manufacture of artificial rubbers. Moreover, the cultivation of rubber-producing trees and shrubs was considerably expanded in the Americas, in Africa, and in Europe. Though in need of re-equipment, the great bulk of the Eastern plantation industry is likely to survive the war. Even if the rehabilitation of this industry should stop considerably short of its prewar size, the world's rubber-production capacity is sure to be more than double the average prewar absorption.

Will absorption expand to the extent of doubling prewar requirements after the rubber-starved world returns to normal? To some producers and industrial consumers of rubber, this question seems to be the crux of the postwar rubber problem. If consumption so expands, it is intimated that the natural- and synthetic-rubber industries can exist satisfactorily side by side, for no important problem of surplus output would arise, and only that of undue price swings will need attention. On the other hand, insufficient expansion of rubber absorption will raise the vexing problem of surplus-production capacity, and it is argued that cut-throat competition, unless prevented by international agreement, will arise between the two industries, and probably be supported by government intervention in the form of tariff protection or more direct forms of subsidization.

This train of reasoning, however, does not comprehend the full complexity of the postwar rubber problem. It is naïve to assume that the mere balance of production and consumption will automatically produce a lasting competitive equilibrium between the plantation- and synthetic-rubber industries. If their respective properties permit natural and artificial rubbers to compete for the same types of uses, active trade competition between them is inevitable unless wholly or partially prevented by government intervention in the form of subsidization or international control. They would compete not only in temporarily depressed markets but also in the long run, and one industry may expand at the expense of the other. In a market unhampered by control and unfettered by subsidization, the outcome of this commodity rivalry would tend to change with changing prices and comparative characteristics of product, and would call for remarkable adaptability on the part of the industries concerned.

The host of rubber problems will be aggravated and perhaps multiplied if aggregate production facilities greatly exceed average requirements. Should unstable prices be uncontrolled, or should their fluctuations be subdued or prevented by export restriction and/or a buffer-stock scheme? Should world-wide or local readjustments of production capacity be left to the harsh working of free competition, or should they be directed by deliberate planning? If the latter course is chosen, which type of regulation is most practicable? Which is most desirable from the viewpoint of all interests involved—producers, industrial consumers, and ultimate consumers?

The issues of unstable prices and ill-adjusted output facilities affect or are affected by such problems as the accrual of foreign purchasing power of different nations, the flow of international trade, the value of foreign investments, the welfare of economically backward countries, and industrial preparedness for war. What would the British Empire, for example, substitute for her huge rubber exports as a source of dollar exchange? How would she replace the rubber-growing industry in the economy of British Malaya? Should the United States write off its wartime investments in Latin-American rubber-development schemes, or scrap its synthetic-rubber industry and again be vulnerable to the foreign conquest or blockade of Asiatic rubber-producing countries? Is the Soviet Union willing to rely for substantial and regular rubber imports on a source of supply which can be cut off by the strongest naval powers of the world? Identical or similar questions apply to other rubber-exporting or -importing countries, large and small, and are likely to become subjects of public policy here and elsewhere.

PLAN OF THIS STUDY

The chief purpose of this study is to examine the social desirability of various forms of international rubber control. Following a summary survey of rubber production and consumption, and the characteristics of the prewar rubber market, the International Rubber Regulation Agreement of 1934—now defunct—is described and analyzed. To apply the experience of the past to future problems, it is then necessary to review the events of World War II that affected the rubber world: the rubber shortage outside Japanese-controlled lands and the rise of a large-scale synthetic-rubber industry. Next, tentative conclusions are advanced regarding the postwar rubber market and its possible problems. Finally, the intricate question of international regulation is discussed.

RUBBER TERMINOLOGY

There are many kinds and types of rubber, varying in chemical and physical properties. Rubber of identical properties, moreover, is often distinguished by different natural or economic origins. It is useful, therefore, to clarify the rubber nomenclature adopted in this study.

The basic distinction is between crude or natural rubber on the one hand, and synthetic or artificial rubbers on the other. *Crude rubber* is of vegetable origin. It is divided into two types: *wild rubber*, collected from naturally occurring trees, shrubs, and vines, and *plantation rubber*, from cultivated plants. For purposes of economic analysis it is useful to distinguish two types of plantation rubber. *Estate rubber* is produced in relatively large capitalistically organized rubber estates, and *native rubber* in relatively small rubber groves cultivated by native peasants.

Strictly speaking, there is no such thing as *synthetic* or *artificial rubber*. A number of synthetic compounds have rubber-like qualities, but they differ from each other and from natural rubber in many physical properties and in chemical constitution. Thus, while all crude rubber has the same chemical composition and roughly the same physical qualities, there is a large and growing variety of synthetic or artificial rubbers. Some scientists have proposed not to apply the name rubber to these at all, but to call them elastomers. However, this term has hitherto failed to find wide currency and is not employed in this study. While it is useful for some purposes to speak of synthetic rubber or rubbers, it should be kept in mind that the reference is to a class composed of different types and kinds—such as Buna-S or Butyl—exhibiting different properties and derived by different manufacturing processes.

Finally, *reclaimed rubber* must be mentioned. *Reclaim*, as the name suggests, is a material gained from discarded rubber products. Its chemical composition and properties are similar to, but not identical with, those of the original rubber, natural or synthetic.

CHAPTER II

RUBBER SUPPLY BETWEEN TWO WARS

Crude rubber is an elastic, coherent solid obtained from rubber latex, a milky emulsion occurring in the roots, stems, branches, and fruit of a wide variety of trees, shrubs, vines, and other plants. In this watery liquid float tiny globules of the rubber hydrocarbon which by proper treatment can be coagulated and made to solidify in the crude natural rubber of commerce.

HISTORICAL INTRODUCTION

Throughout the nineteenth century all crude rubber produced and consumed was wild rubber collected in the tropical forests of Latin América and Africa. In 1850, annual shipments for the first time exceeded 1,000 tons. Para, the port city of the Amazon delta, was the rubber center. In response to growing demand, tapping was extended westward in the Amazon basin and gradually spread to Ecuador, Colombia, Central America, and Africa.

Rubber consumption expanded during the second half of the nineteenth century. The United States, for instance, consumed a mere 1,500 tons in 1859. Thirty years later absorption had increased tenfold, yet the absolute quantities were still small compared with later requirements. Among the various rubber products, footwear remained the leading item until after the turn of the century. Then, with the popularity of the bicycle and especially the advent of the automobile, rubber consumption rose by leaps and bounds.

In 1900, wild-rubber production had been increased to about 54,000 tons a year, but this source of supply was unable to satisfy the ever-growing volume of demand. Prices shot up from the level of about 67 cents a pound in the 1890's to over $1.00 in 1903, and in 1910 averaged $2.09 per pound. Under this potent stimulus, latex collection expanded. Mexico's guayule shrub made its appearance as a new source of wild rubber and contributed 9,000 tons in 1910. Two years later the total wild-rubber output attained its all-time peak with over 70,000 tons, of which 42,000 came from Brazil.

At this stage the supply picture changed entirely. A new source of crude rubber soon relegated wild rubber to a negligible position. In 1876, Henry A. Wickham, an Englishman, brought 70,000 seeds of *Hevea brasiliensis* from Brazil to England where nearly 3,000 were successfully germinated. Young trees soon found their way to Ceylon, British Malaya, and other parts of the East. In the 1880's intensively cultivated plantations were started in southeastern Asia. As indicated in the accompanying tabulation,[1] this industry quickly passed through its period

Year	Total cultivated area (*Acres*)	Total exports (*Tons*)
1899...........	4,000	4
1905..........	127,000	145
1910..........	1,125,000	8,200

of infancy. In 1914, exports of plantation rubber first exceeded those of wild rubber. With sharply expanding supplies, prices dropped and wild-rubber production shrank, while the growing output of the plantations easily kept pace with increasing requirements. By 1922, 93 per cent of the world's rubber supply of over 400,000 tons originated in the Eastern plantations.

The proportion continued to grow. Between World Wars I and II nearly all crude rubber came from plantations (Chart 1). Indeed, even reclaimed rubber surpassed wild rubber in importance. In the middle and late 1930's synthetic rubbers entered the scene. In 1939, exports of plantation rubber amounted to 976,000 tons as compared with wild-rubber shipments of 28,400 tons, while synthetic-rubber production was estimated at about 75,000 tons, and perhaps as much as 100,000 tons of reclaimed rubber (rubber content) were consumed during the year. At the outbreak of World War II, then, all sources of rubber other than plantations were decidedly secondary.

The following sections of this chapter briefly survey the production and supply characteristics of these different sources of

[1] Rubber Manufacturers Association, Inc., *Crude Rubber*, p. 18.

rubber, excepting the synthetics. Before World War II, artificial rubbers were important only in the Soviet Union and Germany. The advent of these novel materials will be discussed in chapter x.

WILD-RUBBER PRODUCTION

Hevea brasiliensis, a native tree of the Amazon Valley, is the outstanding vegetable source of rubber. Though varying somewhat in composition, its latex yields the largest quantity of rubber in proportion to extraneous matter. The rubber-plantation industry uses this species almost exclusively, and the bulk of wild rubber is collected from the several hundred million Hevea trees of the Amazon basin. Wild rubber, however, is gained also from many other American and African trees and from certain vines in tropical Africa and shrubs in Madagascar and Mexico.

CHART 1.—WORLD EXPORTS AND NEW YORK PRICES OF CRUDE
RUBBER, ANNUALLY, 1919–39*

(Thousand tons; cents per pound)

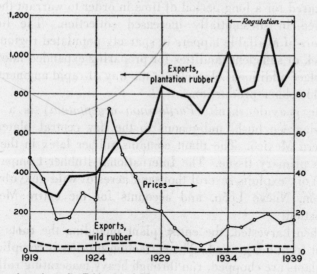

* Data from Appendix Tables I and VI.

Throughout the interwar period, wild-rubber production, secularly on the decline, fluctuated primarily in response to changing rubber prices (Chart 1, above, and Appendix Table I). High prices stimulated increased collection, low prices tended to contract output. The untold millions of Hevea trees in the Amazon basin are scattered over a vast expanse of jungle land. Frequently no more than three or four trees are found on an acre of thick jungle growth. The inaccessibility of the tropical forest never permitted more than a tiny fraction of these trees to be tapped. Tapping expeditions are organized to sweep through jungle areas of varying extent. A high percentage of the itinerant tappers fall victims to malaria and other tropical diseases. Collections are unsystematic, tapping operations crude, and coagulation methods primitive. Despite the low wages paid to native tappers, production costs are high because one man can tap only a few trees in a day's work and transportation costs are necessarily heavy. At times of low rubber prices only the most accessible areas are worked. Since it takes a considerable outlay of capital (in capital-poor countries) to send out collection parties, and because these expeditions are scheduled to be under way for many months and often an entire year, high prices must be assured for a long period of time in order to warrant the risk involved in substantially increased collection. The limited numbers of available tappers in sparsely populated regions and the lack of sufficient facilities for preparing expanded latex outputs place additional obstacles in the way of rapid augmentation of wild-rubber production.

The guayule shrub (*Parthenium argentatum*) is a small grayish-green bush, indigenous to the dry central plateau of northern Mexico. The plant contains rubber latex in the cells of the primary tissue. The International Rubber Company of New York exploits several thousand acres of wild guayule near Torreón, Nuevo León, and accounts for the entire Mexican production.

When harvested, the entire plant including the roots is removed from the ground. The extraction process is complicated. The plants are chopped, run through heavy macerating rolls and grinding mills, and the rubber is finally obtained by successive skimming operations. Production costs are high. Unless the rubber obtained is deresined, an additional cost factor, its impurity restricts its use. In the years preceding World War II, Mexico produced about 3,000 tons of this rubber, nearly all of which was exported to the United States. The International Rubber Company also experimented with the cultivation of domesticated guayule in the Salinas Valley of California, but production was small.

RECLAIM OUTPUT

Reclaimed rubber[2] is gained from discarded rubber articles —such as tires, tubes, and hose—and from waste products accruing in the fabrication of new rubber articles. Much of this scrap contains fabrics, metal, and other alien materials. All of it is vulcanized and intricately compounded, since little natural rubber is consumed in its crude form. In order to serve its ultimate purposes and serve them well, rubber is not only re-shaped but also colored, given various degrees of softness, elasticity, resilience, tensile strength, and tear-, abrasion-, and chemical resistance. All these properties are obtained by the admixture of sulphur and numerous other organic and inorganic chemicals. Besides fabric and metal parts, more than one-third of the weight of a rubber article may consist of substances other than crude rubber.

The reclaiming process, however, is not a reversal of vulcanization. Thus far it has proved technically impossible to devulcanize scrap and recover rubber in its original form. Reclaim is essentially a replasticized and resoftened rubber compound which still contains sulphur and many other ingredients and, in chemical composition and properties, differs from natural rubber. The actual rubber content of reclaim ranges from 30 to 70 per cent and, in the United States, averages from 55 to 60 per cent. Possessing qualities somewhat different from crude rubber, reclaim is only partially competitive with the natural material.

Statistics of production and absorption of reclaimed rubber are not available for the world as a whole. Fortunately there are absorption data for the United States, by far the largest consumer of both crude and regenerated rubber. Here, during

---

[2] On the production of reclaim, see George S. Armstrong and Company, Inc., *The Rubber Industry* (An Engineering Interpretation of the Economic and Financial Aspects of American Industry IV, New York, 1942), pp. 37–40; P. W. Barker, *Rubber: History, Production, and Manufacture* (U.S. Dept. Comm., Bur. Foreign and Domestic Comm., Trade Promotion Series 209, 1940), pp. 37–39; H. L. Fisher, *Rubber and Its Use* (Brooklyn, 1941), pp. 92–93.

1935–39 reclaim absorption averaged over 142,000 tons a year, about 27 per cent as much as crude-rubber absorption— or nearly 15 per cent, if only the rubber content of reclaim is considered. Russian officials have claimed that their country possesses a large capacity for producing reclaimed rubber, but no dependable figures are available to us. The same is true of Germany. Lesser quantities of reclaim are produced and consumed in many other countries. The United Kingdom's consumption averaged 9,000 tons a year from 1935 to 1939. Japan was reported to have absorbed about 8,000 tons in 1938. A few thousand tons were consumed in Canada.

The following tabulation and Chart 2 compare United States reclaim consumption with crude-rubber absorption and prices.

CHART 2.—RATIO OF RECLAIMED TO CRUDE RUBBER CONSUMPTION, AND RUBBER PRICES IN THE UNITED STATES, ANNUALLY, 1920–40*

(Percentages; cents per pound)

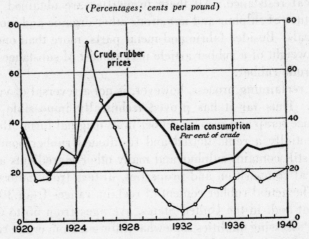

* Based on data in *Survey of Current Business, 1942 Supplement* (U.S. Dept. Comm., Bur. Foreign and Domestic Comm.), p. 160.

Years	Absorption		Percentage of reclaim to crude	New York price of crude rubber (*Cents per lb.*)
	Annual averages			
	Crude rubber	Reclaim		
	(*Thousand tons*)			
1920–24......	261	65	25.8	25.2
1925–29......	406	186	45.7	40.2
1930–34......	382	108	28.5	8.0
1935–39......	528	142	26.9	16.0
1940.........	619	189	30.4	19.9

The expansion of reclaim consumption in the middle and late 1920's and its contraction in the early 1930's indicate that, as with many secondary materials, changes in the price of the primary material directly affect substitution. On the supply side, however, the price-responsiveness of reclaim production is disturbed and reduced by a variable set of conditions.

Immediate responsiveness is limited by the reclaiming capacity existing at any one time. The reclaiming process involves very complex technical operations which are exceedingly capital-intensive and require highly skilled operators. Prior to World War II, investment in equipment was estimated at about $100 per ton of annual capacity. Additional investment, therefore, tends to be undertaken only if a price rise of crude rubber is marked and likely to be sustained over a considerable period. On the other hand, overhead costs per unit of output tend to rise sharply as production is contracted and plants operate much below capacity. These conditions tend to render the response of reclaim supply to the price of crude rubber sluggish and imperfect, as Chart 2 shows. Secular changes in the difference between average production costs of reclaim and crude rubber (including changing costs of collecting scrap rubber as well as shifts in its usability) are other factors determining supply variability.

THE PRODUCTION OF PLANTATION RUBBER[3]

With negligible exceptions, the production of plantation rubber relies on one tree. *Hevea brasiliensis* is a straight-growing tree reaching 40–50 feet in height when mature. It will thrive on a wide range of soils, but requires a warm, moist climate. An equable tropical temperature and a well-distributed annual rainfall of 80–100 inches are most suitable for its cultivation. The

---

[3] In the preparation of this section, the author relied chiefly on Barker, *op. cit.*, pp. 4–20; C. A. Gehlsen, *World Rubber Production and Trade, Economic and Technical Aspects, 1935–1939* (International Institute of Agriculture, Studies of the Principal Agricultural Products on the World Market 7, Rome, 1940), pp. 97–172; D. H. Grist, *An Outline of Malayan Agriculture* (Straits Settlements and Federated Malay States, Dept. Agr., Malayan Planting Manual 2, Kuala Lumpur, 1936), chap. ix; Sir Andrew McFadyean (ed.), *The History of Rubber Regulation 1934–1943* (London, 1944), chaps. i, v; George Rae, "Statistics of the Rubber Industry," *Journal of the Royal Statistical Society* (London), Pt. II, 1938, CI, 317–34; J. W. F. Rowe, *Rubber. Studies in the Artificial Control of Raw Material Supplies* 2 (London and Cambridge Econ. Serv. Special Memorandum 34, London, 1931).

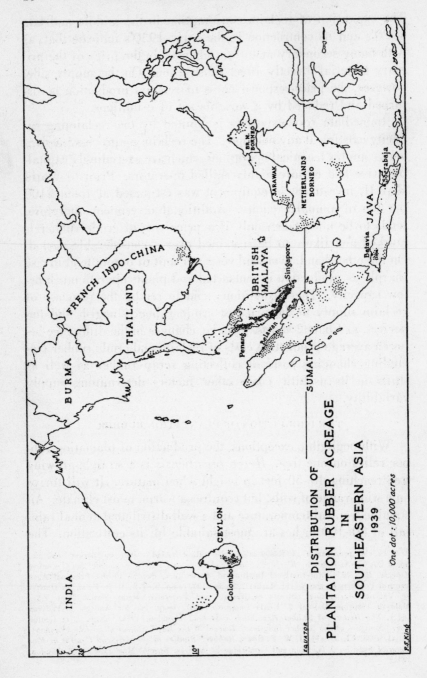

DISTRIBUTION OF
PLANTATION RUBBER ACREAGE
IN
SOUTHEASTERN ASIA
1939

One dot : 10,000 acres

tree therefore flourishes best in the relatively narrow belt within about 10° of the equator, and not over 2,000 feet above sea level.

Before World War II nearly all plantation rubber came from southeastern Asia (see Map). This producing area lies in a tropical belt within 20° north and 10° south of the equator. It extends west to include Ceylon and Malabar in southwestern India, stretches from Indian Assam southeast to Annam in French Indo-China, and down the Malay Peninsula through lower Burma, Thailand, and British Malaya into the Malay Archipelago. We shall refer to the entire region as Malaysia.

Planting and cultivation.—On modern rubber estates, nursery-raised saplings, 100 to over 200 to the acre, are planted in regular rows on thoroughly cleared jungle land. As the trees grow, the stand is gradually thinned out by the elimination of the least healthy plants. By the time they reach bearing age—5–7 years after planting—about 100 trees per acre remain. In the course of time natural causes lead to gradual diminution to between 70 and 80 trees. A stand of less than 70 renders upkeep and harvesting uneconomic.

The yield of a young tree just tappable is only about half that of a fully mature plant of about 13 years. If not excessively tapped, Hevea trees continually renew their latex-secreting bark; once past their prime, however, productivity rates decline. The economic life-span of the tree is as yet unknown. Estimates range up to fifty years and more. Much depends on the suitability of the physical environment and on cultivation and treatment. Rubber plantations are not actually tilled. Routine care consists of weeding, soil conservation, manuring and fertilizing, and fighting plant diseases and animal pests.

Up to about 1930, seeds were obtained from ordinary trees which included both low and high yielders. Then bud-grafting and seed selection were increasingly introduced to raise yields. The practice of bud-grafting is based on the assumption that the high-yielding properties of a selected plant can be transferred to another by grafting buds from it upon a vigorous but unproved young tree. The vegetative progeny thus raised is known as a "clone." Not all high-yielding parent trees transmit their high-yielding properties. Hence it became necessary to make careful selections before arriving at those clones that were worth propagating. Clones which have been submitted to and tested and approved by recognized scientific stations are called "proved" clones. The results of clonal planting have proved truly amazing. While ordinary Hevea trees might yield about 450 pounds of rubber per acre a year, bud-grafted trees have produced over 1,300 pounds.

Other scientists developed the method of generative propagation. This is a highly complicated technique, since the rubber tree is not normally self-fertilizing. Whether the yield characteristics of one or both parents are transmitted to all, some, or none of the progeny can be determined only by planting the resultant seed and testing the mature tree. The generative method now departs from high-yielding clonal seed and proceeds to obtain superior seed both by artificial pollination and by the natural crossing of various families of high-yielding clones. Yields as high as those of bud-grafted trees have been obtained.

The superiority of bud-grafted and seed-selected over ordinary seedling rubber trees is definitely established. It is true that the grafting operation slows down the maturing process by about two years, and that the bark renewal of budded trees is possibly somewhat slower than that of ordinary Hevea strains. Yet these disadvantages are outweighed by greater dependability and uniformity of yield and, above all, by much higher productivity. Although maximum yields obtained in experimental stations have seldom been reproduced under ordinary plantation conditions, bud-grafted rubber trees on efficient estates have yielded two or three times the latex flow of ordinary Hevea seedlings.

Since seed selection was developed much later than bud-grafting, the controversy over the comparative merits of the two methods had not been settled when the Japanese army overran the producing areas of southeast Asia. Although experiment-station results favored bud-grafting, planters on the whole preferred selected seeds. Conservative advice recommended the use of budded stock for half or two-thirds of new plantations, and of high-yielding clonal seed for the remainder.[4] It stands to reason that the postwar plantation industry will employ both techniques

[4] McFadyean, *op. cit.*, p. 69.

until the economic superiority of one is definitely determined for different types of plantations.

Tapping and yields.—Rubber latex is drawn from the tree by making an incision in the bark. Each time the tree is tapped, a thin slice of bark is cut away and the exuding latex collected in a cup hung on the trunk below the incision. A Hevea tree yielding an average of 4 pounds of rubber annually requires about 160 tapping operations a year. The tapping cut, though very quickly accomplished, must be performed with great skill in order not to injure the tree and to maximize the yield, which depends on the depth and angle of the incision.

In earlier days tapping as a rule was ruthless and too frequent. This hindered bark renewal and resulted in strongly diminished yields. Modern tapping is more careful. One-third or one-fourth of the plantation acreage is always resting, while the remainder is usually tapped on some alternative program, such as every other day. Such conservative practice permits ample and speedy bark renewal, keeps up the rubber content of the latex, and thereby reduces tapping costs per operation and per unit of output. While such intermittent rest periods are definitely beneficial, extension beyond three or four months does not affect the subsequent yield curve, because the continuous formation of rubber by the tree occurs in response to the tapping.

Apart from its age, the yield of the Hevea tree depends primarily on its inherent characteristics, and secondarily upon environment. Within limits all these factors can be manipulated by the planter. The biological characteristics of the tree are modifiable by bud-grafting and seed selection. Favorable environmental conditions can be obtained or maintained by proper site selection, efficient cultivation methods, optimal tapping schedules, and the careful selection, training, and supervision of tappers.

Unfortunately, it was not before the late 1920's that the plantation industry concentrated on the task of evolving radically improved planting and tapping techniques. Before that, progress was haphazard and localized, although acreage and output expanded vigorously in response to the growing demand. Thereafter the industry found itself encumbered with surplus output

capacity—under international control—with strict planting limitations. Thus while experimentation with and testing of new
production principles and methods were by no means prevented,
broad and speedy application of results was greatly retarded.

Table 1 shows, in thousand acres, the composition of the
aggregate plantation acreage of all Malaysian producing coun-

TABLE 1.—MALAYSIAN RUBBER ACREAGES, BY TYPE OF PLANTING STOCK,
1940*

(Thousand acres)

Age in years	Ordinary seedling		Bud-grafted		Clonal seed		All kinds	
	Estate	Native	Estate	Native	Estate	Native	Estate	Native
0– 5	160	283	453	19	47	43	660	345
5–10	38	204	249	1	3	..	290	205
10–15	585	1,527	369	..	1	..	955	1,527
Over 15.......	2,604	2,199	79	..	..	..	2,683	2,199
Total	3,387	4,213	1,150	20	51	43	4,588	4,276

* Data from Sir Andrew McFadyean (ed.), *The History of Rubber Regulation 1934–
1943* (London, 1944), p. 224. Countries included are British Malaya, Netherlands Indies,
Ceylon, India, Burma, North Borneo, Sarawak, Thailand, and French Indo-China.

tries at the end of 1940. Three-fourths of the total estate acreage
and nearly all the native plots were planted to ordinary seedling
rubber. Up to the middle 1920's few budded plants were used.
In 1926–30, 61 per cent of new estate acreage was still planted
to ordinary seedlings. In 1931–40 this percentage had declined
to 21 in favor of improved material. The use of clonal seed became of practical importance only in the late 1930's. In the
total picture it still is of little weight.

Employment of bud-grafted trees was always negligible in the
native sector of the industry, for the technique was complicated
and required a large cash investment. Clonal seed, on the other
hand, if made available to the small holder, is well adapted to
native use. The experience in the late 1930's in the Netherlands
Indies reveals this fact. The estate industry of different producing countries resorted in highly varying degrees to improved
planting materials (Chart 3). The Netherlands Indies and
French Indo-China were the most progressive in this respect,

while such countries as Sarawak and North Borneo proved quite conservative.

CHART 3.—COMPOSITION OF MALAYSIAN RUBBER ESTATES BY
TYPE OF PLANTING STOCK, 1940*

(*Percentages*)

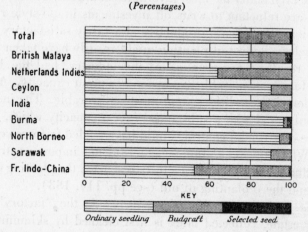

* Based on data in Sir Andrew McFadyean (ed.), *The History of Rubber Regulation 1934–1943* (London, 1944), p. 224.

The prolonged time lag between the discovery of improved plantation techniques and their widespread application explains the slowness with which average yields have risen in the industry. The annual yield of fully mature Hevea trees of unselected stock averages about 5 pounds of rubber. In contrast, budded trees of proved stock average about 16 pounds and, by 1940, clones had been developed that produced an average of 25 pounds a year. This suggests an improvement of several hundred per cent. Yet at the outbreak of World War II, the average estate yield was estimated at from 400 to 525 pounds per acre as compared with from 350 to 400 pounds in the early and middle 1920's. Average yield improvement over two decades was probably about 25 per cent.

Rowe observed in 1931 that rubber production was on the threshold of a veritable revolution in technique.[5] If during the following decade the results of new discoveries did not produce

[5] Rowe, *op. cit.*, p. 80.

revolutionary results, there were good reasons for the delay. In view of the long producing period of rubber trees—brought to maturity at a heavy capital outlay—large-scale application of improved planting methods would necessarily have been a slow process, even under the most favorable conditions. Naturally, investors are reluctant to write off investments in old-style rubber plantations that remain productive at a fairly satisfactory level. Nonetheless, improved planting might readily have taken place, with a resulting rejuvenation of the industry, had the 1930's called for a considerable expansion of output capacity. Actually, underlying conditions were most unfavorable. The industry was confronted with a substantial excess capacity which, in the absence of artificial control, would have tended to force contraction. While the regulation scheme did not impose contraction of production capacity, it carefully restricted the planting of new areas and the replanting of old (see pp. 114, 133).

The preparation of crude rubber.—At the "factory" of a rubber estate, collected latex is first cleaned by skimming and sieving and is then transferred to a coagulation tank. Acid is added to speed coagulation, and aluminum sheets two inches apart are inserted vertically while the latex is still fluid. Overnight the liquid jells to form wet, doughy curds about 3 feet long, 15 inches wide, and 1½ inches thick. After removal of the partitions, the slabs of coagulated latex are taken out, cleaned with water, put through smooth rolls which press out the water, and then passed through a mill with grooved rolls which "rib" the slabs. The ribbed sheets—now about 4 feet long, 18 inches wide and ⅛ inch thick—are again washed and drained. Then they are put into a smokehouse to dry and cure for several days over a smoldering fire of fresh wood and coconut husks. The functions of this smoking process are to hinder the formation of molds and bacteria, and to give the sheets a uniform color. The resulting product, known to the trade as "ribbed smoked sheets," make up about 85 per cent of the estates' rubber production. Most of the remainder is crepe rubber; its preparation requires heavier machinery but omits the smoking process.

The plantation industry.—For purposes of economic analysis, the rubber-plantation industry of the East is divided into two sections: the estate section, comprising plantations of 100 acres and more, and the native section, represented by plantations or rubber gardens of less than 100 acres, owned by Asiatic small holders. Table 2 shows the aggregate Hevea area of the East

TABLE 2.—RUBBER PLANTATION ACREAGE IN MALAYSIAN COUNTRIES, 1940*

(Thousand acres)

Country	Estates	Native holdings	Total
British Malaya	2,107	1,374	3,481
Netherlands Indies	1,567	3,200	4,767
Ceylon	359	280	639
Thailand[a]	...	419	419
North Borneo and Sarawak.	92	281	373
French Indo-China[a]	311	20	331
India	83	54	137
Burma	68	43	111
Total	4,587	4,671	9,258

* Data from McFadyean, *op. cit.*, p. 224. Figures for the Netherlands Indies have been corrected in accordance with revisions in *ibid.*, p. 83, and totals have been increased correspondingly.

[a] Owing to the fact that Thailand occupied part of Indo-China in 1940 there may be some duplication in the figures given for the planted areas of these two territories at the end of 1940. In the case of Indo-China the last official figure received gave the acreage at the end of 1938; the figure given at the end of 1940 is the end-1938 figure plus the new planting in 1939–40 permitted to Indo-China under the Agreement. This estimated acreage at the end of 1940 has been divided between estates and native holdings in the same ratio as the area at the end of 1938. *Ibid.*

nearly equally divided between the two sections of the industry. Native production is particularly important in the Netherlands Indies, Borneo, and Thailand, with approximately 70, 75, and 100 per cent of the total Hevea acreage controlled by small holders. In British Malaya the percentage is nearly 40. Only in French Indo-China is native production insignificant, with 6 per cent of the total rubber acreage.

Rubber estates and native plantations are economically two distinct types of enterprise. Most estates are owned and managed by Europeans. They are highly capitalistic enterprises which operate under conditions of high fixed costs and in many producing areas are dependent on foreign labor supplies. Native rubber gardens, on the other hand, are usually peasant enterprises unencumbered by fixed costs or dependence on migratory workers. To the majority of them, rubber is a welcome cash crop cultivated along with rice and other food crops for their own use.

Rubber estates.—In size, rubber estates range all the way from 100 to 10,000 acres. In British Malaya, for instance, there were about 2,500 estates in 1940. Their average acreage was 841. About 1,900 of these estates, from 100 to 1,000 acres in size, owned only 27 per cent of the country's entire rubber-estate area. On the other hand, the remaining 600 estates, each over 1,000 acres, controlled 73 per cent of the total acreage.[6] There were about 950 rubber estates in the Netherlands Indies of which more than one-fourth, mostly in Java, were interplanted with coffee, tea, and other crops. The average size of estates exclusively engaged in rubber production was 1,300 acres in Java and Madura and 1,620 acres in the Outer Provinces.[7]

It is estimated that nearly one-fifth of the Far Eastern estate acreage is owned by Asiatics (largely Chinese) and four-fifths by Europeans.[8] Most of the small estates are owned by Asiatic planters. Most European estates, far larger on the average, are owned by public or private limited-liability companies of which a large majority were formed in England. Directors and executive secretaries of rubber companies formed in Britain are usually located in and function from London. Such companies frequently operate more than one estate in the East, and a great many companies are more or less closely interlocked by common directorships.

A peculiar institution of British plantation enterprise is the so-called agency system. Its genesis dates back to the early development of tea and coffee plantations in the East. Merchant houses established in the region were employed to act as a vital connecting link between plantation management and directorates located in England. These agents sometimes hire and usually supervise the managerial staff, purchase plantation supplies, and act as shipping agents. Indeed, these firms frequently control the general policy of rubber companies. Since they rarely hold

6 "The Malayan Rubber Industry in 1940," *Malayan Agricultural Journal* (Kuala Lumpur), July 1941, XXIX, 275.

7 Netherlands Indies, Dept. Econ. Affairs, *The Export Crops of the Netherlands Indies in 1938* . . . . (Bull. Central Bur. Statistics 175, Batavia, 1939), pp. 90–103.

8 Rubber Manufacturers Association, Inc., *Crude Rubber*, p. 41.

substantial investments in the operating companies, ownership often is virtually divorced from control.[9] One agency may serve several rubber companies at the same time.

Because of the agents' experience with tropical enterprise, the emerging rubber-growing industry eagerly adopted the system and undoubtedly benefited from it. The 1930's, however, brought increasing criticism against the maintenance of the connection. In addition to a sizable management fee, the agencies were remunerated by their profits as buyers of estate stores and as shipping agents. The lack of competition for these services tended to render them expensive. Moreover, the size of the remuneration did not, except in periods of very high or very low rubber prices, vary with the profits of the rubber companies. This seems unfortunate in view of their control over management. The agencies were interested in lengthening the life of the operating rubber companies rather than in maximizing their net profits at any given price. In general, their influence was one of caution and conservatism rather than of progressive enterprise.[10]

Except in Java, the great majority of Eastern rubber estates rely on outside labor. Estates in British Malaya draw most of their workers from India, China, and Java, those in Sumatra from Java and China, those in southwestern India and Ceylon from southeastern India. The reasons for this dependence on migratory workers are chiefly two: (1) the local natives, such as the Malays in British Malaya, proved reluctant to engage in the type of regular and disciplined work required on modern rubber estates; (2) estates are located in an area, such as Sumatra, which is sparsely settled and therefore does not yield an adequate labor force. Fortunately huge labor reservoirs could be tapped in southeastern India (especially in Madras Presidency), China, and Java, where constant pressure on the population's subsistence provides a potent motive for migration.

The labor forces involved are large, but fluctuate with changing levels of production. British Malaya's rubber estates, for example, employed 292,000 workers at the end of 1935 as com-

<hr>

[9] P. T. Bauer, "Notes on Cost," *Economica* (London), New Series, May 1945, XII, 94.
[10] *Ibid.*, p. 95.

pared with 352,000 at the end of 1940. The country exported 369,900 tons of rubber in 1935, 540,900 in 1940. Rising wages in times of prosperity and falling wages in times of depression help to regulate the inflow and—to a lesser extent—the outflow of immigrant workers in Malaya. The reaction is sluggish, however, and a considerable time lag must be expected. The government therefore manipulates the flexibility of the labor supply by altering the immigration quotas of Chinese coolies as the situation demands; and in times of stress the government may give financial assistance for purposes of prompt emigration or repatriation of foreign laborers.

Nevertheless, dependence on migratory workers from distant areas is necessarily precarious. It lacks flexibility. Adjustment to suddenly altered output schedules cannot be perfect under the circumstances. There always appears a troublesome time lag which prevents rapid expansion of production in response to a booming market, while a sudden contraction of production generates an irksome problem of surplus labor. When the market situation calls for a lowering of the output level, estate managers often hesitate to dismiss workers because they fear being understaffed should a sudden turn in the market occur. Many producers also employ labor on long-term contracts (sometimes several years) in order to prevent workers recruited and trained at the estate's expense from changing to a different employer.

On the average, a little over half of the labor staff of a rubber estate are employed as tappers. Nearly all the rest are field workers and weeders. Only about 2 per cent are needed for factory work. The Chinese, most of them tappers, are more efficient workers than Indians or Javanese. While an Indian tapper may bring in about 11 pounds of rubber a day, a Chinese tapper will collect around 16 pounds. Indian coolies receive a fixed daily wage determined by agreements between the government of British Malaya and India. In 1937 the daily rate was approximately 30 U.S. cents. Chinese laborers, usually employed on a contract basis, obtained about twice that much. Both in British Malaya and in the Netherlands Indies, the governments enforce certain minimum standards of housing, sanitation, and hospitalization.

The formation of powerful labor unions is retarded by divisions of nationality and the migratory character of the majority of the workers. Nevertheless, strikes and other labor troubles are factors seriously and constantly to be reckoned with. The Chinese coolies especially are quick to react collectively to real or imagined grievances. During the late 1930's moreover, unionization increased among Asiatic labor groups, especially in British Malaya.

Total investments in the entire rubber industry of the East are estimated at substantially more than a billion dollars.[11] No reliable data are available. There can be no doubt, however, that the United Kingdom is by far the leading investing country, with considerably more than half of the capital invested in rubber estates, and that the Netherlands ranks second. France and the United States trail far behind. The total investments of all four countries are estimated to exceed 600 million dollars. Chinese and native plantations represent the remaining investment in the industry.

Par capitalization per acre of rubber estate varies prodigiously. The issue of stocks at premiums of widely differing magnitude in part accounts for this divergence. This factor aside, actual investment per acre differs markedly not only from country to country, but also with the specific location of the plantations, the estate size, the configuration of the land, the nature of the estate equipment, wages at the time of planting, and the prevailing interest rate.

In the middle 1930's it was estimated that, including interest, it required from $200 to $400 per acre to plant and raise estate trees.[12] After consultation with the Internationale Vereeniging voor de Rubbercultuur, the Rubber Growers' Association (RGA) issued a report in 1936 on a "costing formula" suitable for the calculation of a "fair and equitable price level."[13] Table 3 presents their estimates of current costs of bringing a fully equipped average estate into bearing, exclusive of interest charges on capital employed during the maturing period. The

[11] U.S. Tariff Commission, *Rubber* (War Changes in Industry Series Report 6, September 1944), p. 35.

[12] Barker, *op. cit.*, p. 7.   [13] Reprinted in McFadyean, *op. cit.*, pp. 187–205.

spread of the cost range from area to area and within one producing country is clearly indicated. Expenditure for bud-grafting adds only around 10 per cent to the investment outlay, while
the average increment in yields should be proportionally much
greater. According to this report, per acre investment in buildings and machinery represents about one-fifth of the total capital
expenditure.[14] In this respect, too, actual costs vary greatly.
Thus it was reported in 1936 that for a rubber estate of 2,000
acres in British Malaya, valued at $210 per acre, estate equip-
ment was estimated at only $9,000, or roughly 2 per cent of the
aggregate investment.[15]

TABLE 3.—ESTATE INVESTMENT IN SELECTED COUNTRIES*

(£ per acre)

Country	Capital expenditure for ordinary seedling rubber			Additional capital expenditure for bud-grafting		
	Highest	Lowest	Average	Highest	Lowest	Average
British Malaya	47.9	35.3	41.9	10.2	2.2	5.6
Ceylon	....	....	50.3	....	...	3.4
India	....	....	51.9	....	...	4.6
Borneo	....	....	29.0	....	...	4.6

* Data from McFadyean, *op. cit.*, pp. 188–89.

High capital investments in rubber estates are reflected in the
financial structure of the industry. A rubber plantation is in-
dubitably a wasting asset. The actual rate of "waste" differs, of
course, with individual producing units. But even an average
rate for the industry is difficult to ascertain. Problems of its
physical life apart, the economic life of the rubber tree depends
not only on the shape of the yield curve as the tree ages, but also
on technical progress. The discovery and application of superior planting material obviously introduces an important element
of obsolescence affecting the economic life of an old plantation.
In the report cited, the RGA recommended an amortization
charge of 4 per cent per annum for purposes of capital replace-

[14] Reprinted in McFadyean, *op. cit.*, p. 192.

[15] *Rubber News Letter* (U.S. Dept. Comm., Bur. Foreign and Domestic Comm., Leather and Rubber Division), Aug. 30, 1936, p. 2.

ment. Rubber trees, in other words, are assumed to have a productive life of 25 years, i.e., 30 years reckoned from the date of planting. A rate of 7½ per cent was suggested to cover depreciation of buildings and equipment.

The structure of estate production costs contains a heavy proportion of overhead charges. An American observer analyzed estate costs f.o.b. port of shipment, as reported by 20 Malayan rubber companies for 1934,[16] the year the International Rubber Regulation Agreement (IRRA) was introduced. Production was fixed at an annual average of 87.5 per cent of assessed capacity. In view of the comparative overassessment of estates (see pp. 122–23) this was close to full capacity. Total f.o.b. costs, including the rubber cess (export duty), averaged 5.52 U.S. cents a pound. About 54 per cent of the total was attributed to direct production costs incurred in the collection, preparation, packing, and shipping of rubber. Overhead expenditure for general cultivation and estate maintenance, upkeep of buildings and machinery, managerial salaries, quit rent, agency fee, and sundry other items accounted for the remainder. Not all of these overhead cost items are invariable. Indeed, total costs are remarkably plastic. In times of depression, cultivation and maintenance work can be reduced and salaries and other expenses slashed. But beyond a certain point and in the longer run, these cost items resist curtailment. These relatively fixed expenditures definitely tend to increase per unit of output as the production level sinks below capacity.

In addition to f.o.b. costs, rubber companies have to meet still other expenditure. So-called "all-in" costs usually include ocean shipping and selling costs, head-office expenses, staff bonuses and—in RGA cost estimates—depreciation and amortization charges. In its 1934 report, the RGA estimated 1.3, .8, and .4 U.S. cents per pound respectively for the first three items mentioned.[17] Shipping and selling expenses vary directly with the export volume. Bonuses—a profit-sharing arrangement for directors and managerial personnel—can be varied in response

---

[16] Harrison Lewis, *Rubber Regulation and the Malayan Plantation Industry* (U.S. Dept. Comm., Bur. Foreign and Domestic Comm., Trade Promotion Series 159, 1935), pp. 35–36.

[17] McFadyean, *op. cit.*, pp. 191–92.

to changing revenues and even omitted in times of depression. On the other hand, head-office expense constitutes a fixed item. Its magnitude differs greatly for different companies and, in general, weighs more heavily on the smaller estates.

Inclusion of charges for depreciation and amortization greatly increases the rigidity of the cost structure. Whether definitely fixed charges of this kind should be regularly included in total estate production costs—as recommended by the RGA—is debatable. Certainly the specific cost formula adopted by the RGA was not employed by operating rubber companies in their published accounts. A wide disparity is found between the figures of these accounts and those of the cost reports that were periodically assembled by the RGA.[18]

In principle, however, the RGA is correct in pointing out that a company which does not set aside funds for capital replacement is either living on accumulated fat or on its capital assets. In prosperous years of the past, rubber companies did set aside such funds to be subsequently used for investment in equipment, and in replanting and plantation extension. If, in years of deep depression, no such funds were accumulated, this merely means that in the shorter run depreciation and amortization allowances can be deferred. These charges, in other words, can also be adapted to business conditions. To a certain extent they are to be considered variable, not fixed. For this reason, total output costs are influenced as much or more by the changing price of rubber as by changing rates of production. Nevertheless, in the longer run the element of rigidity must reassert itself to spare individual enterprises or the industry as a whole the necessity of disinvestment.

Needless to stress, there are vast differences between estates in the burden of amortization charges per pound of output, no matter how or when these charges are actually made. These differences are not solely the outcome of the specific economic life-expectancy of the individual estate. The issue of shares at premiums of varying amount also led to great differences in the par capitalization per acre. When the industry was confronted with severe depression in the late 1920's, many rubber companies

[18] McFadyean, *op. cit.*, p. 197.

were overcapitalized. Balance-sheet values were often quite fic-
titious. They bore no relation to the current market value of the
estate because the capital invested was no longer represented by
equivalent assets. Many schemes of capital reduction were carried through in the 1930's, but there remained many overcapitalized companies whose shareholders refused to accept unpalatable
facts.[19]

The level of average estate production costs underwent many
shifts during the interwar period. Increasing efficiency made for
a secular downward trend of costs. Other conditions at times
stengthened, at times counteracted this general tendency. In
periods of depression and low prices, temporary economies were
effected on top of permanent economies resulting from improved
efficiency. When prices were high and the industry prospered,
temporary cost-decreasing measures were suspended and the
pressure toward utmost efficiency was relaxed. Under conditions
of tight output control, the cost level changed in response to the
prevalent production level, with overhead costs per unit of output
diminishing or increasing as production was expanded or curtailed. Currency manipulation at various times exerted a temporary and, at times, highly disturbing influence on costs. A brief
historical account of estate production costs will be found in
chapter v (pp. 92, 104–05).[20]

Native plantations.—The first Hevea trees owned by natives
were apparently planted in Djambi, Netherlands Indies, in 1904.
The bulk of the total small-holders' acreage was planted between 1910 and 1919 and between 1924 and 1929, both periods
of very high rubber prices. Except perhaps for Thailand and the
Outer Provinces of the Netherlands Indies, the gradual though
at times abrupt extension of the area under native rubber was not
the result of active government encouragement. Hevea trees are
relatively easy to grow. Encouraged by Chinese merchants, the
natives perceived a cash crop whose cultivation appeared both
profitable and congenial. No doubt it had the grave disadvantage of a long wait from planting to bearing age, but, once ma-

---

[19] *Rubber News Letter*, Aug. 30, 1936, p. 2.

[20] For an excellent and detailed account, see E. G. Holt, *Prewar Costs of Production for Plantation Rubber*, in U.S. War Production Board, Office of Rubber Director, *Special Report on the Synthetic Rubber Program* (Aug. 31, 1944), Appendix A, pp. 13–26.

ture, rubber trees promised a larger income in proportion to the work involved than any other known alternative.

The organization of native rubber production is by no means homogeneous. Small holdings differ greatly in size and serve different purposes in the income situation of different types of native producers. Plantations of less than 100 acres are classified as small holdings, but the average area of planted rubber per native holding is about 3 acres. It is somewhat larger in British Malaya and somewhat smaller in the Netherlands Indies. In 1935, about 700,000 Malay holdings in British Malaya averaged about 4 acres, while an additional 567,000 small holdings, owned by Chinese and Indians, were about four times as large. A census taken in the Netherlands Indies in 1936 showed 788,000 native holdings with an average of a little over 2 acres per holding. But variation is considerable. While some small holders cultivate 40 or 60 acres, many others own diminutive patches with only a few dozen trees.

The majority of small holders in British Malaya and a small proportion of the native owners in the Netherlands Indies depend on the income derived from their rubber gardens. On the other hand, to the large majority of small holders in the Netherlands Indies, rubber production is a cash-crop enterprise accompanying rice cultivation. In the sparsely populated Outer Provinces, where jungle land is freely obtainable, the native clears each year about two acres on which he grows rice, his staple food. After harvesting one or two crops from this rice patch, he abandons it and makes another. While formerly the deserted land reverted to jungle before it was cleared again, now the patch is planted with rubber. This practice is part of the so-called "ladang" system of agriculture.

Unlike the capitalistic enterprise of the rubber estate, the small holder needs neither managerial staff nor offices. As a rule he acts as his own manager and, with some exceptions, especially in Sumatra, he is also independent of migratory labor. In British Malaya the owner and his family normally constitute the whole labor force. If needed, additional workers can be hired in his village and are paid a small wage per pound of rubber collected. In the Netherlands Indies, too, most holdings are operated as a family enterprise. Under the ladang system, rubber cultivation is often carried on in spare time, and rubber production tends to decline temporarily when the natives cultivate and harvest rice.

If the holding is too large for this type of enterprise—as in some districts of Sumatra—additional workmen, either locally recruited or migratory Javanese, are employed. In lieu of a wage payment, these laborers usually receive a certain portion of the rubber they collect. Their pay, therefore, varies with the price of rubber and in times of low rubber prices they may insist on a larger share of the rubber produced. Whether or not outside labor is employed depends not only on the size of the holding, but also on the price of rubber. During periods of high prices, owners with only 5 or 10 acres or even less may find it pleasanter to hire tappers than to do the work themselves. They decide to take part of the profit in leisure. When prices are very low over a longer period of time, migratory labor, because of the unattractive remuneration, may be scarce. Accepting the inevitable, the owner and his family then will do the work themselves. Thus there is a great deal of flexibility in this variegated system.

The economy of the native holding is entirely different from that of the estate. The Hevea gardens of the natives represent very small capital investments. In British Malaya the owner has to pay a small fee for his land. In Sumatra and Borneo the land is made available to the native merely for settling and clearing it. Ordinarily the owner's equipment consists of a few pans or old oil cans for coagulating the latex and one or two simple and cheap rollers. While many of the larger native plantations have a smokehouse of their own, the overwhelming majority of native owners use public smokehouses on payment of a small fee. Their chief investment is their own labor.

Conditions and practices of cultivation are much less uniform among small holdings than among estates. Generally speaking, cultivation is scanty and primitive and the vast majority of native plantations are qualitatively inferior to estates. For example, in the Netherlands Indies it was estimated in 1936 that only 4.2 per cent of the entire acreage under native rubber can be classified as "good" and 17.8 per cent as "fairly good"; of the rest, 40.3 per cent is "mediocre," 21.5 per cent "poor," and 16.1 per cent "neglected."

The average number of trees per acre in small holdings is much greater than on estates. Ranging up to 500 trees, average planting density is about 150 on Ceylonese, 220 on Malayan, and 350 on Netherlands Indies native plantations. Except for accidental elimination by wind and disease, there is no thinning out of the relatively poorer trees. Ordinarily, native producers give little attention to general maintenance work, disease fighting, and weeding. The amount of upkeep depends to some extent on the price of rubber; but even when high prices make rubber production seem attractive, rough clearance along the lines of the patch is usually considered sufficient.

The tapping operation is generally performed with little skill. Trees are often injured and bark renewal thus retarded. As a rule most small holdings are now operated on some system of alternate tapping. Before the introduction of control, natives were inclined to overtap their trees in response to the market. Yet, contrary to early prophecies, neither scanty cultivation nor occasional overtapping has in the long run ruined the average native plantation. The Hevea tree apparently stands a lot of rough treatment and neglect. With the dense planting customary with the native grower, he can also afford to lose many a tree from disease and still have left enough to make continued tapping worth while.

Despite the inferior quality of native holdings, their per acre output exceeds estate production. This is so because their planting density is twice or thrice that of estate plantations, and because natives are inclined to tap their trees more rigorously. As compared with estates, the average yield of the small holding is smaller per tree, but larger per acre. In 1935, for instance, the average yield per native acre was estimated at approximately 500 pounds as compared with around 375 pounds per estate acre.

The average product put out by the native producer compares poorly with the better grades of estate produce. The larger of the small holdings frequently prepare their product for exportation much as do the estates. The operation, however, is usually much more crude. Often old troughs discarded by estates, or even kerosene cans, are used as coagulating pans. Instead of four pairs of machine rollers, only one or two hand-operated rollers are employed for milling. In the absence of a smoking shed the product is sometimes smoked over the kitchen fire—if it is smoked at all.

If the native applies painstaking effort, he may be able to turn out very good quality sheet. Usually, however, his rubber is considerably inferior in purity to that of the average estate. Notwithstanding government efforts to induce the native to prepare a better product, natives tend to continue the production of lower-grade rubber because the price differential between a superior product and one of lower grade does not appear sufficiently attractive to make the extra effort worth while. Thus, in spite of the erection of numerous public smoke cabinets in some Malayan districts, the small holders persist in preparing unsmoked sheet because of the low premium obtainable for the higher-grade material. In the Netherlands Indies a large number of natives do not even take the trouble to mill their rubber, and simply sell thick slabs of wet coagulum which is then sent to milling factories in the Indies or in Singapore and Penang.

Native rubber is sold, usually once a month, to local dealers, many of whom are Chinese. These dealers in turn sell the commodity to larger export dealers. The small holder obtains a lower price for his produce than the estate producer. Thus, when estate-produced ribbed smoked sheet sells for an f.o.b. price of 21 Straits cents a pound, the native will get about 18 cents for roughly the same product and correspondingly less for inferior grades. Middlemen and milling factories receive the difference.

Unlike estate producers, the native rubber grower has made slow progress in adopting improved production techniques. Aside from lack of investment funds, the chief barriers are the natives' illiteracy, their deeply ingrained conservatism, and their reluctance to engage in any extra work that does not immediately and tangibly result in a higher income. Beyond a certain point, the money needs of many natives also fail to furnish an adequate stimulus. Finally, the native producer had little to fear from estate competition. He has always been in a position to produce more cheaply than the capitalistic estate.

Still, some technical advancement has been achieved by the small holder and in the late 1930's the rate of progress was markedly accelerated. Many natives gained experience by direct contact with estate enterprise either as neighbors or as estate workers. The ubiquitous Chinese dealer indirectly provided a potent incentive toward an improvement in native production. His practice of importing and displaying for sale new articles for consumption inspired in the natives novel wants which could be satisfied only by augmenting their cash income. Some new techniques are more adaptable to native enterprise than others. Thus the bud-grafting technique failed to spread to the native section of the rubber industry, while small holders evinced considerable interest in selected seed in the late 1930's. In part this is to be explained on the ground that the use of selected seed is technically less complicated than bud-grafting.

Governments could perhaps have done more than they did to propagate superior production methods. Such efforts as were made met with slow but definite success. During the 1930's in British Malaya, for example, the Small Holders' Advisory Service carried on a great deal of propaganda aimed at arousing native interest in replanting and in the use of high-yielding material. Field work was carried on by Asiatic rubber instructors who gave numerous lectures and demonstrations. Much attention was given to weeding practices, soil-maintenance work, and the manner in which latex is prepared for export. The agricultural stations of the Department of Agriculture supplied large quantities of selected seeds and budwood for the use of the small holder. The establishment of small-holders' co-operatives proved a promising development. In 1937 as many as 253 such co-operatives were in operation. In addition to the bulk-purchasing of fungicides and coagulants, they were engaged in bettering production and marketing methods. A similar and perhaps even more determined effort was made by the government of the Netherlands Indies. There also, the native producer was aided by the distribution of selected seed, and tapping schools were opened in several districts.

As may be inferred from the foregoing, it is impossible to say anything precise about the average small-holder's production costs. Owing to the services rendered by middlemen, the cost of marketing is obviously higher for the native peasant than for the estate. Taxes levied on exports are the same for both types of producers. On the other hand, if the small holder receives a lower price for his inferior product, his costs of preparing rubber for shipment are much lower, too. Indeed, apart from marketing costs and export duties, all other cost items are lower for the native than for the estate.

The native grower has no capital charges comparable to those borne by the estate enterprise. He may be servicing debts to local dealers, money-lenders, or banks, and his holding may be mortgaged; but such debts have rarely been incurred on capital account. Cash outlays for planting and cultivation are very small. If the native producer employs tappers, his labor costs are often paid with the product itself, and vary directly with the price of rubber. Nor does he have to go to the expense of bringing employees from India, furnishing living quarters and hospital care, or hiring a European manager. Directors' fees, home-office expenditure, agency fees, upkeep for buildings, machinery, and roads—these items do not exist for the small holder.

Comparing production costs for the capitalistic rubber estate and the native peasant holdings, three significant conclusions can be stated. (1) The estate's cost structure is complicated, while that of the small holder is simple. The difference between the price he receives for his produce and his small cash outlays are remuneration for the labor he and his family perform. (2) In the absence of relatively fixed overhead expenses, the native's production costs per unit of output do not tend to rise as production is curtailed. (3) The native rubber grower can produce rubber more cheaply than the estate—how much more cheaply depends primarily on the value he places on his labor.

CHAPTER III

TRADE AND USES

THE WORLD RUBBER TRADE

As far as crude rubber is concerned, the product of the Hevea plantations will predominate after World War II as it did before.

About 99 per cent of all plantation rubber came from southeastern Asia. The tiny remainder was produced by the Firestone estates in Liberia and a few smaller plantations in Africa, Latin America, the Philippines, and Oceania. Chart 4 and Table 4

CHART 4.—CRUDE RUBBER EXPORTS BY COUNTRIES AND REGIONS,
AVERAGES, 1929–33 AND 1937–41*

(Thousand tons)

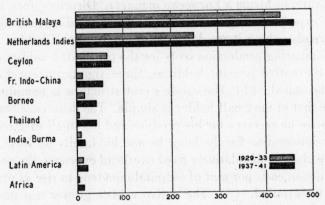

* Based on data in Appendix Table I.

indicate the ranking of the more important exporting countries of Malaysia. British Malaya, the foremost exporter, is very closely followed by the Netherlands Indies. These are the Big Two. Their combined exports in 1938–40 averaged over 78 per cent of total Malaysian shipments. The next three in rank,

Ceylon, French Indo-China, and Thailand, shipped 16.4 per cent, bringing the total for the five leading countries to 95 per cent. All producing areas under British rule or control shipped 51.4 per cent of aggregate exports. It is easily seen that, politically speaking, the United Kingdom and the Netherlands dominate the trade.

TABLE 4.—RUBBER EXPORTS, WORLD AND MALAYSIAN COUNTRIES, AVERAGE 1938–40*

Exporting country	Annual net exports	
	Tons	Percentage
World total (including wild rubber)........	1,085,420	....
Malaysia total	1,047,086	100.00
British Malaya	415,918	39.7
Netherlands Indies	402,745	38.5
Ceylon	66,421	6.3
French Indo-China	62,937	6.0
Thailand	42,437	4.1
Sarawak	25,657	2.5
North Borneo	13,000	1.2
British India	10,261	1.0
Burma	7,710	.7

* Compiled from data in McFadyean, *op. cit.*, pp. 228–29.

There are cogent reasons for this striking concentration of production in one region of the world. No doubt the enterprise of the British and Dutch, their experience with tropical agriculture, and their free capital funds go far toward explaining the early success of this Malaysian industry. British power and Dutch and British administrative skill insured settled political conditions for many decades. The physical environment is eminently suited to the cultivation of the Hevea tree. Soils and temperatures are favorable, rainfall is adequate and well distributed. The major producing areas are located close to the sea and rail and road facilities are good. Transportation, therefore, is relatively inexpensive. Most important of all, perhaps, is the proximity of huge reservoirs of labor in the densely populated areas of British India, China, and Java where poverty furnishes a strong motive for migration. Not only is labor plentiful and relatively cheap; compared with other populations in the tropical zone it is skilled and adaptable as well.

Chart 5 presents a graphic picture of the distribution of crude-rubber imports. The pre-eminence of the United States is impressive. In 1937–39 this country consumed as much rubber as the rest of the world combined (see Table 5). The United

CHART 5.—CRUDE-RUBBER IMPORTS BY PRINCIPAL IMPORTING COUNTRIES, AVERAGES, 1925–29 AND 1935–39*

(Thousand tons)

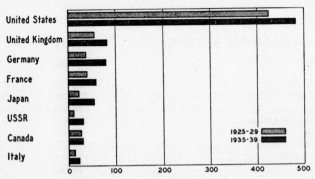

* Based on data in McFadyean, *op. cit.*, pp. 234–35.

TABLE 5.—ANNUAL RUBBER ABSORPTION IN IMPORTING COUNTRIES, AVERAGES OF SELECTED PERIODS, 1920–39*

Period	Thousand tons					Percentage			
	Total	U.S.A.	United Kingdom	Continental Europe	Rest of world	U.S.A.	United Kingdom	Continental Europe	Rest of world
1920–22 ...	326.2	228.4	17.6	53.8	26.3	70.0	5.4	16.5	8.1
1927–29 ...	694.2	425.8	55.1	141.4	71.8	61.3	7.9	20.4	10.4
1937–39 ...	1,042.0	524.2	114.8	272.0	131.0	50.3	11.0	26.1	12.6

* Compiled from data in McFadyean, *op. cit.*, p. 236. U.K. data, 1920–29, are net imports corrected for changes in warehouse stocks; 1937–39 average represents total absorption estimated from returns received by the IRRC from the majority of U.K. rubber manufacturers. Data for Continental Europe and Rest of World are merely totals of net imports.

Kingdom, Germany,[1] France, Japan, the Soviet Union, and Italy follow in that order. The table also indicates that the interwar

[1] It should be noted that in 1937–39 Germany's imports increased abnormally over those of the preceding decade. The accumulation of strategic stockpiles was undoubtedly the main factor in this expansion.

period witnessed marked shifts in absorption of crude plantation rubber. In the early 1920's the United States absorbed as much as 70 per cent of the world's imports. Tremendously as United States absorption grew in the succeeding two decades, that of the rest of the world increased relatively much faster.

The highly industrialized and wealthy countries are naturally the leading importers and consumers of rubber. They use large quantities of the material in industrial equipment and consumers' goods. Above all, they can afford the widespread system of individual transportation which is implied in the large-scale use of motor vehicles. A comparison of per capita rubber imports would reveal even more strikingly the vast differences between poor and wealthy countries. However, such a comparison would be statistically somewhat misleading, since it disregards the importance of the international trade in rubber-containing goods, especially automobiles and tires.[2] Nevertheless, it is noteworthy that in 1937–39 per capita rubber consumption in the United States averaged 9 pounds as against one-half pound in the rest of the world. The United Kingdom absorbed 5.4 pounds per person, Italy only 1.2, and Chile a little more than one-tenth of a pound. For vast areas of the world the figure would be negligible.

A survey of the distribution of world exports and imports of crude rubber reveals the clear-cut geographical separation of the main producing and consuming centers. Production is concentrated in the tropical zone of southeastern Asia; the chief consumption centers are located in the temperate zones of North America and Europe. This circumstance meant long shipping routes and, during the interwar period when no substantial alternative supply of rubber existed, the prospect of a precarious dependence on distant sources of supply in time of war.

The chief ports of departure were Singapore, Penang, and Port Swettenham in British Malaya; Belawan, Batavia, and Soerabaja in the Netherlands Indies; and Colombo in Ceylon. About two-thirds of all Malaysian rubber was shipped in burlap bales weighing up to 250 pounds each, the remaining third in

---

[2] Per capita rubber consumption would appear understated in the industrially backward countries as well as in wealthy but small countries.

plywood cases of 5 cubic feet, ten cases equaling a long ton of rubber. Small quantities of liquid latex were shipped in special tanks or steel drums. Before World War II, ships were routed principally via the Suez Canal and the Mediterranean. The Italo-Ethiopian war and subsequent war scares caused the bulk of the rubber shipments to detour around the Cape of Good Hope. After the outbreak of war, shipments were increasingly routed via the Panama Canal.

Occasionally, freight rates on rubber from Singapore to New York have been as low as $8.00 per ton, but the average peacetime rate ranged from $15.00 to $18.00, or ½ to ⅝ of a cent per pound. Rates tended to increase with rising rubber prices, and to fall with declining prices. With the re-routing of shipments over a longer haul in the late 1930's, and later with the war-induced shipping shortages, freight rates rose steeply. They averaged $21.50 a ton in 1940 and $27.00 in 1941. Insurance charges for ordinary marine risks were a small cost item ranging from 1/20 to 1/40 of a cent per pound.

Before World War II, British vessels carried over half of all Malaysian rubber exports, and United States, Dutch, Japanese, and Norwegian bottoms most of the rest. The location of the major rubber-goods manufacturers determined the port of entry in the United States. More than 40 per cent of all crude rubber consumed in this country was processed in Ohio (mainly in Akron), about 25 per cent in California, Massachusetts, Pennsylvania, and New Jersey, the remainder in a large number of states. Approximately four-fifths of all United States imports, therefore, entered Atlantic Coast ports, chiefly New York, Baltimore, and Boston. A little over one-tenth, consumed in California, entered at Los Angeles.

Rubber's vital importance as a commodity and, during the interwar period, the absence of a satisfactory substitute that could be produced in the chief consuming countries, prevented any widespread erection of tariff barriers. Rubber entered all but a few countries duty-free. Indeed, in the Anglo-American trade agreement which became effective in January 1939, the United States bound itself to maintain the duty-free status of rubber.

France, which imported altogether about 50,000 tons of rubber but less than 20,000 tons from French Indo-China, in 1931 imposed a customs duty of 30 centimes per kilogram on all imports. This revenue fed a compensation fund from which producers in French Indo-China were paid subsidy premiums ranging up to 3 francs per kilogram. The purpose of this duty was to maintain the French plantation industry on a sound financial footing throughout the depression. In order to stimulate the use of domestic wild rubber, Brazil maintained high taxes on all imported rubber. In 1937, the German government decreed a high import tax on rubber for the purpose of protecting its infant synthetic industry. Complete state control of economic affairs in Soviet Russia prevented competition between cheap imported and more expensive domestic rubber.

THE INTERNATIONAL RUBBER MARKET

In the forms in which it enters international trade, natural rubber is consumed exclusively by manufacturers of rubber articles. Considering the large quantity of rubber that is traded and thus consumed, industrial purchasers are relatively few. In the United States, nearly two-thirds of all crude rubber was consumed by the five biggest rubber-goods manufacturers. Similar conditions prevailed in Europe and Japan. Contrasted to this striking concentration of industrial consumption is the multiplicity of producers.

It is the function of the rubber market to bring producers and industrial consumers together, and to facilitate their trading operations. Local dealers buy up the output of the native producers and pass it on to larger export merchants or the milling factories in the chief ports of exit. Estates commonly sell on their own account, but utilize the services of well-established agency houses. However, the 1930's saw a definite trend toward the centralization of the bulk of the trade in a relatively small number of powerful trading companies.

Seeking to reduce the margin between the price received by producers and the price manufacturers pay in the importing countries, some of the larger industrial consumers set up their own purchasing organizations in the East. Middlemen, however, still handle the bulk of all rubber. Before World War II, rubber-goods manufacturers in the United States bought about three-fourths of their requirements from importers and dealers, mostly in New York, and to a lesser extent through European traders.

Outside New York, the chief rubber markets of the world are located in London, Amsterdam, and Singapore. Hamburg, Antwerp, and Paris in Europe, and Colombo and Batavia in the East, are of definitely minor importance. Until World War I, London was by far the outstanding trading center and entrepôt. With the overwhelming growth of United States imports, London was gradually superseded by New York as the leading market.

Trading is organized in rubber exchanges of the principal rubber markets. The Rubber Exchange in New York, established in 1926 but closed during World War II, deals only in futures contracts. Contracts were traded in for delivery in the current and eleven succeeding months. The contract unit was 10 long tons. Quotations were in cents and hundredths of a cent per pound. During any one day transactions were not permitted at prices varying more than 2 cents above or below the previous closing price. General recognition of many precisely defined grades of the raw material greatly facilitated trading.[3]

The futures market in rubber tended to restrain extreme price fluctuations somewhat and, to some extent, allowed rubber producers and industrial consumers to shift the risks involved in highly unstable prices. It collected and interpreted information on supply and demand trends invaluable not only to the trader but also to the industrial consumer and rubber producer. Nevertheless, its usefulness did not approach that of many other futures markets for it was too small to permit hedging operations by the big rubber-goods manufacturers.

THE USES OF RUBBER

Crude rubber is a remarkably versatile raw material and therefore finds application in the fabrication of a wide variety of goods. In many articles—tubes, hose, boots, waterproof

---

[3] Rubber Manufacturers Association, Inc., *Crude Rubber*, pp. 29–30.

clothing, bathing utensils, contraceptives—rubber is used because of its impermeability to liquids and gases and its singular plasticity. In the electrical field, rubber is applied primarily because of its remarkable resistance to electrical currents. Its elasticity is utilized in the field of mechanical rubber goods. In combination with other qualities, rubber's abrasion-resistance allows the making of satisfactory tires, soles, and conveyor belts. The fabrication of rubber-containing sanitary goods utilizes the ease with which the material can be cleansed with water and antiseptics. Imperviousness to many chemicals makes rubber indispensable in the modern laboratory.

Only a negligible quantity of natural rubber is ultimately consumed in its crude form. In spite of its unique and generally useful qualities, some shortcomings of the material would drastically restrict consumption if articles were made from raw rubber. Its extreme sensitivity to temperature changes and its high chemical reactivity and propensity to age are such shortcomings. If unaltered, even some of rubber's very virtues, such as plasticity, elasticity, and softness, become vices in many forms of use. The arts of vulcanization and compounding wholly or partly remove these undesirable properties and, in addition, impart additional desirable qualities (see p. 13). Many rubber goods contain fabrics and metal parts which give body and shape to the articles and render them more durable.

The first step of the rubber-goods manufacturer is to enhance the plasticity of rubber by "breaking it down." This process is performed by a mechanical operation called mastication. Compounding machines, operating on the principle of a dough mixer, then mix the masticated material with sulphur, gas black, and a great variety of chemicals. The composition of these ingredients depends on the manufacturer's formula for the end-product. Next the compound is shaped into its desired form. If it needs to be sheeted for the further fabricating process, the mass is run through a calender, a machine which consists of three or more smooth steel rolls. The warm plastic is squeezed through these rolls—sometimes, as in tire-building, around a textile fabric. For the manufacture of tubular rubber articles, an extruder machine is used. Often diverse parts thus processed must be assembled. In tire-making, for example, layers of cord fabric are built up over collapsible drums. Finally, the resultant product is vulcanized under pressure and heat.

Different rubber articles contain various amounts of crude rubber. Excluding fabric and metal parts, a bathing cap contains about 83 per cent, in weight, of crepe rubber, a tire carcass 80 per cent of crude rubber (usually three-fourths smoked sheet and one-fourth crepe), a hard comb 67 per cent of smoked sheet, a tire tread 62 per cent of smoked sheet, a black heel 30 per cent of smoked sheet plus 30 per cent of reclaim, black matting 3 per cent of smoked sheet and 42 per cent of reclaim. As most rubber goods also contain fabrics and metal parts, the finished articles contain an even smaller proportion of crude rubber. Thus the average good-quality automobile tire, weighing 22 pounds, contains about 11 pounds of crude rubber and one pound of reclaim. The rest consists of fabric, compounding ingredients, and bead wire.

Statistical information on the division of rubber consumption among various classes of uses is unfortunately quite fragmentary. Detailed and relatively complete data for a number of years have been collected only for the United States. No exact world picture of rubber consumption in various uses can therefore be assembled. Yet a study of United States consumption permits conclusions covering one-half of total world absorptions.

No less than 76.6 per cent of all crude rubber consumed in the United States from 1938 to 1940 went into tires, inner tubes, and tire sundries (see Table 6). The large bulk of this was used in pneumatic tires and tubes. In 1940, for eample, 337,747 tons of crude rubber were consumed in this particular field. Pneumatic automobile tires accounted for about 85 per cent of the total, automobile inner tubes for 12, and farm-tractor tires and tubes for 3 per cent. In 1938–40, production of mechanical rubber goods, such as belting, hose, tubing, insulation products, valves, and gaskets consumed another tenth of the total. Boots and shoes, and rubber heels and soles, took nearly 6½ per cent. The remainder was dispersed over a great variety of articles. Rubberized fabrics include automobile fabrics, raincoats, and hospital sheeting; hard-rubber goods include such items as battery jars and combs; druggists' and medical sundries include water bottles, syringes, nipples, and so forth.

TABLE 6.—UNITED STATES CRUDE-RUBBER ABSORPTION BY PRINCIPAL PRODUCTS, AVERAGE 1938–40*

Article	Metric tons	Percentage of total
Grand total	406,397	100.00
Pneumatic tires and tubes (automobiles and farm tractors)	298,283	73.40
Bicycle tires and tubes....................	2,522	.62
Airplane tires and tubes...................	380	.09
Solid cushion tires........................	626	.15
Tire sundries and repair materials........	9,554	2.35
Total, tires and tire sundries...........	311,364	76.61
Other rubber products:		
Mechanical rubber goods..................	37,506	9.23
Insulated wire and cable compounds.......	6,291	1.55
Rubber flooring	1,160	.29
Sponge rubber	5,764	1.42
Auto and other rubberized fabrics.........	4,253	1.05
Hard rubber goods........................	2,588	.64
Druggist, medical, and surgical supplies...	3,435	.85
Stationers' rubber goods..................	2,044	.50
Bathing apparel and rubber clothing.......	1,100	.27
Boots and shoes...........................	14,709	3.62
Heels and soles...........................	11,376	2.80
Sporting goods, toys, and novelties........	2,082	.51
Miscellaneous rubber sundries.............	2,724	.67
Total, other rubber products...........	95,032	23.39

* Compiled from data in *Statistical Bulletin* (International Rubber Regulation Committee, London), October 1941, VII, 20. See also Appendix Table X.

The diversity of use of crude rubber shifted conspicuously in the interwar period. Even during the decade from 1931 to 1940 such secular changes in specific consumption rates are quite noticeable, despite the simultaneous influence of cyclical factors (see Appendix Table X). Although, with few exceptions, all uses shared in the absolute rise of United States crude-rubber absorption, relative to the entire field some uses declined and others expanded. The reasons for these changes merit brief examination, since they exemplify and shed light on significant transformations in the world rubber demand and its variability.

Perhaps the most striking shift is that, in the recent past, United States crude-rubber consumption has grown much more slowly in the tire-and-tube field than in other fields of rubber use. In the late 1920's the manufacture of tires and inner tubes accounted for about 85 per cent of aggregate absorption. In the late 1930's, this proportion had fallen to about 75 per cent. Conversely, crude-rubber consumption in the aggregate of all other uses increased vigorously. Not all use-groups in this field participated in the general expansion (see Appendix Table X). Consumption in bathing apparel, rubber clothing, and automotive fabrics contracted, while rubber boots and shoes, heels and soles, rubber flooring, stationers' rubber articles, and sporting goods held their own in the general increase of crude-rubber consumption. On the other hand, the use of rubber in the making of insulated wire and cable compounds, druggists' sundries, and some rubberized fabrics showed a proportionate increase. The most conspicuous expansion took place in the fields of mechanical rubber goods, hard-rubber articles, and sponge rubber.

A detailed account of these changes cannot be given here. It must be realized that all these different use-groups comprise many diverse single items and that the consumption trends exhibited by these items may have differed in direction and strength from the composite group-trend.

The general factors responsible for these divergent trends are manifold. Where consumption rose rapidly, new uses were discovered or old uses expanded for a variety of reasons. The quality and, therefore, the usability of the rubber article may have been improved, its price cut, its popularity enhanced; or the use may have expanded automatically with the consumption of the entire commodity of which the rubber article is a constituent part. This combination of causes applies particularly in the field of mechanical rubber articles and sponge rubber. Where consumption remained relatively stationary, the secular growth of consumption may have come to an end, the market became satiated, and production was for replacement demand only. Rubber boots and shoes, heels and soles, and stationers' rubber articles are good examples of this stage. Where consumption declined, specific crude-rubber uses may have met with the competition of better and/or cheaper rival materials, such as plastics and reclaimed and artificial rubbers, or technical improvements of fabrication either improved the durability of the article or permitted a reduction in the amount of crude rubber required to give equally satisfactory service.

CHART 6.—UNITED STATES TIRE AND TUBE PRODUCTION, SHIPMENT, AND STOCKS, AND INDEX OF INDUSTRIAL PRODUCTION, ANNUALLY, 1921–40*

(Million units; per cent of 1935–39 average; logarithmic vertical scale)

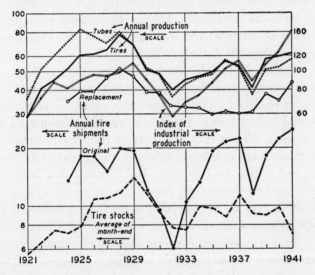

* Data from *Survey of Current Business, 1942 Supplement*, pp. 7, 161.

The operation of changing and diverse trends affecting crude-rubber consumption in the United States can also be observed in the tire-and-tube field, still by far the outstanding use-group. Identification of these trends will help to explain why consumption growth in this field slowed down in the 1930's. This deceleration is, of course, reflected in the production of automobile tires and tubes (see Chart 6). With the advent and growing popularity of the motor vehicle, tire- and tube-production rose by leaps and bounds during the first two decades of the present century. Making due allowance for fluctuations in stocks, the rapid expansion of tire production culminated just before the onset of the Great Depression in 1929–30. Thereafter the output curve flattened out and even declined slightly.

Tire shipments are conveniently broken down into three classes: original equipment for new automobiles, replacement equipment for used vehicles, and exports. Chart 6 shows clearly that tire shipments for original equipment flattened out after the late 1920's but suggests the continuation of a slight average increase. On the other hand, tire shipments for replacement and export definitely contracted in the 1930's. The decline in replacement sales reflects the fact that the life expectancy of the average tire was enhanced. Though fluctuating with the trend of business conditions, the average age of the registered car increased during the last decade.

The secular decline in the production of inner tubes is far more conspicuous than the slight contraction of tire production. The output of tubes attained its climax as early as the middle 1920's and subsequently exhibits a striking downward trend. In 1922 about 15 per cent of all crude rubber consumed in the United States went into inner tubes. Fifteen years later the percentage had fallen to less than 10.[4] Again, the development reflects a marked increase in the durability of the average tube.

A brief survey of the variable underlying conditions of tire and tube consumption corroborates and further elucidates these trends. To a considerable extent the rapid expansion of tire production into the late 1920's and the subsequent slight contraction was paralleled by changing production rates in the automobile industry of the United States (see Chart 7). The swift rise of passenger-car output during the first quarter of the century was climaxed by a peak in the late 1920's followed by a small average decrease. Including 1941, no single year surpassed the production record of 1929, nor does any subsequent two- or three-year period average a larger output than that of the late 1920's. In the phase of the 1930's the market for new passenger automobiles had become saturated. Roughly speak-

---

[4] P. W. Barker, *Rubber Industry of the United States, 1839–1939* (U.S. Dept. Comm., Bur. Foreign and Domestic Comm., Trade Promotion Series 197, 1939), p. 25.

ing, new production was for the replacement market. The
growth trend in passenger-car manufacture thus approximates
the growth trend in tire production.

CHART 7.—UNITED STATES MOTOR VEHICLE PRODUCTION AND
REGISTRATION, AND INDEX OF INDUSTRIAL PRODUCTION,
ANNUALLY, 1900–40*

(Thousand units; per cent of 1935-39 av.; logarithmic vertical scale)

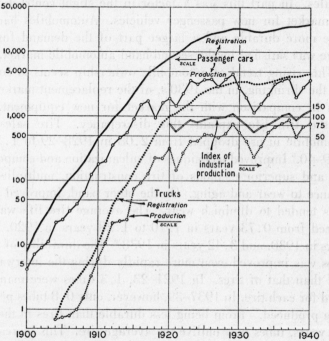

* Data from Automobile Manufacturers Association, *Automobile Facts and Figures, 1941*
(Detroit), pp. 4, 11; *Survey of Current Business, 1942 Supplement*, p. 7.

On the other hand, the production of motor trucks did not
cease expanding in the late 1920's (see Chart 7). Following
the Great Depression, expansion continued in the 1930's. In
1925–29 trucks accounted for 13 per cent, in 1937–41 for
nearly 20 per cent of all motor vehicles produced. Since more
crude rubber is absorbed in the average truck tire than in the
average passenger-car tire, the continued rise in truck production tended to increase rubber absorption in the tire-and-tube

field. However, other factors, to be mentioned shortly, offset this trend.

Chart 7 also reveals that the growth of automobile ownership continued beyond the 1920's. The total of registered automobiles in the United States was larger in the late 1930's than in the corresponding period of the preceding decade. Again, the increase is greater for motor trucks than for passenger automobiles. In part this was a factor in the slight contraction of the market for new passenger vehicles. Automobiles had become more durable and a larger part of the demand for car usage was satisfied by the second-hand automobile market.

This rising trend of automobile ownership seems to contradict the shrinking, in the 1930's, of the replacement market for tires in comparison with the market for new equipment. Increased tire life explains this discrepancy. Tire sales per automobile in use dropped from 2.08 in 1928–29 to 1.17 in 1939–40.[5] Improved techniques of vulcanization and compounding, and superior methods of tire construction, multiplied resistance to wear and aging. On the other hand, improved highways tended to diminish wear. The average tire life was enhanced from 0.73 years in 1910 to 1.28 years in 1920, 2.47 years in 1930, and 3.42 years in 1938.[6] The durability of inner tubes was improved even more rapidly during the interwar period than that of tires. In 1921–23, 1.3 tubes were manufactured for each tire. In 1937–39, however, only 0.8 tubes per tire were produced.[7] From being less durable than tires in the earlier years, tubes now outlive the average tire. This increase in the life-expectancy of tubes is predominantly responsible for the decline of crude-rubber absorption in the tube field in the 1930's (see Appendix Table X).[8]

In addition to superior tire-manufacturing techniques, improvement in tire-repairing techniques also increased the life-

---

[5] E. B. Alderfer and H. E. Michl, *Economics of American Industry* (New York, 1942), p. 277.

[6] *Rubber News Letter*, Oct. 15, 1939, p. 199.

[7] Data from *Survey of Current Business* (U.S. Dept. Comm., Bur. Foreign and Domestic Comm.), successive issues.

[8] Inner tubes also benefited from the fact that in consequence of better tire and automobile construction they were decreasingly exposed to strain.

expectancy of the average tire. The advent of tire reconditioning is especially noteworthy. Only beginning in the middle 1930's were recapping and retreading techniques perfected and facilities introduced on a large scale. It has been estimated that 3.6 million tires were retreaded in 1937, 5.6 million in 1939, and about 7 million in 1941.[9] In peacetime, the chief retreading material (camelback) was made of reclaim and crude rubber. This development was, therefore, accompanied by a notable increase of crude-rubber consumption in tire-repair materials (see Appendix Table X).

Two other factors negatively influenced the consumption of crude rubber in the tire field. One was the partial substitution of reclaim for crude rubber. No data are available that would permit an approximate appraisal of this trend. But compared with the early days of tire construction, the admixture of reclaim to the tire mixture in the late 1920's and in the 1930's tended to reduce crude-rubber requirements. The other factor was the gradual disappearance of the use of solid and cushion tires for trucks and busses. In 1922 about 7.5 per cent of all crude rubber consumed in the United States went into this use.[10] By 1940 the percentage had fallen to 0.18 (Appendix Table X).

These consumption-decreasing factors would have produced a far greater diminution of crude rubber use in the tire-and-tube field, had it not been for the simultaneous operation of circumstances tending to increase rubber consumption. In the 1930's, these conflicting elements largely offset each other.

Most important in the rising consumption trend was the gradually increasing total and rubber weight per tire and tube. While the diameter of the wheel became smaller, the tire in contrast became bulkier and heavier. From 7.72 pounds of rubber in 1922 the average rubber weight was increased to 13.73 pounds in 1937. Similarly, the rubber weight of the average inner tube grew from 1.78 to 2.20 pounds over the same period.[11] The increasing use of heavy motor trucks operated in the same direction.

[9] *Rubber News Letter*, Jan. 31, 1940, p. 20, and Sept. 15, 1940, p. 160; U.S. Tariff Comm., *Rubber*, p. 12.

[10] Barker, *op. cit.*, p. 25.   [11] *Rubber News Letter*, Nov. 15, 1938, pp. 6–7.

Improved automobiles and better roads permitted and encouraged faster driving and so increased tire wear. This tended to expand the replacement demand for tires. Furthermore, while fluctuating somewhat with the broad trend of business conditions, the average mileage covered annually by the average motor vehicle increased markedly throughout the interwar period. The gradual rise in gasoline consumption per automobile confirms this trend and suggests its weight (see Chart 8). The

CHART 8.—INDEXES OF UNITED STATES GASOLINE CONSUMPTION PER CAR, RATIO OF TRUCK TO PASSENGER CAR REGISTRATION, AND INDUSTRIAL PRODUCTION, ANNUALLY, 1920–40*

(*Average 1920–40 = 100*)

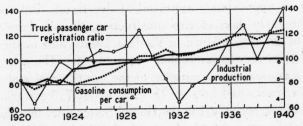

* Based on data from *Automobile Facts and Figures, 1941*, pp. 11, 45; *Survey of Current Business, 1942 Supplement*, p. 7.

ᵃ Actual consumption in hundred gallons shown by inset scale at right.

average annual gasoline consumption per motor vehicle was 484 gallons in 1920–22, but it was 724 in 1938–40. Part of the increase was undoubtedly due to expanding proportion of motor trucks and busses in the total automobile fleet of the United States. This qualification, however, still allows for a considerable net increase in the gasoline consumption of and, hence, annual mileage traveled by the average motor vehicle (see Chart 8).[12]

Finally, the expanding use of airplanes opened up a new field of tire-and-tube consumption. Yet though this use-field grew rapidly in importance in the 1930's (see Appendix Table

[12] It might be contended that modern automobiles are heavier and operate at higher speeds than earlier models and that these factors accounted for the increase in gasoline consumption. Yet these conditions were offset by the improvements effected in fuels and in engine construction and operation.

X, its capacity for crude-rubber absorption remained negligible compared with total consumption. In 1940, only 0.14 per cent of all crude rubber absorbed in the United States went into airplane tires and tubes.

The division of crude-rubber consumption in other industrially advanced countries is very roughly similar to but by no means identical with that in the United States. Exact data are unavailable. But it is estimated that in the middle 1930's only about 60 per cent of all rubber absorbed outside the United States went into tires and tubes,[13] as against about 76 per cent in the United States. Outside the tire-and-tube field, other uses in these countries more nearly approached their corresponding level in the United States. A very rough computation reveals that in 1933–35 United States consumption of crude rubber other than in tires and tubes was approximately 1.6 pounds per capita while it was 5.5 pounds in the tire-and-tube field. On the other hand, in a sampling of industrially advanced European countries,[14] the respective per capita figures were 0.9 and 1.4 pounds.[15]

This striking discrepancy between the two sets of consumption figures reflects the marked difference in national wealth and per capita real income. Crude rubber is a relatively inexpensive material and most rubber articles are relatively inexpensive consumer goods (e.g., rubber-impregnated clothing, boots, soles and heels, hose, druggists' sundries, stationers' supplies). Automobile tires and tubes, on the other hand, are constituent parts of a relatively very expensive consumer commodity. The lagging use of passenger automobiles outside the United States is, indeed, primarily a consequence of lower per capita real incomes. Other major contributing factors are the much higher costs of automobiles as well as of operating and servicing ex-

[13] George Rae, "Statistics of the Rubber Industry," *Journal of the Royal Statistical Society* (London), 1938, Vol. CI, Pt. II, p. 341.

[14] The sample includes the United Kingdom, Germany, France, Italy, Sweden, Norway, Denmark, Belgium, the Netherlands, Switzerland, Austria, and Czechoslovakia. Together with the United States these countries accounted for 91 per cent of world rubber absorption.

[15] Rubber data from Appendix Tables III and IV; *Statistical Bulletin* (International Rubber Regulation Committee, London), Dec. 1937, III, 16. Population data (estimates for Dec. 31, 1935) from League of Nations, Economic Intelligence Service, *Statistical Year-Book, 1936/37,* 1937. II. A. 7 (Geneva, 1937), pp. 15, 18.

penses. In addition, there are miscellaneous minor factors varying from country to country. Some countries show a relative lack of serviceable roads. In others the need for individual transportation may be less urgent because of abundant public means of conveyance and shorter distances to be covered. Easy forms of instalment-buying are usually less developed than in the United States. The possession of an automobile as a symbol of prestige is socially more restricted than in the United States. There may also be differences in spending patterns and consumption preferences.

The size of national automobile fleets varies with the incidence of these complex factors. The density of automobile ownership in the United States—one car for every four persons—is closely approached only in such comparably wealthy countries as New Zealand, Australia, and Canada. There are six persons per automobile in New Zealand and eight each in Canada and Australia. But the corresponding figure is 17 for France, 388 for Japan, 1,283 for Bulgaria, and 6,782 for China. Where vehicles serve as a means of production rather than consumption, as do motor trucks, the difference between the United States and the rest of the world is revealingly less conspicuous. In 1939, for example, 71 per cent of the world's passenger automobiles, but only 54 per cent of the world's trucks, were registered in the United States.

Both the bicycle and the motorcycle are stronger competitors of the automobile in Europe than in the United States. Bicycles afford a cheap form of individual transportation, and quite frequently they are used because their operation is cheaper than the use of public means of conveyance. The motorcycle again offers a means of individual transportation which is less convenient but cheaper than automobile use. Not only are operation and service costs lower than for automobiles, but the cost of the motorcycle in relation to the cost of an automobile is lower in Europe than in the United States.

While this tremendous difference in automobile usage explains the structure of world rubber consumption, the progressive shrinking of the difference during the interwar period is equally important for the understanding of world consumption trends. Chart 9 shows that in the middle and late 1920's the total registered stock of passenger automobiles in the rest of the world expanded faster than that in the United States. In the 1930's, moreover, when expansion in the United States occurred at but a slow and halting pace, it continued strongly outside this country. Though slowing down in 1938, the last prewar year, the growth trend in the rest of the world exhibited no sign of ending. The same conditions prevailed with motor trucks.

CHART 9.—MOTOR VEHICLE REGISTRATION IN THE UNITED STATES AND OTHER COUNTRIES, ANNUALLY, 1922–39*

(Thousand units; logarithmic vertical scale)

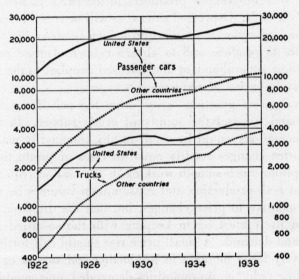

* Data from *Automobile Facts and Figures, 1940*, p. 21.

It may be concluded that crude rubber is used in a complex variety of consumption fields, that the structure of consumption varies from country to country all over the world, and that structural changes in consumption patterns have taken place throughout the history of rubber use. All these factors have significant implications for the variability, over time, of the world's demand for rubber.

CHAPTER IV

ECONOMIC CHARACTERISTICS OF THE RUBBER MARKET: VARIABILITY OF SUPPLY AND DEMAND

Concern over extremely low and, at times, wildly fluctuating prices gave rise to insistent demands for control measures on the part of crude-rubber producers in the early 1920's and in the early 1930's. Depressed prices, as will be seen in chapter v, were the consequence of disequilibrium between the world's capacities to produce and to absorb rubber. Output capacity had become superabundant and released supplies to the market generally in excess of requirements.

Violent price gyrations arose from the peculiar nature of the demand for and the supply of crude rubber. In theory, price fluctuations would be small in any commodity market in which price changes readily equalize rates of production and consumption. Such smooth working of the market requires not only that both production and consumption volumes be reasonably responsive to price changes, but that the direction of the response itself must be in keeping with the so-called law of supply and demand. A small price rise should call forth either a relatively large increase in production and supply or a corresponding reduction in quantities demanded, or a combination of the two. Similarly, a fall in price should bring about inverse responses.

The purpose of the present chapter is to explain why the crude-rubber market does not work along the lines of the postulated market mechanism and why prices, therefore, tend to exhibit considerable swings. We shall see that, facing a falling price level, production fails to contract materially and, confronted with rising prices, its expansion is relatively slow and confined in scope to the limits of existing output capacity. On the other side, rubber consumption is very unresponsive to

58

changes in the price of rubber. Variations in the total consumption volume are determined chiefly by the changing level of industrial activity and by growth trends in the different fields of rubber use. World stocks may for a time absorb differences between the rates of production and consumption, but this capacity is limited.

THE NATURE OF SUPPLY

Crude-rubber production is a variable affected by many diverse conditions. Major and minor, regular and irregular, short-term and long-term influences determine the flow of supplies from the producing areas. For convenience the following discussion focuses first on the short-run and then on the longer-run factors. The former comprise conditions affecting production rates, the latter those affecting basic production capacity. The two pictures must, of course, be viewed as superimposed one upon the other. Both sets of conditions are at work simultaneously; the dividing line between them is uncertain, and one flows imperceptibly into the other.

Short-term variability of supply.—Rubber differs essentially from most other tree crops. Once Hevea trees have attained maturity, and until they die, latex production is not periodic but continuous. Unlike fruit and most agricultural crops, moreover, rubber shows no variegated sequence of poor and good crops. The flow of latex is relatively even from year to year.

To be sure, the factor of periodicity is not completely absent, but its effect on the supply of crude rubber from the producing areas is not of major importance. During the "wintering" period which follows soon after the dry season and lasts from three to six months, Hevea trees shed their leaves and grow new ones. Then yields decline while latex is drawn into the new foliage, but production does not cease. It has been calculated, for example, that monthly estate output in British Malaya averages 7.5 per cent of annual production during "wintering" and 8.8 per cent during the remainder of the year.[1] Such sea-

---

[1] Data from U.S. Dept. Comm., Bur. Foreign and Domestic Comm., *Seasonal Trends of Rubber Production* (Trade Information Bulletin No. 804, 1932), p. 23.

sonal differences in production are more pronounced in Ceylon and British India than in the major producing countries of British Malaya and the Netherlands Indies.

With a time lag of about two months, these seasonal variations in output show up slightly in the flow of exports. Only when maximum production is required does the total effect become very marked. Since "wintering" is of regular occurrence, estate producers and dealers can anticipate it and normally arrange for fairly regular shipments throughout the year. The effect of "wintering" on total crude-rubber exports is also subdued because it does not take place simultaneously in all the producing areas. Varying with geographical location, it occurs from December to February in Ceylon and British India, from February to April in British Malaya, northern Sumatra, French Indo-China, and Thailand; from July to October in Java; from August to October in southern Sumatra; and from March to June in the Amazon Valley.

In nearly all fields of agricultural production, a crop unharvested is a crop lost. Substantially this is also true of crude-rubber production, since the continuous formation of latex by the tree occurs in response to tapping. Yet intermittent suspension of tapping "rests" the tree and, when tapping is subsequently resumed, the latex flow is for a time greater in volume and richer in solid rubber particles. This phenomenon is called "flush production." To this slight extent, the tree can store a crop. However, the extra yield accruing in flush production normally does not make up for the latex not harvested during "resting." Furthermore, a rest period lasting beyond three or four months has no effect on the subsequent yield.

In addition to these biological conditions, miscellaneous minor factors may regularly or occasionally influence rubber production. There are, of course, certain vagaries of nature. Drought conditions tend to make "wintering" more severe, since refoliation is retarded. Rain in the morning interferes with tapping, because it coagulates the latex as it exudes from the incision and stops the flow. Very rainy periods may encourage pests and plant diseases which, in turn, decrease latex production. The periodic holding of native festivals and the occurrence

of epidemics and labor troubles, particularly strikes, also influence output.

Economically most important is the response of producers
to marked and protracted changes in prices. Here we must distinguish between estate producers and two categories of small
holders whose behavior is typically different. Such behavior
classifications are of course rough, since there are diverse individual reactions within each group.

How does the average estate producer behave in the face of
a sharply falling price level? According to the simple dictate
of the law of supply and demand, producers should curtail supplies to the market and thus exert an upward pressure on prices.
Chart 10 shows that the average estate producer in 1929–32 did

CHART 10.—ESTATE AND NATIVE RUBBER PRODUCTION IN MALAYA AND
THE NETHERLANDS INDIES, AND CRUDE-RUBBER PRICES AT
SINGAPORE, ANNUALLY, 1929–34*

(Thousand tons; Straits cents per pound; logarithmic vertical scale)

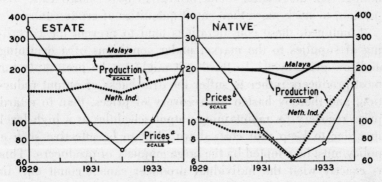

* Data from George Rae, "The Statistics of the Rubber Industry," *Journal of the Royal
Statistical Society* (London), 1938, vol. CI, Pt. II, p. 324.

  a Ribbed smoked sheets.
  b Medium blanket.

not follow this policy pattern. Supplies coming forth from estates in British Malaya remained substantially at the same level
throughout the period 1929–34. The minor adjustment exhibited by estate production in the Netherlands Indies must be attributed largely to the fact that a sizable number of Dutch estates have rubber interplanted with other crops. There are

several weighty reasons for this reluctance to diminish outputs of rubber estates.

(1) Foremost is the high proportion of relatively rigid overhead costs in total production costs (see pp. 28–30). They can be compressed, but there are limits to their plasticity. Per unit of output, these "sticky" cost items diminish as production expands, and mount as output is reduced. (2) Except for the minor benefit of "flush production," latex untapped is latex irretrievably lost. (3) Reliance on coolie workers, usually recruited at producers' expense from a distance and often employed under long-term contracts, renders estate producers reluctant to disband part of their labor staff. Should a sudden turn in the market occur, they would lose time and incur expenses in recruiting and training new workmen. (4) The difficulty of forecasting the trend of the rubber market not only prevents planned and quick adjustments in estate labor forces, but also makes the accumulation of estate stocks a hazardous undertaking. On the whole, estate producers have shown little disposition to stock more than small quantities of crude rubber.

Combined, these considerations tend to prevent the curtailing of supplies to the market under conditions of a declining and low price level. In theory, it might yet be preferable for most producers rather to suffer the drawbacks of output reduction, and thereby hasten the recovery of prices, than to retard price recovery by maintaining output schedules at a high level in order to keep unit costs down. But to be effective such a policy must be adopted by the large majority of producers. This is exactly what the individual producer cannot count on. In view of the multiplicity of producing units scattered over half a dozen major producing countries and comprising distinct types of enterprises, concerted action is almost impossible to achieve on a voluntary basis. Even when, in the past, planters' associations organized tapping holidays, such efforts were abortive because of insufficient participation and inadequate observance of accepted rules (pp. 92, 106–07).

The cumulative result of all these circumstances is that declining prices fail to check the flow of supplies substantially. As the price of rubber falls toward the level of prime or direct costs, steps are taken to reduce the less rigid items of fixed costs. Maintenance work is curtailed, staff bonuses are suspended, salaries are slashed. Prime costs also are lowered by cutting wage rates and reducing tapping costs per unit of output, sometimes by selectively tapping high-yielding trees or stands only, sometimes by maintaining tapping operations on a maximum scale, sometimes even by resort to overtapping. The area for adjustment of costs is large. Only when all costs have been depressed to a minimum and prices fall to the level of drastically reduced prime costs is, theoretically speaking, the limit of this area reached.

As we have indicated, not all estates follow identical policies. But even relatively fixed costs are, in practice, subject to considerable manipulation. Many may suspend tapping on all or part of their acreage or lengthen periods between tapping operations. Yet reluctance and failure to contract output in the face of falling prices is predominant—exactly how predominant and how persevering depends on the specific situation of industry and market. Thus the general conclusion seems justified: estate-rubber production is highly unresponsive to a falling price of rubber. In practice, costs are much more responsive than supply.

The estate industry's responsiveness to a rising market is basically more in keeping with theoretically correct market behavior, but it too is limited in total scope and speed. The scope of adjustment to a rising market is, of course, limited by existing production capacity. Expansion of capacity requires many years, and biological factors militate against a rigorous overstraining of existing plantation capacity. Lest they exhaust and harm their trees, producers are loath to resort to severe tapping schedules. It must also be realized that, beyond a certain point, output expansion may become unprofitable for the individual producer since some direct costs tend to rise with increasing production schedules, especially in times of generally expanding business activity.[2] This is particularly true of the costs of recruiting additional labor.

[2] See Bauer, "Notes on Costs," *Economica*, New Series, May 1945, XII, 93–94.

Confronted with a sudden expansion of the total demand volume and suddenly rising prices, supply response tends to be slow because it takes time to recruit additional labor forces over a great distance. Again, the difficulty of forecasting the future of the market may act as a retarding factor. Employers are inclined to be cautious if they apprehend a sudden reversal of the market situation by the time they would have incurred recruiting and training expenses for the expansion of their labor staff. Beside the ordinary time lag between increased production and increased supplies in the consuming countries, it is this "sticky" labor situation which tends to make supply relatively slow to expand in the face of sharply rising prices.

Unlike estate producers, native small holders do not carry the burden of large fixed investments, unless the necessity of making a living is so regarded. Invariable overhead costs, if not entirely absent, are small. Nor do they employ labor forces recruited at their expense from distant areas. The conditions which prompt their behavior toward a changing market, therefore, differ materially from those that fashion the reactions of estate producers.

There is, however, no approximate identity of response among the native rubber planters of Malaysia. One rather finds two basic types—with gradations between—whose outlook is determined primarily by the extent to which their livelihood depends on the sale of crude rubber (see p. 32).

(see p. 32)

The majority of small holders in British Malaya, and in other producing countries under British control, derive their living chiefly or wholly from the sale of crude rubber. In addition, they have to meet small fixed charges (quit rent and taxes) in cash. Confronted with a sagging price level, this type of peasant planter is inclined to maintain output and, for a time, even perhaps expand it through more severe tapping. He wants to maintain a minimum cash income, and to this end is willing to put in more effort. Since his costs are reckoned chiefly in his own labor, his "cost" level is remarkably flexible.

He hesitates to shift to the production of food for two reasons. First, in many producing areas there is little suitable land available for the growing of rice, his staple food. Second, the price of rice, like that of rubber, falls during a period of general business depression. Thus, with the exception of 1932, the small holder of western and southern Malaya could, throughout the Great Depression, secure more rice by producing rubber than by growing rice himself. Only at the bottom of the slump did this type of native planter curtail production to some extent. Then he tried to get along with less income and, in numerous cases, devoted part of his labor outlay to the production of food crops. Chart 10 shows this resistance to output curtailment during the depression years of the early 1930's. By and large, production on the part of this type of small holder is only slightly more responsive to a protracted price fall than is estate production.

The native producer who grows rubber only as a source of supplementary cash income makes a quite different response to a falling market. The majority of the native rubber planters in the Netherlands Indies belong to this category. Their fixed costs are virtually nil. As rubber prices become less and less rewarding, these producers gradually contract output and, finally, may stop production altogether. The pursuit of diversified farming, and especially the growing of rice, gives them an economically strong position which, in turn, affords scope for adjustment. Two additional factors reinforce this pattern of reaction. Since tappers are hired locally on the basis of sharing in the total quantity of the rubber harvested, low prices tend to become gradually so unattractive that they discontinue tapping. Furthermore, prices received for their produce by the natives in Sumatra and Borneo are generally lower than those received by the small holders in British Malaya and Ceylon, because of higher transportation costs and inferior quality. As rubber prices decline, therefore, they become unremunerative in the Netherlands Indies sooner than in British Malaya and Ceylon.

As a result of these factors, there is a gradual tapering-off of production as prices drop. Charts 10 (p. 61) and 11 bring out clearly how price-responsive the production of this type of small holder is. The sharp contraction of their output in the early 1930's is all the more remarkable because their productive capacity in terms of total Hevea acreage rose throughout the period considered.

CHART 11.—TAPPABLE RUBBER AREA, RUBBER EXPORTS, AND CALCULATED PER UNIT INCOME OF NETHERLANDS INDIES NATIVE PRODUCERS, ANNUALLY, 1931–36*

(Thousand acres; thousand tons; U.S. cents per pound; logarithmic vertical scale)

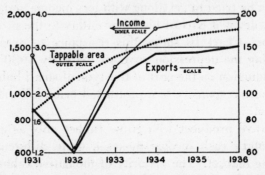

* Data from Rae, *op. cit.*, p. 320; E. G. Holt, *Pre-war Costs of Production for Plantation Rubber*, in U.S. War Production Board, Office of Rubber Director, *Special Report . . . . on the Synthetic Rubber Program* (Aug. 31, 1944), Appendix A, p. 17.

The response of native production as a whole to a rising price level also differs from that of estate production. Since small holders are not generally dependent upon labor recruited over large distances, their output will rise more swiftly in response to rapidly rising prices. (See Chart 10, p. 61.) Temporarily, some native producers may even resort to overtapping. As a rule, however, the native cannot be counted upon to keep production at a maximum level for long periods of time. In this respect cultural traits cause the native to behave differently from the capitalistic estate. The modesty of his needs and desires beyond what he is accustomed to expect in prosperous years, and his relative unfamiliarity with the institution of saving combine to check prolonged maximum efforts.

Viewing crude-rubber production as a whole, one may conclude that supply to a *falling* market is relatively unresponsive to price and so accelerates the downward trend of prices. Response to a *rising* market is also somewhat sluggish and therefore often fails to arrest sharp price rises in time. During the interwar period, native producers who responded readily to price changes contributed too little to the total production to affect the aggregate supply situation materially. Similarly, the supply of wild rubber, also relatively price-responsive (see pp. 11–12), was so small as to be negligible in the total picture.

Long-term variability of supply.—This involves adaptability of supply capacity to secular changes in world absorption. The question concerns not only variability of supply but also, ultimately, variability of investment in production capacity. Under free-market conditions, inadequate capacity will lead to a rise in price and redundant capacity to a decline, thus evoking the immediate producers' reactions described above. What are the ultimate reactions?

TABLE 7.—NEW RUBBER PLANTINGS AND NEW YORK CRUDE RUBBER PRICES, AVERAGES 1900–1933*

Period	Additional planted area annual average (*Thousand acres*)		Average annual price (*Cents per pound*)
	Estates	Natives	
1900–09	439[a]	78[a]	109.8
1910–14	219	117	123.4
1915–19	174	169	63.8
1920–24	88	95	25.4
1925–28	215	375[b]	63.0
1929–33	130	78[b]	9.2

* Compiled from George Rae, "Statistics of the Rubber Industry," *Journal of the Royal Statistical Society* (London), 1938, Vol. CI, Pt. II, p. 320; *Commodities in Industry: The 1940 Commodity Year Book* (Commodity Research Bur., Inc., New York, 1940), p. 529.

[a] Total area under plantation, 1909.
[b] Underestimated (see McFadyean, *op. cit.*, p. 83.

As Table 7 indicates, there is a direct relationship between new plantings and the long-run trend of rubber prices. A high price level encourages, a low one discourages, additions to total plantation capacity. The apparent simplicity of this pattern, however, is somewhat illusory. Within the quarter-century preceding World War I, the rubber-plantation industry passed quickly through the phases of infancy and adolescence. Yet, growing by leaps and bounds, it was scarcely able to keep pace with the swift secular rise in consumption. On the whole, investment seemed without risk and profits were spectacular.

By the end of World War I, production capacity had caught up with absorption capacity. Both continued to grow thereafter, but it became increasingly clear in the early 1920's that the speed with which output capacity expanded was out of proportion to the concurrent rise of absorption. Increments in production capacity were the automatic outcome of new plantings made at least five or six years earlier. It is this time lag between the planting and maturing of trees that renders price a rather inadequate guide for investment in additional capacity. Indeed, the time lag is even more considerable than is suggested by the average age of tappability—from five to six years after planting—for the yield per tree gradually increases until it reaches full maturity.

Under such circumstances, investment in new capacity becomes a very speculative affair. This is especially true for the estate producer, whose capital outlay is exceedingly large. He cannot be certain that a particular price situation on which he bases his decision to invest will obtain six to twelve years later, or that average prices will be high enough to make his investment profitable. Another factor renders price an unreliable regulator of investment. This is the tendency to overcompensation which results from the relative similarity in reaction patterns, information, and outlook of a great multiplicity of producers. A simultaneous response leading to capacity expansion will easily result in overexpansion.

Both these factors were at work in the large plantation additions made in 1925–28. The high prices of the period by no means reflected inadequate supply capacity. They were mainly the result of an artificial scarcity of supplies created by the Stevenson control scheme (see pp. 98–101). Nevertheless, new plantings were undertaken on a very large scale both by estate and native producers. Overcompensation was obviously involved. By the time these new acreages came into production, in the early 1930's, rubber prices were exceedingly low because of temporarily depressed absorption and excess capacity.

The increase in native plantations in the middle and late 1920's is amazing. As the table (p. 67) indicates, the native rubber planter, like the estate producer, was guided by changes in the price level. Indeed, being less able or less inclined to speculate on the future trend of the market, his planting activities are more likely to be determined by current profit than those of the estate producer. Although he risks no large capital outlays when planting additional land to Hevea, he shuns the necessary labor when current rubber prices seem unrewarding. However, a price level which appears relatively unattractive to the investor in rubber estates may still seem profitable to the average small holder.

The importance of adequate information on consumption and production trends is another lesson of the investment boom of 1925–28. While forecasting would remain a hazardous undertaking in any case, the collection, publication, and scrutiny of rubber absorption data in major consuming countries would somewhat improve the estimates of the forecaster. Assembly and analysis of planting and production data would help in estimating accretions of production capacity from year to year. Detailed and well-publicized information on current planting activities should blunt the tendency toward overcompensation. Unfortunately, these sources of information were unavailable or not conveniently accessible in the late 1920's.

Throughout the 1930's the rubber-plantation industry was encumbered by excess production capacity, even though from 1934 new planting and replanting were strictly limited by international regulation. It should be emphasized that, because of the increasing use of vastly improved planting stock, replenishment or expansion of output capacity cannot be measured by acreage alone. Replanting to improved budded stock or selected seeds of a plantation formerly in ordinary seedlings results in an increase of yield per areal unit and hence of output capacity.

Once total production capacity exceeds average absorption, capacity contraction is not easily accomplished. The estate plantation represents very large investments. This capital is fixed, since a rubber plantation obviously cannot be converted to other uses. The "economic life" of the trees, representing the great bulk of the investment, is very long. Abandonment of an estate therefore would mean prodigious losses to investors.

Among native producers, the majority see no alternative uses for their land planted to Hevea. For a while, when prices are abysmally low, they may temporarily abandon their plantations but, even over a period of time, this does not result in substantial reduction of output capacity. Adjustment was all the more difficult during the period concerned, since only very small acreages of Hevea became obsolete on account of old age.

The existence of marked surplus capacity in the early 1930's led to a fight for survival. All cost items were compressed to the barest minimum and available financial reserves were used to continue the struggle. Even when the relatively poor-yielding plantations of an estate were left unharvested, this was a temporary measure only. As soon as prices improved sufficiently to cover prime costs, it would again become profitable to tap these stands. Nevertheless, while many estate companies operated at a loss, few went bankrupt.

In addition to the fear of disinvestment involving capital sacrifice, the determined struggle of estate companies for survival was also spurred by the hope that consumption would eventually catch up with production capacity and that the intervening period might be made more bearable by international export restriction. Compulsory regulation became a reality in 1934, but average consumption did not catch up with output capacity during the 1930's.

There can be no profitable speculation on what exactly would have happened in the absence of the International Rubber Regulation Agreement (IRRA). It is safe to surmise, however, that the less efficient and financially weaker estate companies would have succumbed after a prolonged period of distress for the entire industry. Even so, wholesale bankruptcy would not have meant destruction of the output capacity of the companies concerned. Most if not all of their plantations would have been taken over by other interests and, with greatly reduced fixed costs, returned to production as soon as the new cost-price relationship permitted. Also, very low prices over a long period should have engendered some widening of rubber use.

It may be concluded, then, that capacity curtailment of the rubber-plantation industry faces powerful obstacles. Large capital investments, the longevity of the rubber tree and, once mature, its ability to exist without much care, render such contraction a very slow process. On the other hand, expansion of consumption may be seriously retarded because of the length of time required for the "growing" of additional capacity. As the history of rubber prices indicates, this happened early in the present century, but there has been no repetition since plantation rubber became well established.

VARIABILITY OF ABSORPTION

The long-term variability of crude-rubber absorption was discussed in the preceding chapter (pp. 47–57). The secular trend of rubber consumption in the aggregate and in various use categories was surveyed and significant factors were brought out which tended toward expansion or diminution of consumption. The following discussion is therefore confined largely to the problem of short-term variability. Which factors determine variations in consumption volume? Is price, in particular, an important or unimportant determinant?

Only a negligible proportion of crude rubber is consumed in raw form. The large bulk is used as one material among others in the fabrication of rubber articles which, in turn, often are only a part or parts of finished producers' and consumers' goods. Long-term factors apart, variations in the volume of consumption of crude rubber will primarily depend, first, on the relative proportion of the value of the finished product represented by the cost of rubber; second, on the substitutability of reclaim for crude rubber; and, third, on the nature of the demand for the finished products that contain rubber.

These problems will be examined with primary reference to the United States, since the fragmentary data are more abundant for this country than for others. Also, rubber consumption in the automotive field will be appraised separately from other uses of the material. Accounting for more than three-fourths of United States rubber absorption, consumption in tires and tubes is of preponderant concern. Unfortunately, many of our conclusions will have to be based on *a priori* reasoning because of the complexity of the factors which determine rubber consumption and which, on account of the scarcity of data, cannot be statistically separated from one another.

Even aside from inventory problems, changes in the price of crude rubber are of great importance to the manufacturers of tires and tubes. In six biennial census years from 1929 to 1939, the cost of rubber ranged from 13 to 33 per cent of the total factory sales value of tires and tubes. Chart 12 shows

CHART 12.—VALUE OF RUBBER USED RELATIVE TO VALUE OF RUBBER MANUFACTURES, AND INDEXES OF COST OF RUBBER AND OF TIRE PRICES IN THE UNITED STATES, BIENNIALLY, 1929–39*

(Percentages; indexes on 1929–39 base)

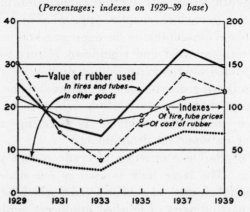

* Data from U.S. Dept. Comm., Bur. Census, *Biennial Census of Manufactures,* successive issues; *Survey of Current Business, 1942 Supplement,* p. 20.

that this proportion fluctuated closely with the cost of crude rubber to the manufacturer. However, these fluctuations appear only slightly and temporarily reflected in changes in the wholesale price of tires. Indeed, a significant mathematical correlation between crude-rubber and tire-and-tube prices cannot be found. A host of additional factors—changes in total production rates, changes in tire-and-tube construction, changes in the price of labor and of other materials, alterations of distribution channels, competitive price-cutting—affect tire-and-tube prices and defy comparable measurement.[3] Multiple correlation analysis is impracticable for lack of data.

[3] L. E. Carlsmith, *The Economic Characteristics of Rubber Tire Production* (New York, 1934), pp. 122–23.

If markedly low or high rubber prices are sustained over a lengthy period of time, the quantity of reclaim per average tire may be altered by the manufacturer. Thus, excessively high rubber prices in 1925–27 led to increased use of reclaimed rubber. The somewhat poorer quality of the average tire, in turn, resulted in a perceptible expansion of the replacement market.[4] Ordinarily, however, fluctuating rubber prices, while they may affect tire-and-tube prices, are not accompanied by corresponding changes in total tire-and-tube production, and therefore do not significantly affect crude-rubber consumption in this field. The reason for this lies in the nature of the demand for tires and tubes.

This demand is a conspicuous example of a joint demand. Motor vehicles and tires and tubes are complementary goods. Neither is of any utility without the other. However, as far as price considerations play any part in determining the demand for automobile usage, the price of tires and tubes is of minor importance. The proportion of the sales value of an automobile represented by the value of tires and tubes is no more than between 5 and 8 per cent. The value represented by the crude rubber contained in this equipment is ordinarily at most one-third of the total value of tires and tubes. Obviously no conceivable change in rubber prices could affect the demand for new automobiles. Price considerations are likely to be of slightly greater, though still decidedly minor, weight in determining the replacement demand for tires and tubes. Factors other than price predominantly account for fluctuations in the tire-and-tube renewal market (see pp. 47–57).

The conditions which dominate variations in tire-and-tube consumption become discernible upon an examination of the demand for automobile usage. For purposes of analysis it is important to distinguish between the market for original equipment arising from the demand for new automobiles and the market for renewal equipment arising from automobile usage in general.

Strictly speaking, the demand for automobiles, whether new

---

[4] *Ibid.*, p. 107.

or second-hand, is a derived demand.[5] The primary demand is predominantly for individual transportation. Demand for the automobile as a form of "conspicuous consumption" and a symbol of social standing is a secondary consideration, of declining importance in the United States. A passenger automobile is a durable consumer good. The enjoyment of the transportation service it affords can be obtained for a long period of time without acquisition of a new vehicle. Indeed, the demand for new automobiles is only a small part of the aggregate demand for car usage.

The effective demand for new automobiles, as reflected in production figures, is far more erratic than the demand for automobile usage in general, as reflected in registration figures. Since automobile production and sales are closely related, there is a close correlation between the sales of new vehicles and the level of business activity (see Chart 7, p. 51). Business conditions largely determine the income of automobile purchasers and exert a strong psychological influence upon automobile purchasers because potential buyers anticipate changes in their income.

The correlation between automobile sales and national income is, however, somewhat less close than that between sales and general business activity. Sales tend to rise more rapidly than national income increases and to fall faster than national income contracts. Two factors are responsible for this discrepancy. There is a time lag between changes in the payment of certain types of income (interest, dividends, salaries) and changes in general business conditions. Movements of national income therefore fluctuate more narrowly than movements of industrial production. The individual recipients of incomes of the slowly changing kind, however, purchase products like automobiles less on the basis of current than on the basis of anticipated income. Secondly, it is obvious that not all of the income of the potential automobile buyer is available for the acquisition of such durable consumer goods as automobiles. Only that

[5] The following analysis is based largely on the excellent papers by S. L. Horner, C. F. Roos, Victor von Szeliski, A. T. Court, and S. M. DuBrul in General Motors Corporation, *The Dynamics of Automobile Demand* (New York, 1939).

portion is so available which is left after the payment of taxes and ordinary living expenses. The remainder may be called supernumerary income. The magnitude of supernumerary income is influenced by changes in the cost of living and in taxes which, in general, lag behind changes in the national income. When, as a result of expanding production, national income rises, the slower rise of living costs tends to permit supernumerary income to increase more rapidly than total income. The reverse effect is observable when national income declines.

As determinants of the volume of automobile purchases, all factors other than supernumerary income are of distinctly lesser rank. Changes in the price of motor vehicles and anticipations of such changes have only a minor effect. Indeed, they are eclipsed in importance by the amount of average monthly payments (not their number) required, e.g., by the terms of the instalment contract. Among other minor factors are the price of used automobiles, which affects trade-in allowances and hence the net price of new automobiles; style factors; and the replacement pressure which is a variable function of the size of the total automobile fleet and its mechanical condition or age structure.

The general demand for automobile usage is met by the total car stock of the country. As Chart 7 (p. 51) shows, the automobile fleet of the United States was still growing at the outbreak of World War II, though the rate of expansion had markedly declined since the 1920's. As would be expected, however, the chart also indicates that fluctuations in the purchase of new automobiles are reflected in the number in the total fleet. In depression periods, such as in 1930–33 and 1938, the American fleet declined because the contraction of supernumerary income led to a sharp diminution of new-car purchases. While the abandonment of obsolete units may be postponed and while obsolescence itself is retarded because of more sparing operation, the shrinkage of replacement units will eventually result in a contraction of the total car stock. This condition gradually raises the replacement pressure and, as supernumerary income rises with an upturn in the business cycle, this pressure is relieved by the purchase of new vehicles.

The nature of the demand for motor-truck usage and for new trucks does not substantially differ from that for passenger automobiles. Since these vehicles are producer goods, the correlation between the trend of general business activity and new purchases as well as changes in total registration is as close as for passenger cars (see Chart 7).

The demand for rubber absorbed in tires and tubes for original equipment is directly determined by the number of new automobiles produced. This section of the demand for crude rubber is totally unrelated to changes in the price of the material. It is highly responsive to the trend of business activity and fluctuates even more widely. Hence it tended to be extremely erratic during the interwar period.

The demand for rubber absorbed in the replacement market is a trifle more responsive to changes in the price of crude rubber, but the difference is definitely minor if not negligible. The reflection of changing rubber prices in changing prices of tires and tubes is subdued and irregular (see p. 72). When

CHART 13.—INDEXES OF CRUDE-RUBBER, TIRE-AND-TUBE, AND WHOLESALE
PRICES IN THE UNITED STATES, ANNUALLY, 1919–40*

(*Average 1935–39 = 100*)

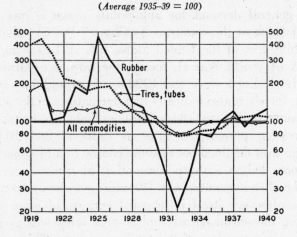

* Based on data in *Survey of Current Business, 1942 Supplement*, pp. 18, 20, 160.

a pronounced increase in price occurs, automobile owners can be assumed to get more wear out of obsolescing equipment, to

repair damaged equipment, and, perhaps, to purchase somewhat lower grades of renewals. The trend of the replacement
market is also predominantly determined by the course of business conditions, but fluctuations are much less pronounced. This
relationship arises not only from the changes that take place in
the total automobile fleet, but also from accompanying fluctuations in the mileage driven by the average car owner. Again,
it is reduced income rather than increased prices of tires and
tubes which leads to the endeavor to extract as much service out
of obsolescing equipment as possible. But a residual price responsiveness must be presumed.

The replacement market is about twice as large as the market for original equipment, and fluctuations in the volume of
total car usage are far milder than those in the volume of automobile production. Rubber consumption in the replacement
market, therefore, has a strikingly steadying effect on the fluctuations of total rubber consumption in the tire-and-tube field,
despite the marked influence of secular improvements in tire
durability. This fact is brought out clearly in Chart 6 (p. 49).

Lack of data makes it impossible to examine in detail the
variability of the demand for rubber in the different use categories outside the tire-and-tube field. Each category is a composite of numerous single-use items which differ in economic
behavior and, throughout the interwar period, were subject to
varying secular growth trends (see pp. 47–49). Chart 14 shows
that, except for these secular trends, total rubber absorption in
all categories fluctuated quite closely with consumption in the
tire-and-tube field, and hence was correlated chiefly with the
course of business activity. The chart also compares rubber consumption in mechanical rubber goods and insulated wire and
cable compounds with that in rubber clothing, shoes, boots,
heels, soles, stationers' supplies, and sporting goods. Absorption in the former group, predominantly represented by producer goods and durable consumer goods, exhibited more violent fluctuations in response to the business cycle than rubber
absorption in the second group in which semidurable articles
predominate.

Except in the long run, crude-rubber consumption outside

the tire-and-tube field did not prove substantially more responsive to changes in the price of crude rubber than did consumption in tires and tubes. Lack of data prevents the citation of

CHART 14.—INDEXES OF VOLUME OF RUBBER USED IN VARIOUS
MANUFACTURED GOODS, AND OF INDUSTRIAL PRODUCTION,
ANNUALLY, 1931–40*

(*Average 1931–40 = 100*)

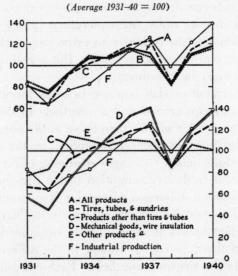

A – All products
B – Tires, tubes, & sundries
C – Products other than tires & tubes
D – Mechanical goods, wire insulation
E – Other products ᵃ
F – Industrial production

* Based on data in Appendix Table X, and *Survey of Current Business, 1942 Supplement,* p. 7.

ᵃ Boots, shoes, heels, soles, sporting goods, stationers' goods, and rubber clothing.

conclusive evidence, but reasoning by analogy appears to support the contention. Nearly all rubber articles are more or less
durable goods whose replacement can be postponed. The share
in the factory sales value represented by the cost of crude rubber is much lower outside than in the tire-and-tube field. In
the six biennial census years from 1929 to 1939, the percentage
ranged from 5 to 14 in the former as compared with from 13
to 33 in the latter field of rubber use (see Chart 12, p. 72).
The incidence of changes in crude-rubber prices, therefore,
tends to be less important to the manufacturers of miscellaneous
rubber goods than to tire manufacturers.

Whatever small differences may exist between the price-responsiveness of crude-rubber consumption in these two fields

arises from the greater adaptability to the use of reclaim in the manufacture of articles other than tires and tubes. Biennial census figures on the activities of the United States rubber-manufacturing industry suggest that substitution of reclaim for crude rubber responded more vigorously outside than in the tire-and-tube field.[6]

Speed and range of response are confined by such conditions as the necessity for altering manufacturing specifications, the varying suitability of reclaim for different purposes, the cost of collecting scrap rubber, the capacity of existing reclaiming facilities, and the presumably small degree to which the consumption of most rubber articles outside the tire-and-tube field is itself responsive to price changes. Calculated on the basis of crude-rubber content, about half of these articles are integral parts of automobiles, airplanes, electrical and other machinery, houses, and so forth. The demand for others, such as stationers' supplies, rubber heels and soles, and many druggist sundries, is fairly insistent. Such small changes in the price of these articles as might be caused by changes in the cost of crude rubber can in neither case be assumed to entail substantial increases or decreases in consumption.

Viewing total crude-rubber absorption in the United States, one may infer that the short-term price-elasticity of the demand for rubber in all rubber articles, while not zero, is very slight. Variations in the aggregate volume of consumption are caused primarily by changes in general business activity and income and by the growth factor exhibited by the individual use items. While these growth trends are in turn largely the result of technological factors or of secular trends in the consumption of the numerous finished rubber goods that contain rubber parts, sustained changes in the price of crude rubber can also be assumed to exert a marked influence. High crude-rubber prices sustained for a considerable length of time encouraged increasing use of reclaim during the interwar period and discouraged the search for new uses of the material. Sustained declines of the rubber price level made for reverse tendencies. The violence of fluctu-

---

[6] U.S. Dept. of Comm., Bur. Census, *Biennial Census of Manufactures*, successive issues.

ations in the absorption of crude rubber is brought out in Chart 15. The close correlation between these fluctuations in the United States and changes in the level of industrial production is somewhat marred by the secular increase in rubber consumption. Outside this country, cyclical fluctuations in consumption appear overshadowed by the striking expansion of rubber use.

CHART 15.—RUBBER ABSORPTION AND INDEXES OF INDUSTRIAL PRODUCTION IN THE UNITED STATES AND EUROPE, ANNUALLY, 1919–39*

(Thousand tons; indexes on 1934–38 base)

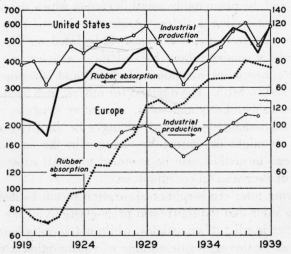

* Data from McFadyean, *op. cit.*, p. 236; *Survey of Current Business, 1942 Supplement*, p. 7; League of Nations, Economic Intelligence Service, *Statistical Year-Book 1938/39*, 1939. II. A. 9 (Geneva, 1939), p. 180.

Chiefly for this reason, but also because of the divergence of the fluctuations in industrial production in different countries, the massive dependence of the world rubber market on United States consumption proved a highly unsettling factor throughout the interwar period.

A minor influence on long-run rubber absorption must be ascribed to the changeability of rubber prices rather than to their level during any period of time. Rubber-goods manufacturers are aware that the violent fluctuations of rubber prices in themselves have in the past discouraged its adaptation to new uses. It is probably largely for this reason that the auto-mobile-manufacturing industry of the United States has opposed the large-scale use of sponge rubber in car seats.

CRUDE-RUBBER STOCKS

Crude-rubber stocks have the function of connecting production and consumption by providing reserves which absorb sudden changes in demand before the rate of production can be adjusted to the change. In other words, the world rubber market relies on world rubber stocks for bridging the period of supply rigidity which must elapse before changes in production rates are reflected in corresponding changes in supplies to industrial consumers. Under ordinary conditions this time lag was estimated at a minimum of two-and-a-half months. Roughly one month was considered requisite for tapping, collecting, milling, packing, and shipping rubber to the ports of exit; nearly one month and a half for loading, maritime transit, unloading, and clearing in the ports of entrance; and several days for transit to the rubber-manufacturing plants. The exact length of the period depended chiefly on the fluidity of the labor supply in the producing areas. Extraordinary circumstances, such as the rerouting of shipping around the Cape of Good Hope in 1936, will also affect the time lag.

With proper care and adequate facilities, crude rubber—especially high-quality grades—can be stored for many years. Because crude rubber turns hard and brittle at low temperatures and tacky at high temperatures, it must be stored at an even temperature of around 70° F. To avoid deterioration through aging, the raw material should not be exposed to direct sunlight. The most serious problem of storing rubber is the prevention of mold which lowers its quality and entails marked loss of weight. Since dampness and poor ventilation encourage mold growth, it is generally advised not to store rubber on concrete floors but to raise it on wooden supports that afford ample clearance for air circulation. Rubber storage in temperate zones is obviously easier, less risky, and cheaper than under tropical conditions.

The three main categories of rubber stocks are those in the producing countries, rubber afloat, and stocks in the consuming countries. Appendix Table V presents a breakdown of the composition of these stocks.[7] Within the producing areas rubber statisticians make a distinction between stocks in the ports of exit and those held by producers and dealers outside these ports. Statistics on port stocks are available only for Para and Manaos in Brazil and for Singapore and Penang in Malaya. Brazilian port stocks, fed by wild-rubber collection in the Amazon basin, are quite small. The much larger stocks in Singapore and Penang average about three-quarters of the gross exports from British Malaya during any one month. The singling out of these four ports is rather arbitrary; but stocks data for other ports in Malaysia, Latin America, and Africa are unavailable.

Other stocks in the producing countries consist of rubber on estates and native holdings, dealers' stocks, and stocks in transit. Information on the size of these categories is fragmentary.[8] No records exist for stocks in transit or for small-holders' stocks. It is assumed that native producers carry very little of their produce, usually less than one week's output. Outside the ports, the large bulk of dealers' stocks consists of native rubber, not processed. Their total is relatively large in the Netherlands Indies and British Malaya, small in the other producing countries.

In British Malaya, monthly estate stocks have been recorded and published since 1928. For other producing countries such data did not become available before the introduction of the IRRA in 1934. On the whole, Malaysian estate stocks average normally about three-quarters of a month's output. Under the first IRRA, producers were allowed to carry stocks of ready rubber up to the equivalent of two months' permissible exports, dealers up to six weeks' permissible exports. The second IRRA, 1938, provided that producers might carry up to 25 per cent of their standard production for the preceding year.

However, producers carried far smaller stocks than permitted under these liberal rules. Actual stocks usually ranged from one-fourth to one-half of permitted producers' stocks. Besides,

---

[7] For an excellent discussion of rubber stocks see Rae, "Statistics of the Rubber Industry," *Journal of the Royal Statistical Society*, 1938, Vol. CI, Pt. II, pp. 346–56.

[8] For estimates and recorded data see successive issues of the *Statistical Bulletin* (International Rubber Regulation Committee, London), Section C.

whenever producers increased their stocks, dealers decreased theirs and vice versa.[9] On the whole, producers' and dealers' stocks inside the producing countries represented merely the necessary working stocks of the industry, and thus varied primarily with the current rate of output. Producers as well as dealers were reluctant to accumulate sizable stocks beyond working requirements. The majority lacked requisite financial resources and adequate warehousing facilities. Moreover, rubber storage in the tropics is relatively expensive and the accumulation of large stocks speculative and risky.

Stocks afloat comprise all rubber declared as exports from the exporting countries but not yet declared as imports in the importing countries. No exact data are available on the size of these stocks. The International Rubber Regulation Committee (IRRC) simply estimates rubber afloat at one-and-a-half months' world shipments from the producing countries. This customary measurement arises from the assumption that rubber shipments from Malaysia to the United Kingdom or the United States are about six weeks in oceanic transit. The mechanical nature of the estimate renders it a very rough indicator of actual quantities afloat.

Relatively complete data on stocks in the consuming countries exist only for manufacturers', importers', and dealers' stocks in the United States,[10] stocks in public warehouses at London and Liverpool, and, since 1934, manufacturers' stocks in the United Kingdom. Statistics on stocks carried in other importing countries are unavailable. However, disregarding government stocks, these countries usually operated on short supplies. Throughout the interwar period their stocks have therefore never played an important part in the world rubber situation. The stocks at London and Liverpool are regarded as the world's ultimate reserve of raw rubber and, when it cannot be sold elsewhere, rubber is sent thither.

Consideration of world stocks ordinarily is confined to con-

[9] *Rubber News Letter*, Mar. 31, 1939, p. 71.

[10] These three classes of stocks in the United States are usually considered as a total. Sooner or later dealers' and importers' stocks become manufacturers' stocks and a large portion of dealers' stocks are usually held against forward sales to rubber-goods manufacturers.

sideration of all types of stocks including port stocks but excluding stocks inside the producing areas. Since data on British manufacturers' stocks became available only in 1934, these are often excluded from historical reviews of world rubber stocks. Unless otherwise specified, this practice is followed in the present study. In view of their incompleteness, it is obvious that the figures on total world stocks can give only a very rough picture of the actual position at any time.

CHART 16.—"WORLD" STOCKS AND NEW YORK PRICES OF RUBBER, MONTHLY, 1934–40*

(Thousand tons; cents per pound; logarithmic vertical scale)

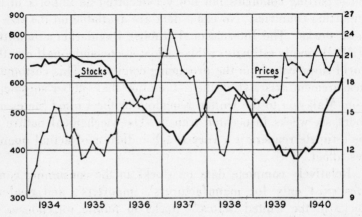

* Data from *Survey of Current Business, 1938 Supplement*, p. 148, and *1942 Supplement*, p. 160. "World" stocks include stocks in London and Liverpool, United States, British Malaya, and afloat. For details see notes in source.

A glance at Chart 16 reveals the inverted relationship prevailing, in general, between rubber stocks and prices. The smaller world stocks are in relation to the current volume of rubber demanded, the higher rubber prices tend to move, and vice versa. Because the volume of rubber demanded is predominantly determined by the changing level of industrial production, there is a close correlation between the movement of stocks and the business cycle. A business recession tends to produce a contracting volume of demand, accumulating stocks, and falling prices. An upward swing of business activity has the opposite effect. But the stocks position is also affected by disturbing developments on the supply side. Thus, the accumulation of surplus output capacity in the late 1920's combined with the marked unresponsiveness of supply to falling prices resulted in rapidly increasing world stocks. Owing to the price-unresponsiveness of consumption, no relief of this pressure was forthcoming from the demand side.

Since the size of absolute stocks must be appraised in the light of current absorption, some rubber statisticians have focused their attention on the ratios of year-end stocks to average monthly consumption during the year. Thus, world consumption in 1937 totaled 1,095,000 tons or about 91,000 tons per month. Year-end stocks were 510,000 tons. The stock ratio, therefore, amounted to about 5.5, meaning that year-end stocks would have met 5.5 months' average absorption. Chart 17

CHART 17.—RATIOS OF END-YEAR RUBBER STOCKS TO AVERAGE MONTHLY ABSORPTION, "WORLD" AND UNITED STATES, AND NEW YORK RUBBER PRICES, ANNUALLY, 1923–40*

(*Prices in cents per pound; ratios as explained in text; logarithmic vertical scale*)

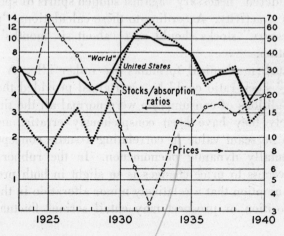

* Based on data in McFadyean, *op. cit.*, pp. 236, 237, 239.

shows the ratios of world stocks to world absorption, and of United States stocks to United States absorption. The changes in these stock ratios are striking. The world ratio fluctuated between 3.2 and 10.4, the United States ratio between 1.6 and

13.5. This method of appraisal, however, affords but a very crude yardstick of the changing stocks position. Year-end stocks are not necessarily representative for the midyear, quarterly, or monthly stocks position. Nor is their correlation with a preceding twelve months' period of consumption particularly revealing.

The question of what might be considered "normal" or "necessary" stocks has agitated the minds of observers from time to time. Such calculations were usually undertaken in terms of a stock ratio stating how many months' absorption current world stocks should afford at any one time. According to some appraisals,[11] "necessary" stocks should allow for one month for the collection, preparation, and shipment of crude rubber to the ports of exit, two weeks for handling in the ports of exit, six weeks for maritime transit, one month for movement through dealers' channels, an average of two weeks for transit to manufacturing plants, and a month for working stocks at the manufacturing plants. In addition, one-and-a-half-months' supply was considered "necessary" against sudden spurts of speculative or business activity. According to these calculations, "normal" or "necessary" stocks should cover about six months' current consumption.

Yet such mechanical formulas are rather idle. A relevant "normal" stock ratio could be ascertained provided the underlying conditions of consumption were normal all the time. Unfortunately they have been conspicuously erratic, and there seems to be scant value in correlating a static concept with a fundamentally dynamic phenomenon. In the rubber market responsiveness to price changes is so slight in both production and consumption that a relatively minor alteration in the world-stocks position or prospect may entail serious fluctuations of price.

Not only the size but also the distribution and ownership of rubber stocks is of importance in determining the position of world stocks. As far as industrial consumers are concerned, the maintenance of large rubber inventories requires commensurate financial prowess such as is enjoyed only by a few big manu-

[11] Rae, *op. cit.*, pp. 352–53; Heinz George, *Kautschuk* (Leipzig, 1938), p. 109.

facturing concerns. In the United States the Big Four (United States Rubber, Goodyear, Goodrich, Firestone) and Dunlop in Britain follow a policy of large rubber inventories in order to protect themselves against possible shortages. In addition, these big manufacturers often hold title to varying quantities of forward purchases in the hands of dealers as well as stocks afloat and in the ports of exit. The large majority of small and medium-sized manufacturers, on the other hand, carry relatively small working stocks. Even when total world stocks are large, there may be relative undersupply of free spot rubber because the leading rubber-manufacturing concerns hold title to a large portion of these stocks.

CHAPTER V

THE CRUDE-RUBBER MARKET UNTIL 1934

The purpose of the present chapter is to review briefly the broad history of the crude-rubber industry and market before the establishment of the IRRA in 1934. The main forces and conditions which led to the drafting of that agreement will be set forth and analyzed. Incidentally, it will be shown that the history of the rubber market is replete with efforts of the producers to protect and advance their interests by intervening in the free rubber market.[1]

EARLY SCHEMES

During the second half of the nineteenth century, while the reign of wild rubber was unchallenged, rubber prices ordinarily fluctuated between 50 cents and $1.00 a pound. To attract larger rubber supplies from the jungles, the price level gradually rose with expanding consumption. The continuity of this trend was disturbed only by business booms and depressions which temporarily drove prices sharply up and down.

The first decade of the twentieth century brought two momentous developments: the advent of plantation rubber and the vigorous growth of automobile production and usage. Since the impact of the automobile somewhat preceded the establishment of a substantial plantation industry, rubber prices shot up and, from 1905 to 1912, fluctuated above $1.00 per pound. Soaring prices, in turn, further stimulated the expansion of the plantation industry in the East. In 1914, supplies from this source for the first time topped shipments of wild rubber. The expansion of total supplies was meanwhile reflected in falling

---

[1] This chapter is based mainly on the following sources: P. W. Barker, *Rubber Statistics 1900–1937* (U.S. Dept. Comm., Bur. Foreign and Domestic Comm., Trade Promotion Series 181, 1938); McFadyean, *The History of Rubber Regulation 1934–1943*, chap. ii; Rowe, *Rubber*; C. R. Whittlesey, *Government Control of Crude Rubber* (Princeton, 1931); and Howard and Ralph Wolf, *Rubber* (New York, 1936), Books II–III.

rubber prices. From an annual average of $2.07 a pound in 1910, the price of crude rubber fell to about 65 cents in 1914.

The nineteenth century witnessed several schemes, undertaken by private speculators, to "corner" the rubber market; but these maneuvers were shortlived. The early twentieth century brought the first government schemes to support rubber prices.

In 1903, the Brazilian government issued a decree permitting the formation of syndicates in agricultural industries "for the defense of their interests." A half-hearted attempt in 1905, providing for government loans to producers to enable them to carry rubber until prices reached an "attractive" level, temporarily drove the price up. Yet the government was financially too weak to weather the period of slackening demand occasioned by the business recession of 1907, and the plan had to be discontinued.

Late in 1908, the state of Para authorized the establishment of a rubber syndicate headed by the Banco do Brasil. At times of relatively low prices, exports of wild rubber were to be restricted by storing rubber until prices improved. Advances by the bank to members of the syndicate were to implement the project. Under this plan rubber prices climbed to new heights, attaining a peak of over $3.00 per pound in April 1910. Again success was shortlived, as ever larger supplies were shipped from the East. For a while the Banco do Brasil tried to stem the resulting downward trend of prices, reportedly losing ten million dollars in this abortive attempt. Eventually its resources were exhausted, and the scheme was abandoned before the end of 1910. The Brazilian syndicate had to liquidate its stocks and the inflated price level abruptly collapsed. An attempt at resuscitation of this valorization scheme in 1911 was stillborn.

Belatedly realizing the menace of cheaper plantation rubber, the Brazilian government in 1912 announced a new project called Defesa da Borracha (Rubber Defense). This plan was to insure survival of Brazilian rubber production in competition with the East. Among other provisions, the program envisaged the encouragement of a Brazilian plantation industry by establishing experiment stations, paying premiums for the planting of rubber trees and the construction of milling factories, improving transportation facilities by water and rail, and promoting food production in the Amazon Valley. This ambitious scheme, too, was doomed to failure. The financial, managerial, scientific, and administrative resources of the country were totally inadequate for the task. Rubber prices continued to decline and, by the end of 1913, most of the enterprises started under the plan ceased operations. A last valorization scheme, providing for price support by open-market operations on the part of a Brazilian government bank, was rejected by the Brazilian Senate in 1914.

WORLD WAR I AND AFTERMATH

With the outbreak of war in 1914, the rubber world entered upon a period of abnormal market conditions. Prices advanced from around 65 cents a pound in 1914–15 to about 72 cents in 1916–17. This interruption of the generally descending price trend, noticeable since 1910, was caused by rapidly expanding absorption. In a brisk war boom, United States production of motor vehicles trebled from 1914 to 1917. Traders and industrial consumers, moreover, increased stocks as insurance against unfavorable shipping developments.

The year 1918 brought a sudden change in this picture. The automobile industry in the United States was largely converted to war production. Absorption contracted and, in view of large existing inventories, the volume of demand for rubber shrank sharply. Finally, restrictions were imposed on rubber imports by the Allied governments in order to save shipping space and to prevent rubber from reaching the Central Powers. As a consequence, stocks of crude rubber rapidly piled up in the East. Confronted with this adverse situation, talk of output restriction gained ground swiftly.

In 1918, the Council of the Rubber Growers Association in British Malaya, representing the bulk of estate production, proposed the first scheme to "adjust" supply to demand by concerted action. Members of the Association agreed to a voluntary restriction of production to 80 per cent of their 1917 outputs. However, while not futile, this measure could not give

substantial results since other producers, notably in the Netherlands Indies and Ceylon, declined to co-operate. In the middle
of 1918, Malayan estate producers asked their government to
appoint a committee with a view to elaborating a compulsory
restriction plan in which the Dutch estate industry should be
requested to participate. The Malayan government appointed a
commission to draft a suitable project. However, negotiations
with the government of the Netherlands had barely been initiated when the Armistice was signed. Since the termination
of hostilities was sure to ease the shipping shortage and since a
basic disequilibruim between the world's supply and consumption capacities was suspected by few, the scheme was promptly
abandoned. Yet, though it never passed beyond the blueprint
stage, it constituted a significant precedent for subsequent endeavors to obtain government support for compulsory restriction.

A brief post-Armistice boom relieved the congested supply
condition in the East. The price of crude rubber recovered to
over 50 cents per pound. This improvement was shortlived.
Exports soon consistently exceeded absorption. World stocks
consequently rose to record heights—at the end of 1921 equivalent to over 9 months' world absorption during the year. Prices
dropped to a low of 11.5 cents that summer.

This predicament must be attributed to several factors. The
post-Armistice boom was quickly followed by the severe business depression of 1920–21. Yet this event only aggravated the
existing disequilibrium between supply and consumption. Disregarding fluctuations in absorption caused by the business
cycle, the secular rise in consumption was far outstripped by
constantly increasing shipments from the producing areas. On
the one side, the introduction of the far more durable cord tire
slowed down the trend toward increased rubber consumption
inherent in the growth of automobile usage. On the other side,
ever new stands of Hevea attained tappable age while those that
had become tappable earlier yielded more rubber as they further
matured.

Under these circumstances, talk of output restriction quickly
revived. British and Dutch interests, representing over 70 per

cent of the mature estate acreage in British Malaya and the Netherlands Indies, adopted a voluntary restriction plan for the period from November 1920 through December 1921. The scheme provided for an output curtailment to 75 per cent of estimated normal monthly production. Exports in 1921 indeed fell by 12 per cent from their 1920 volume. But this was insufficient to check the price collapse. Again, voluntary restriction proved a failure and the scheme was not prolonged beyond 1921. Native producers as well as estate producers not party to the agreement continued uncurtailed production, and many estates which supported the scheme did not fully live up to their commitments. To be effective, it seemed, restriction must be comprehensive and compulsory.

A few salient facts need be cited to characterize the frame of mind prevalent in planters' circles. Only a dozen years earlier, the industry had been expanding against the background of a steadily rising market which absorbed progressively larger supplies. Prices were high. There was no need to strive for low costs. Inefficient and extravagant estate management was encouraged. An unbroken number of fat years had generated such unbounded optimism that nobody took seriously the possibility of lean ones. In general, the industry was regarded as a gold mine to be exploited to the limit. The universal practice had been to pay out stunning dividends while providing little for reserves.

The problems of the war had been viewed as of strictly temporary nature. The unexpected slump of the rubber market in the early 1920's therefore acted as an unexampled shock. While all-in costs of production had averaged around 40 cents a pound before the war, now the price of rubber ranged as low as 14 and 15 cents. As late as 1919, dividends of British rubber companies averaged over 22 per cent. Two years later they averaged 2.1 per cent only and in 1922 four-fifths of all companies were unable to pay any dividends at all.[2] Facing financial ruin, the industry now made frantic efforts to slash production costs. Indeed, some of the economizing measures were so drastic as to jeopardize the future capacity of the estates.

[2] Annelise Schulz, *Der Plantagenkautschuk in Britisch-Malaya* (Berlin, 1936), p. 33.

In these years the industry also experienced the price-unresponsiveness of rubber supplies in a falling market. Despite progressively declining prices, readjustment of output and absorption failed to materialize. Estate managers, company directors, stockholders, and local government officials searched desperately for a way out of this plight. No wonder that projects for compulsory restriction or the trustification of the industry were rife in the planters' and investors' community. Literally dozens of plans were propounded and discussed. The Rubber Growers' Association (RGA) and the Rubber Shareholders' Association, formed in the fall of 1921, were the most potent pressure groups advocating compulsory regulation. The Stevenson scheme was the eventual upshot.

THE STEVENSON SCHEME

Various explanations have been offered to explain the decision of the British government to embrace the cause of commodity control. In retrospect the United Kingdom after World War I seems definitely to have moved toward discarding its classic free-enterprise position. But in the early 1920's the country was still regarded as the champion of laissez-faire against the spreading wave of government interference with business affairs. Questioned about its attitude toward rubber control, a spokesman for the Lloyd George Government stated as late as May 1921 "that no legislation for compulsory restriction of output should be introduced by the Government, as the policy . . . . would necessitate undue Government interference in economic policies . . . . [and] that conditions must be allowed to right themselves."[3] Yet within six months this position was reversed.

What prompted the government to change its attitude between May and October 1921? Perhaps the most important reason was the strong pressure of influential persons and groups and of the local colonial administrations. The Malayan government was deeply concerned over the depression of the rubber industry which brought distress to European and Chinese planters, depleted its revenues, and threatened large-scale dismissal of

---

[3] Great Britain, *Parliamentary Debates, Commons, 1921*, Vol. 141, col. 1,077.

Indian laborers who would have to be repatriated at public expense. In addition to such pressures and the possible influence of powerful individuals, two factors appear to have contributed to the reversal of policy. One was the fear, widespread in the early 1920's throughout Europe, of the financial imperialism of "Uncle Shylock." Specifically, it was feared that American interests would buy up a bankrupt British rubber-plantation industry.[4] Finally, the British government was perturbed over the foreign-exchange position of the country, an anxiety only reinforced by the United States' unflinching insistence upon repayment of the war debts.[5]

In October 1921, Winston Churchill, as Secretary of State for the Colonies in Lloyd George's cabinet, appointed the Stevenson Committee. Of the eight members, five were directors of rubber companies and members of the RGA, two were civil servants, and the Chairman, Sir James Stevenson, was personal commercial adviser to Mr. Churchill and likewise financially interested in the rubber-growing industry. The composition of the committee was heavily weighted in favor of the demands of the industry.

The Stevenson Committee issued two reports.[6] In the first, submitted in May 1922, it summarily reviewed the rubber situation. As of January 1, 1922, it estimated surplus stocks above "necessary" stocks (equivalent to eight months' absorption) at 110,000 tons, and assumed that during the year exports would exceed consumption by 100,000 tons. Various ways of balancing production and absorption were investigated. The committee found that the approach through stimulation of new and extended uses of rubber would not provide an immediate solution of the problem. The laissez-faire method was rejected because of the hardships it would necessarily inflict upon "the many tens of thousands of shareholders in this country alone, and the many thousands of European and Asiatic owners and shareholders resident in the countries of production." These hardships would be prolonged because abandoned plantations "would remain a

---

4 George, *Kautschuk*, p. 126; see also the statement of J. H. Thomas in Great Britain, *Parliamentary Debates, Commons, 1924–25*, Vol. 187, col. 104.

5 *Ibid.*; Rowe, *Rubber*, p. 43.

6 Reprinted in Whittlesey, *op. cit.*, pp. 204–14.

potential source of rubber and would be brought into production again by someone as soon as a margin of profit can be secured." Voluntary restriction of output was deemed impracticable in view of past experiences.

"Fully aware of the grave objections to government interference with industry" and "only with reluctance and with a lively apprehension of the dangers," the Stevenson Committee therefore advocated "compulsory restriction as an alternative to what seemed to be worse evils." The committee calculated that British dependencies accounted for 72 and the Netherlands Indies for 25.5 per cent of the total production of plantation rubber. It insisted that a system of compulsory restriction could be recommended only if the Netherlands government was willing to participate.

The governments of the British producing countries approved the scheme but the Netherlands government was not found amenable. It explained its negative decision on the grounds that it would be unwise and undesirable to introduce government intervention in the rubber industry, that restriction was artificial and unnatural, that it would tend to buttress inefficiency and extravagance in production, and that, unless control were made permanent, a fight for the survival of the fittest must develop sooner or later while, in the meantime, efficient producers would be hampered by being asked to support inefficient ones. Finally, the Dutch government declared that it did not wish to incur the displeasure of the United States government. In this attitude the Netherlands authorities were backed by the majority of Dutch estate producers.

Upon receipt of the Dutch refusal to support the scheme, the Stevenson Committee resumed its deliberations and, in October 1922, issued a second report. Reversing its former opinion, the committee now recommended application of its plan regardless of Dutch non-collaboration. The RGA had pressed for this decision after it had secured assurances of voluntary support by a number of British and Dutch estate producers in the Netherlands Indies. Mr. Churchill had curtly refused to discuss the scheme while the committee deliberated. Upon receipt of its second report, he immediately obtained its approval in the last

minutes of a meeting of a cabinet on its way out of office. Later
Mr. Churchill remarked that "evidently the Cabinet either felt
that the scheme was so excellent that it required no discussion,
or that it was so complicated that discussion was impossible."[7]
The plan was never submitted to or debated in Parliament. Approved by the cabinet, the scheme was quickly passed by the
local legislative councils of British Malaya and Ceylon. It went
into effect on November 1, 1922.

The scheme was implemented as follows. Exports were to be
limited to a prescribed percentage of the standard production of
each producer. With certain qualifications, the quantity of
rubber produced by an estate in the year ending with October
1920 was regarded as its standard production. Where no production records of this base year were available, as in the case
of the small holders, standard production was assessed according
to an arbitrary scale that fixed output capacity per acre on the
basis of the age of the trees. A prohibitive scale of export duties
was imposed on exports exceeding the prescribed percentage
of standard production. Quarterly coupons were issued for the
exportable quota of each producer. Alterations in the percentage were to be governed by changes in the average quarterly
price of rubber.

The pivotal price was fixed at 1s. 3d. per pound. In order to
achieve equilibrium at this price level, the committee decided
that the initial exportable percentage should remain at 60 as
long as the average quarterly price ranged between 1s. and 1s. 3d.
a pound. Should the price during the second or any subsequent
quarter average less than 1s., the exportable percentage was to
be cut by 5 in the ensuing quarter, and this automatic adjustment was to be repeated until the pivotal price range was reached.
Similar provisions were made for a gradual increase in the exportable percentage if the quarterly price averaged more than
1s. 3d. Thus, the mechanism of control was completely automatic. Once set to work, changes in the rate of supplies depended upon a complicated mathematical formula rather than
on human judgment and decision. In evaluating the pivotal price
it should be noted that its equivalent in United States currency

[7] Quoted in Whittlesey, *op. cit.*, p. 28.

changed in consequence of the instability of exchange rates between the pound sterling and the dollar. In April 1925, the United Kingdom returned to the gold standard at prewar parity. At this time, the equivalent of 1s. 3d. was 30 U.S. cents as compared with 28 U.S. cents in November 1922.

Chart 18 shows the broad trend of the rubber market under the Stevenson scheme. Though much higher than in 1921–22,

CHART 18.—ANNUAL WORLD RUBBER EXPORTS AND ABSORPTION, END-QUARTER STOCKS, AND QUARTERLY AVERAGE NEW YORK AND LONDON PRICES, 1922–28*

(Quantities in thousand tons)

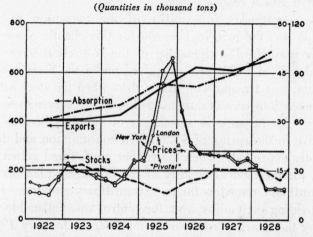

* Data from McFadyean, *op. cit.*, pp. 230, 236; J. W. F. Rowe, *Rubber. Studies in the Artificial Control of Raw Material Supplies 2* (London and Cambridge Econ. Serv. Special Memorandum 34, London, 1931), p. 84. Stocks in United States, United Kingdom, and afloat.

ᵃ Outer scale (cents per pound) for New York; inner scale (pence per pound) for London and "pivotal." The two scales represent very nearly a par relationship; the British series would be raised 1.4 per cent if converted at par.

in the first two years prices generally stayed below the pivotal range. World absorption expanded during the period but exceeded total exports by only a small margin, because restriction in the British producing countries was largely offset by increased shipments from the other producing areas. Stocks therefore declined only gradually. By the end of 1924, however, they had contracted to 165,000 tons, only four months' absorption at the preceding twelve months' rate. Prices had been relatively low during the summer. Industrial consumers, traders, and speculators, expecting a further price decline, had followed a policy of short stocks. At the same time the percentage of permissible exports from the control countries was reduced from 60 to 55 in August and to 50 in November 1924.

With world stocks critically low and restriction increasing, consumption suddenly expanded vigorously in 1925. A spectacular increase in automobile production was the chief cause. World stocks dwindled rapidly. The market turned panicky and rubber prices shot up sharply. In July 1925 they averaged no less than 103.1 cents a pound.

The straitjacket inflexibility of the Stevenson restriction formula was the principal reason for this chaotic phase of the rubber market. The tightening of the restriction screw in the second half of 1924, while required under the Stevenson price formula, was fraught with grave risks when the stock situation was taken into consideration. Owing to the very nature of the scheme, the progressive restriction of supplies became really effective in the spring of 1925 when consumption and demand abruptly expanded. When the rubber market had gotten out of hand, the mechanical rigidity of the Stevenson plan prevented extraordinary remedies for an extraordinary situation. Instead of providing swift adjustment, the control automatism blocked it. During the quarter from November 1924 to January 1925 the restriction rate stood at 50 per cent of standard outputs. A 10 per cent increase of permissible exports was generally expected. In the last days of the quarter, however, prices remained just low enough to make the quarterly average fall short of the necessary 1*s.* 6*d.* by 0.0017 of a penny. The export quota was therefore raised only 5 per cent.

The events of 1925 generated a rising flood of indignant protests in the United States, which then accounted for about three-fourths of the world's rubber consumption. Under the leadership of Herbert Hoover, Secretary of Commerce, and Harvey S. Firestone, Sr., anti-control sentiment was organized in a powerful campaign. The British were flatly charged with pursuing a policy of deliberate monopolistic exploitation. Official protests through diplomatic channels yielded no results.

Soc

The British Colonial Office remained adamant in its refusal to apply special remedial measures.

In the United States, therefore, a program of rubber conservation was undertaken, new reclaiming facilities were built as quickly as possible, and a world-wide search was initiated to locate adequate new sources of crude rubber outside the British control area. Conservation of rubber articles led to a temporary diminution of United States rubber consumption in 1926. Production and use of reclaim expanded rapidly; while the high volume of 1925–26 was not sustained, there was a permanent gain over the pre-1925 level of reclaim production. The newly-established American rubber plantations in Liberia and Brazil could, of course, have no immediate effect on the rubber situation.

With rubber prices skyrocketing, shipments from non-control countries increased and the Stevenson restriction rate was gradually relaxed in 1925. In January 1926 the rate of permissible exports was raised to 100 per cent. At last in response to pressure, the Stevenson scheme was amended in April 1926 to give it more elasticity, by providing for 10 per cent instead of 5 per cent alterations in permissible exports within a range between 60 and 100 per cent of standard production.

At the same time, however, the pivotal price was raised from 1s.3d. to 1s.9d. per pound. No explanation was offered for this unexpected step. British advocates of restriction had considered the old pivotal prices sufficiently rewarding. Critics in the consuming countries attributed its arbitrary increase to plain profiteering. It is quite possible, however, that the reason for this step is to be found altogether outside the rubber field. One observer suggests that the British Treasury, feverishly bent on supporting the gold standard, was in urgent need of additional dollar exchange and instigated the raising of the pivotal price.[8]

Increasing supplies in 1926 permitted gradual replenishment of world rubber stocks. Prices receded from their excessive level but averaged about 50 cents in 1926. In the following year the price continued to fall slowly, although the rate of permissible exports from the control countries was cut to 60 per

[8] Rowe, *op. cit.*, p. 43.

cent. It became increasingly evident that the restricting countries ceased to command a degree of monopoly power sufficient
to render the Stevenson plan workable. By reducing the total
standard production of British Malaya and limiting the use of
unexpired export permits, restriction was in effect still further
tightened in 1927. Prices, however, continued to fall; from an
annual average of 38 cents a pound in 1927, they fell to less than
20 cents in the spring of the following year. Exports from the
nonrestricting areas had begun to exceed total shipments from
the British producing countries. The British government realized
that it had lost control of the market. In April 1928 Prime Min-
ister Stanley Baldwin declared that the Stevenson plan would
be abandoned on November 1.

A critical appraisal of the Stevenson scheme need not be undertaken in this study. Two excellent analyses, one by an
American and one by an English economist, are available.[9] Today no one defends the clumsy machinery of the scheme. The
issue of restrictive commodity control versus a free commodity
market will be taken up in connection with the appraisal of a
subsequent control plan—the IRRA. It is necessary, however,
to point to certain effects of the Stevenson scheme which were
not wiped out by its termination.

The Stevenson plan did not regulate the planting of new and
the replanting of old plantations. The high prices which resulted
from restriction, and especially the excessive prices of 1925–26,
stimulated new planting in all rubber-producing areas but comparatively more so in the unrestricted than in the restricted
countries. Particularly vigorous was the expansion of native
plantations in the Netherlands Indies. Indeed, the total acreage
of small holders there was more than doubled and probably
trebled while the scheme was in operation. Expansion in British
Malaya was less than one-fourth of that in the Netherlands
Indies. For this reason, it was soon to become evident that the
share of the British producing countries in the world's capacity
to produce rubber had diminished. It also appeared that the
share of the native producers relative to the estate industry had
expanded. Yet the most important and the most deplorable

⁹ Whittlesey, *op. cit.*, chaps. v–x; Rowe, *op. cit.*, chaps. iii–iv.

consequence of the Stevenson scheme was the tremendous increase in total capacity which was to accrue from 1930 to 1934. The marked surplus capacity which then plagued the industry resulted largely from the exorbitant prices of the middle 1920's.

At the same time this high price level had acted like a protective tariff for the infant reclaiming industry. The world's reclaiming facilities were greatly augmented in 1926–27; reclaiming processes were improved, and rubber-goods manufacturers became more adept at substituting reclaim for crude in many uses. The ratio of reclaim to crude-rubber consumption naturally contracted as rubber prices fell to an unprecedented depression level. But there can be no doubt that it had received a lasting lift.

INTERIM BETWEEN CONTROLS: RUBBER DURING THE GREAT DEPRESSION

The Stevenson scheme was terminated on October 31, 1928. The International Rubber Regulation Agreement came into operation on June 1, 1934. For about 6½ years, the rubber market was left to find its own course—to the rubber planters a disheartening one. Unfortunately, the greater part of this period coincided with the severest depression the rubber industry had ever known. Two factors were responsible for this calamity: the Great Depression, which brought a contraction of rubber absorption, and a growing production capacity, which was then far in excess even of normal requirements. The rubber market was turned free at a most unpropitious time.

Chart 19 summarily shows the development of the rubber market during the interim period. Contrary to gloomy expectations, the first year after the abandonment of the Stevenson scheme was quite satisfactory to the industry. Shipments, especially from British Malaya and Ceylon, increased markedly, but the frantic business boom of 1929 carried the rubber market along. Rubber consumption experienced a stupendous and unexpected increase, particularly conspicuous in Europe, and prices rose to a profitable level although world stocks were signally expanding.

The break occurred in October 1929. The great business

boom was suddenly followed by a depression of unprecedented depth and protraction. The rubber market participated in this swing of the business cycle. From 20.2 cents a pound in September 1929 the monthly average price of rubber declined almost without interruption to 2.7 cents in June 1932. World

CHART 19.—ANNUAL WORLD RUBBER EXPORTS AND ABSORPTION, END-
QUARTER STOCKS, AND QUARTERLY AVERAGE NEW
YORK PRICES, 1928–34*

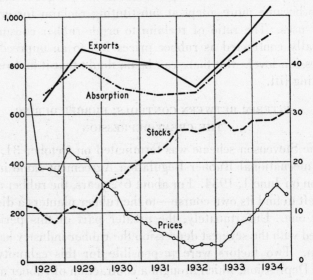

* Data from McFadyean, *op. cit.*, pp. 230, 236; *Survey of Current Business,* successive supplements.

rubber stocks grew from about 300,000 tons in the fall of 1929 to over 600,000 tons in the spring of 1933. Curiously enough, world absorption did not diminish spectacularly. It had attained a record volume of about 800,000 tons in 1929. In 1931 and 1932, at the depth of the depression, it had fallen only 120,000 tons below this boom level. This decline was relatively far smaller than the simultaneous diminution in the consumption of other major industrial raw materials. Contraction occurred almost entirely in the United States (see Chart 15, p. 80). Outside this country, the rate of secular growth in rubber use was so vigorous that rubber consumption diminished very little, as in Europe, or expanded, as in the rest of the world.

The depression-induced shrinkage of rubber consumption, relatively small as it was, was sure to cause a slump in rubber prices even if production capacity and average consumption capacity had been in approximate balance. In view of the marked unresponsiveness of supply to price, small disequilibria between supply and demand volume are sufficient to bring about sharp price fluctuations. Still, it must be inferred that the severity of the rubber crisis was less an outcome of the sudden change in the volume of industrial production than a result of the pressure of excess output capacity.

In these years the industry became quite conscious of the fundamental disequilibrium existing between normal production and consumption capacities. More and more Hevea tracts, planted in the prosperous years of the middle 1920's, attained tappability and afforded yield increases as they further matured. Moreover, since superior planting material had been widely utilized, these new plantations had much greater productive capacity than the older plantations. The estate industry also became conscious of the increasing and unexpectedly vigorous competition of native production. A disproportionately larger share of the new plantings had been undertaken by small holders. This knowledge gave rise to the fear that the entire industry was "going native." The main rivalry, it was realized, no longer lay between British and Dutch estate producers but between the capitalistic estate under European management and the native peasant producer.

The responsiveness of supply to sagging prices was by no means zero. Except for French Indo-China, where producers received direct subsidies, shipments from all countries decreased. Supplies from the wild-rubber collecting countries and from the native plantations in the Netherlands Indies contracted very sharply. Native output in other Malaysian producing areas declined to a varying but distinctly lesser degree. Measured on the basis of 1929 production, the contraction of estate output was negligible (see Chart 10, p. 61). However, since the total producing acreage had been increasing since 1929, production relative to capacity declined much more between 1929 and 1932 than a comparison of actual output data for the two years indicates. Still, while aggregate world shipments fell off in 1931–32, the decline was far from enough to make consumption and shipments balance and thereby to prevent the accumulation of huge stocks and the accompanying collapse of rubber prices.

The primary obstacle to substantial curtailment of estate production in the face of exceedingly low prices lay in its peculiar cost structure (see pp. 62–63). There were additional reasons. Hopes, never completely abandoned, of a sudden improvement of the rubber market made estate producers hesitant to dismiss too many of their laborers. Expectations of a new restriction scheme, raised by the onset of depression, made them maintain production at a high level in order to receive a large standard assessment.

More revealing than their willingness to maintain output at a high level was the ability of estates to do so and to survive the severe slump of prices. This ability rested on a reduction of production costs nearly as drastic as the decline of prices itself. Chart 20 compares the average sales price received by a large number of Malayan estate companies with their average net costs of production. From 1928 through 1933, each successive year brought a new record of low costs. Even compared with the pre-boom level of the early 1920's, costs were cut in four by 1932. Among the dollar companies registered in British Malaya, the all-in costs of the cheapest producer in 1929 were 60 per cent above those of the highest-cost producer in 1932.[10] The industry's incapacity to adjust output to descending prices was paralleled by a remarkable capacity for reduction in costs.

Only at the bottom of the depression did such drastically slashed production costs exceed the average sales price. Yet even this crisis was safely weathered by the industry. It did not lead to a competitive struggle for survival. Nearly all estates, high- and low-cost, survived. Of all British rubber companies only a few had to be reorganized by additional call on the shareholders and only two were foreclosed by debenture holders.[11]

[10] Bauer, "Notes on Cost," *Economica*, New Series, May 1945, XII, 92.

[11] Rae, "Statistics of the Rubber Industry," *Journal of the Royal Statistical Society*, 1938, Vol. CI, Pt. II, p. 325.

The explanation is that in 1931–32 almost all rubber companies lived more or less on their capital and on reserves which had been set aside in the prosperous years from 1925 to 1927.

CHART 20.—COST OF PRODHCTION AND SALES PRICE OF RUBBER,
MALAYAN ESTATES, ANNUALLY, 1921–33*

(Pence per pound; logarithmic vertical scale)

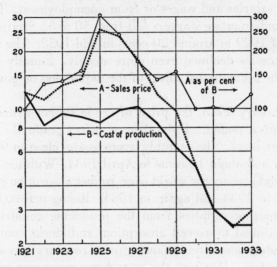

* Data from Holt, *op. cit.*, p. 15.

Some reductions of production costs were of a strictly emergency character, others represented genuine economies that were to survive the crisis. To the first category belong the lowering of directors' and agents' fees, the cutting of salaries and wages, the overworking of reduced managerial and labor staffs, and the reduction of maintenance work to the barest minimum. Among genuine cost economies were the adoption of improved tapping systems, the substitution of the superior forestry method of cultivation for the expensive practice of clean weeding, and general improvement in the efficiency of labor utilization. Some estates also reduced managerial costs by providing for the joint management of several plantations and by employing Asiatic supervisors under the control of a European superintendent. A few smaller estates were combined for the purpose of cutting overhead costs.

While the industry survived practically unchanged in composition and capacity, investors, managers, labor, and the producing countries as a whole experienced a succession of desperately lean years.[12] Investors felt the impact of the crisis in the absence of dividends (see Chart 22, p. 143) and the deflation of share values. Managers and laborers suffered grievously from low salaries and wages or from unemployment. The daily wage of Indian estate workers fell from 50 to 55 Straits cents at the end of 1929 to around 20 cents in mid-1932. The wages of Chinese coolies declined even more steeply. Equally devastating was the accumulated effect of the depression on government revenues.

In February 1933, the price of crude rubber averaged less than 3 cents a pound. From then on prices gradually mounted to a higher level. The monthly average was close to 9 cents in December and about 12 cents in April 1934. With the recovery of industrial activity the world over, rubber absorption expanded markedly in 1933 and again in 1934. Rising prices, however, drew increasing supplies from the producing countries, shipments continued to exceed absorption, and stocks continued to grow. Under these circumstances, price recovery was sustained by two factors. One was the restocking movement among industrial consumers. The other was the anticipation of renewed restriction and a period of generally higher rubber prices.

British estate producers had commenced a new drive for restriction shortly after the Stevenson scheme was discarded. When the rubber market suddenly deteriorated late in 1929, representatives of the British and Dutch estate industries organized an Anglo-Dutch Liaison Committee. Plans for voluntary output curtailment led to an agreement in April 1930. In order to avert the continued accumulation of rubber stocks, the month of May was declared a "tapping holiday." About four-fifths of the estate producers of British Malaya, Ceylon, and the Netherlands Indies adhered to the plan and suspended production in May. Yet an attempt to secure the collaboration of small holders was abortive. With half of the Malaysian producing ca-

---

[12] P. T. Bauer, "Some Aspects of the Malayan Rubber Slump, 1929–1933," *Economica*, New Series, November 1944, XI, 191–94.

pacity under native control, the tapping holiday proved a dismal failure.

The result was a renewed clamor for compulsory regulation. In June 1931, the Anglo-Dutch Liaison Committee issued a public statement. Its chief points were that without restriction the industry was doomed to ruin, that no voluntary scheme could avert this result, and that government intervention was imperative. Sentiment and agitation for compulsory control grew rapidly. Hundreds of plans were put forward and discussed. At this stage, however, the Netherlands government, pointing to its long tradition of laissez-faire, again rejected the principle of compulsion. Actually Dutch unwillingness to embrace international regulation had ceased to be a matter of principle for, early in 1931, the Netherlands government had agreed to participate in control schemes for sugar and tin and, in October 1932, took the initiative in proposing a tea agreement to the British. The administrative difficulty of enforcing a compulsory plan on the many native producers scattered over the Outer Provinces, and the opposition of the numerous rubber planters, were the decisive reasons for Dutch non-co-operation.

In April 1933, however, the government of the Netherlands Indies reversed its attitude and announced that it favored compulsory restriction, provided it was possible to devise a practicable scheme that could be enforced on the small holders. Under the relentless impact of protracted world depression, opposition to compulsory regulation had declined and the entire economic structure of the Indies had been undergoing a profound change. In tune with world-wide reaction, the sixty-year-old policy of free trade and the Open Door had given way to a policy of extreme protectionism and government intervention in economic affairs.

Now government delegates, on the one hand, and rubber planters' associations, on the other, resumed parallel parleys. In March and April 1934, an agreement was drawn up and approved by the associations. The governments approved, and in April the International Rubber Regulation Agreement was duly ratified by the governments of Great Britain, the Netherlands, France, India, and Thailand.

CHAPTER VI

THE INTERNATIONAL RUBBER REGULATION AGREEMENT

The IRRA, the first comprehensive and compulsory scheme for the strict control of rubber supplies to the world market, was a treaty between the five signatory governments. The producing countries covered were British Malaya, Ceylon, British India, Burma, North Borneo, Sarawak, the Netherlands Indies, Thailand, and French Indo-China. Together these countries furnished 98.7 per cent of the world's rubber exports in 1934. The agreement came into force on June 1, 1934, and, unless renewed, would come to an end on the last day of 1938.[1]

OBJECTIVES

The avowed purposes of the IRRA are stated in its preamble. The signatory governments agreed "that it is necessary and advisable that steps should be taken to regulate the production and export of rubber in and from producing countries with the object of reducing existing world stocks to a normal figure and adjusting in an orderly manner supply to demand and maintaining a fair and equitable price level which will be reasonably remunerative to efficient producers . . . ."

This statement contains a somewhat bewildering mixture of reference to basic means as well as to secondary and ultimate objectives. Reordered, the elements of this declaration of policy appear as follows. The parties to the agreement aspired to the maintenance of "a fair and equitable price level" that would be "reasonably remunerative to efficient producers." Toward this ultimate end surplus stocks were to be reduced to a normal level and supply and demand adjusted "in an orderly manner." The

---

[1] The text of the agreement and subsequent amendments is reprinted in International Labour Office, *Intergovernmental Commodity Control Agreements* (Montreal, 1943), pp. 104–16. All quotations from the Agreement are taken from this source.

"regulation of production and export" was considered necessary to accomplish the agreement goal.

However, even such logical restatement of the IRRA objectives fails to yield a satisfactorily clear formulation of its real aims. This, like many other preambles, was among other things a vehicle of propaganda. The scheme had to be "sold" to the world at large. In some aspects the statement of objectives is confusingly vague. In others, the formal meaning appears to cover a real meaning. Some policy aims are implicit rather than explicit, and at least one is not stated at all. To get at the real purposes of the scheme it must be reviewed in the light of the reasons that doomed the industry to continued depression, of the heated debate of numerous control plans that preceded the adoption of the IRRA, of comments subsequently made by representatives of the industry, and of the authorship of the plan.

Regardless of the willingness of governments to approve of and back the new control plan, and regardless of the support received from a considerable but indeterminable number of small holders, the scheme embodied in the IRRA was the work of estate producers' associations. Under the leadership of the British RGA, these producers' groups had most vociferously and effectively promoted the cause of compulsory control. Their members had put forward most of the numerous schemes which were widely discussed before the adoption of the IRRA. Most important of all, the draft of the agreement was devised by representatives of the British, Dutch, and French estate producers' associations.

It seems a plausible assumption that anxiety over the fate of the estate industry was the primary *raison d'être* for the new control project. Under a system of relatively free enterprise, such as characterized the interwar period, investors and entrepreneurs naturally strive to maximize their incomes. The state of the rubber-growing industry in the early 1930's frustrated this drive. When the world slowly emerged from the paralyzing effects of the Great Depression, the future of the estate industry remained extremely critical. Although consumption expanded vigorously, production expanded still faster.

The profitability of investments in the estate industry was

nullified and the investments themselves were threatened by the persistence with which excess supplies were released by the redundant production capacity of the rubber-growing industry as a whole. The estate industry, in particular, suffered also from the growing competition of the native rubber planter. The profound apprehension, prevalent at the beginning of the depression, that the entire industry might "go native," had somewhat lessened in view of the remarkable accomplishment of the estate industry in reducing production costs. But it had by no means disappeared. In 1933 and 1934, moreover, the estate industry experienced the disturbing consequences of the marked price responsiveness of rubber supplies coming from the majority of native producers in the Netherlands Indies. While prices were utterly depressed, these producers sharply curtailed production, but increased it as prices began to recover. Thus, in 1933, the output of estates in British Malaya and the Netherlands Indies exceeded their 1932 output by only 12,000 tons. The native growers of these two countries exceeded theirs by no less than 130,000 tons. It was quite evident that a price level barely profitable to the average estate producer would attract increasing supplies from the native small holders.

The planned elimination of an adequate number of relatively inefficient producers or of the least productive Hevea acreage would have been an ideally economic solution of the problem of surplus output capacity. Legally and politically, such a bold step was perhaps impracticable, and it was never considered. Indeed, the IRRA studiously refrained from referring to surplus production capacity, although it constituted the chief source of the troubles to be remedied. Focusing attention on surplus stocks, the consequence of surplus capacity, the planners indicated that the entire estate industry, as it then existed, was to be saved and its earning prospects bettered.

As an alternative to the reduction of capacity, the authors of the plan chose to immobilize all but that portion of capacity which was required to satisfy the current demand volume at a price level profitable to the industry. This is what the scheme essentially amounted to. Partial immobilization of output capacity, of course, implied restriction. Yet, for propagandist reasons, the agreement carefully avoided this term and through-out spoke more vaguely and inoffensively of "regulation." Since rubber consumption is a highly variable entity, the margin of productive capacity that was to be immobilized would be varied accordingly. The rate of restriction had to be modified according to the course of the rubber market. The authors of the scheme undoubtedly hoped that in the long run the world's capacity to consume crude rubber would catch up with the full existing capacity to produce the material. In order to accelerate this slow equilibrating process, planting and replanting were to be strictly limited and efforts were to be made to stimulate new uses of crude rubber.

Output control also made it possible to suspend the menace arising to the estate industry from native competition. The status quo between the two groups of rubber producers could be effec-tively "frozen." Regulation of output increases permitted the encouragement of a profitably high price level without at the same time attracting increasing supplies from many small holders. As will be pointed out below, the initiation of control likewise allowed the relative underassessment of native and overassessment of estate capacity. The agreement is completely silent on this aim of regulation. But in 1936 the chairman of the British North Borneo Company declared frankly "that one of the primary objects of the Rubber Control Scheme was to protect European capital in plantation companies in Malaya, Borneo, and the Netherlands East Indies from competition arising from the production of rubber by the native at a fraction of the cost involved on European-owned estates." He affirmed "that the opinion is being freely expressed that, in addition to being pro-tected by the Scheme, the estate has the added advantage of en-joying a rate of assessment much higher than that given to the small holder."[2]

The earning prospects of the rubber-producing industry are determined by sales volume, unit costs, and the price received for its product. The IRRA aimed at insuring prosperity by "maintaining a fair and equitable price level." No attempt was made to define what a "fair" or "equitable" price was. Surely,

[2] Quoted in *Rubber News Letter*, Sept. 30, 1936, p. 2.

to say that it is a price "reasonably remunerative to efficient producers" is only to add vagueness to vagueness. No criterion was suggested that would allow efficient producers to be distinguished from inefficient ones. To carry out this price program, the controlling body devised a very elaborate system of cost accounting on the basis of which estate producers were requested to report their production costs. The official history of the scheme declares, without deliberate irony, that "the existence of reliable costing data . . . . coupled with the life-long experience and profound knowledge which many members of the Committee possessed . . . ., enabled it to take decisions which, in intention at least, were invariably directed towards the realization of the objective so succinctly [*sic!*] stated in the preamble."[3] However, in an appendix the same document[4] reprints official correspondence that suggests how utterly arbitrary was this costing formula (see p. 30). The value of the cost data as a guide to the controlling body is extremely doubtful. In the final analysis, the determination of a price "reasonably remunerative to the efficient producers" depended on the *ad hoc* judgment of those who held control.

The attempt, through regulation, to subdue the violent fluctuations of rubber prices must be regarded as a secondary objective of the IRRA. Concern over undue price gyrations greatly exercised the proponents of compulsory control. In the agreement it finds expression only in the declaration that demand and supply were to be adjusted "in an orderly manner." Implicitly this subsidiary objective is also contained in the wider goal of maintaining a "fair and equitable price level," at least in so far as fluctuations below such a level are regarded as undesirable.

CONTROL DEVICES AND MACHINERY

The over-all control devices were simple in conception. Each participating country was assigned a basic production quota roughly representative of its output capacity. These quotas were fixed for each successive year in order to make allowances for new Hevea acreages that were attaining tappability. The Inter-

---

[3] McFadyean, *The History of Rubber Regulation, 1934–1943*, p. 51.

[4] *Ibid.*, pp. 187–205.

national Rubber Regulation Committee (IRRC), in charge of administering the scheme, was instructed to announce from time to time the percentage of the basic quotas that could be exported by each agreement country. Since the aggregate standard quota of all agreement countries increased from year to year, every percentage of permissible exports allowed shipments of slightly increasing volume in successive control years.

TABLE 8.—BASIC EXPORT QUOTAS OF AGREEMENT COUNTRIES, ANNUALLY, 1934–38*

(Tons)

Country	1934	1935	1936	1937	1938
Straits Settlements, Federated Malay States, Unfederated Malay States and Brunei	504,000	538,000	569,000	589,000	602,000
Netherlands Indies	352,000	400,000	443,000	467,000	485,000
Ceylon	77,500	79,000	80,000	81,000	82,500
India	6,850	8,250	9,000	9,000	9,250
Burma	5,150	6,750	8,000	9,000	9,250
State of North Borneo	12,000	13,000	14,000	15,500	16,500
Sarawak	24,000	28,000	30,000	31,500	32,000
Siam (Thailand)	15,000	15,000	15,000	15,000	15,000

* International Labour Office, *Intergovernmental Commodity Control Agreements* (Montreal, 1943), p. 106.

The basic quotas shown in Table 8 were fixed, for all territories except French Indo-China, roughly on the basis of average exports from 1929 to 1932. However, the test of past performance could not be applied rigidly. The supply from the different producing areas had been more or less responsive to changing prices during the base period. Besides, allowances had to be made for immature and partially mature planted areas. Since information on these matters was quite fragmentary, it was often found necessary to rely on estimates. Thus the final result was the product of established fact, conjecture, and—natural under the circumstances—haggling.

With two exceptions, the percentage of the basic quota that would determine the "permissible exportable amount" was to be applied uniformly to all agreement countries. As they had done under the International Tin Control Scheme of 1931, French Indo-China and Thailand were able to bargain for special concessions. French Indo-China remained free to export rubber up to 30,000 tons per annum or up to the limit of French net imports, with certain penalties attached should the country ship rubber in excess of these limits. Thailand was guaranteed a minimum percentage of her basic quota amounting to 50, 75, 85, 90, and 100 per cent for the five control years from 1934 to 1938. Despite this liberal concession, the Thai parliament refused to ratify the agreement, insisting on an increase in its basic quota from 15,000 to 40,000 tons and complete freedom of new planting. In effect, this amounted to nearly complete freedom of action. These demands were not granted immediately, and the restriction scheme was started without Thailand's participation. Yet her position was so strong, both on account of her expanding production capacity and a geographic location eminently suitable as a smuggling base, that the country's basic quota was increased as demanded for the years from 1935 to 1938, and Thailand also was permitted to extend its rubber plantations by a total of 31,000 acres.

The agreement provided that in any control year the net exports of a signatory country should not exceed the permissible exportable amount by more than 5 per cent. Such excess shipments, moreover, were to be deducted from the country's permissible exports in the following control year. On the other hand, underexports up to 12 per cent of the permissible amount were to be added to the country's permissible exports in the following year. In order to facilitate compliance with these rules, the total stock of crude rubber in any agreement country was, with some exceptions, limited to a quantity not exceeding 12½ per cent of its permissible exports for the control year. Each individual producer, furthermore, was forbidden to carry stocks in excess of one-fifth of the quantity produced during the preceding twelve months or, alternately, twice the amount he was entitled to export during any one month.

In order to prevent further expansion of production capacity, new planting was prohibited. For experimental purposes only, each territory was allowed to plant a total area not exceeding one quarter of one per cent of its entire Hevea acreage. Replanting was strictly limited. Upon special permission by the local control administration, a producer might replant an area not exceeding 10 per cent of his total acreage in any one control year or a total not exceeding 20 per cent during all five control years. The exportation of any planting material from the agreement countries was prohibited.

The IRRC was composed of delegations representing the various agreement countries. Fourteen members and ten substitute members were to be nominated on the basis of the following scale:

Country	Members	Substitute members
British Malaya	4	2
Netherlands Indies	3	2
Ceylon	2	1
India and Burma	1	1
French Indo-China	1	1
North Borneo	1	1
Sarawak	1	1
Thailand	1	1

It is revealing to study the connections of the committee members that were nominated. A complete list is presented in the official history of the scheme.[5] The representatives of British India, Sarawak, and Thailand were civil servants or diplomats respectively. Of the eighteen members and alternates of British Malaya, the Netherlands Indies, Ceylon, French Indo-China, and North Borneo, eleven were business men recruited from rubber-producing or -exporting countries and the remaining seven were colonial civil servants. Representation was thus entirely confined to producing interests and the interests of the producing countries. It can be assumed, furthermore, that the influence of the committee members directly connected with estate companies was even larger than is indicated by this numerical breakdown. Their knowledge of rubber production and the rubber market doubtless surpassed that of the average civil servant on the committee.

The list of committee members also indicates the emergence

[5] McFadyean, *op. cit.*, pp. 177–86.

in the 1930's of a new élite of commodity controllers with inter-locking memberships in different control bodies. Members and alternates of the IRRC at the same time held three memberships in the International Tin Committee, four in the International Tea Committee, one in the International Sugar Council and one in the Wheat Advisory Committee. Sir John Campbell, the chair-man of the IRRC, was also chairman of the International Tin Committee. Professor J. van Gelderen, head of the Economic Section of the Netherlands Ministry for the Colonies and leading member of the Dutch delegation, was at the same time vice-chairman of the International Tin Committee.

Mindful of the eyes with which industrial consumers and the trade were likely to view the establishment of another restriction scheme devised and controlled by the interests of the producing countries, the IRRA provided for an advisory panel of three representatives of the world's rubber-goods manufacturers. Rep-resentatives from the United Kingdom, Germany, and the United States were duly selected. They had no voting right on the IRRC but were invited to tender advice "as to world stocks, the fixing and varying of the permissible exportable percentage of the basic quotas, and cognate matters affecting the interests of rub-ber manufacturers" (Art. 18).

The agreement contained elaborate rules for the working of the IRRC. Each delegation would vote as a unit and possess a number of votes calculated on the basis of one vote for every complete 1,000 tons of the basic quota assigned to their country. Thus, of a total of 1,114 votes in 1935, British Malaya would command 48 per cent and the Netherlands Indies 36 per cent. Excluding Sarawak, the British agreement countries possessed 58 per cent of the total votes. The presence of four delegations was required for a quorum. A three-fourths majority of the votes of all delegations was necessary for the fixing of the per-missible exportable percentage of the basic quotas and for the modification or abrogation of the procedural rules laid down in the agreement. All other decisions would be carried by an un-qualified majority of the votes.

The principal office of the IRRC was to be maintained at London. The various participating governments or administrations would provide for the remuneration and expenses of their delegations. The expenses of the committee were to be defrayed by all the agreement countries, save Sarawak and Thailand, in proportion to their respective basic quotas. Finally, the IRRC was directed to set up and maintain research and statistical services, and the participating governments were requested to supply the committee with precise information on planted areas and related matters.

The IRRA embodied a far less rigid control scheme than the earlier Stevenson plan. While the method of restriction was fundamentally the same, the procedure for the changing of the restriction rate was much more flexible. Instead of having recourse to an awkward mechanical formula, as the Stevenson scheme did, the IRRA relied on the judgment of a controlling body which was authorized to change the exportable percentage of basic quotas at any time and to any extent and thus could act quickly in the face of disturbing market trends.

Practical considerations, of course, limited the degree of flexibility institutionally so accorded to the controlling body. Too frequent alterations of the restriction rate would unduly hamper both local control enforcement and the organization of rubber production in the individual enterprise. As a general rule, therefore, the IRRC fixed percentages for successive control quarters. The period of supply rigidity necessitated a considerable lapse of time before alterations in the restriction rate would be reflected in supplies to the market. These unavoidable elements of rigidity placed a premium on the committee's ability to forecast correctly the trend of the rubber market.

The new scheme was also more flexible than the Stevenson plan in that it was not bound to a specific pivotal price. Both projects were intended to bring about and maintain a desirable price level by the manipulation of supplies. But the IRRA left the definition of a desirable price level to the discretion of the controlling committee.

In view of the great power extended to the IRRC, the success of the new plan depended in large measure on the judgment of its members and their ability to co-operate. The official history of the scheme affirms that the committee worked very smoothly throughout. Indeed, most of the rules set for its deliberations were usually held in abeyance. A quorum was always present. During 58 meetings held over a control period of about 9 years only three matters were actually voted upon.[6] Yet commendable as such a record is, it does not mean that agreement was independent of the distribution of voting power. Obviously, the committee members were fully aware of it. As long as the delegations of British Malaya and the Netherlands Indies were in agreement, they could determine all committee decisions.

It is also reported that, except in the early days of the agreement, the delegations were normally not pledged or bound to any particular course of action by their governments.[7] They were usually left at liberty to depart from their instructions. Beyond doubt, such practice greatly facilitated the smooth functioning of the IRRC. But it also augmented the power of the committee members over the fate of the world's rubber market. The official history of the scheme also emphasizes that of the leading members of the delegations who cast the votes, all but one were government officials and that the committee, therefore, had an essentially governmental character.[8]

However, apart from the fact that the delegates were apparently not bound to their instructions—if indeed they received instructions—it must be emphasized that the government officials on the delegations of British Malaya, the Netherlands Indies, Ceylon, and India were all members of the colonial office or the local administrations, and that in knowledge of rubber production and the rubber market they were likely to be excelled by their businessmen colleagues. The presumption is that, in view of the identification of the delegates with the rubber-growing industry and the rubber-growing countries, they were not likely to base their judgments with objective detachment on the interests of all sections of the rubber world. In this connection it must be remembered that rubber consumption was in all agreement countries either negligible or definitely inferior in economic importance to rubber production. The sole positive restraints on the preoccupation of the IRRC with the problems and interests

[6] McFadyean, *op. cit.*, p. 52.
[7] *Ibid.*, p. 53.   [8] *Ibid.*, p. 54.

of the rubber growers were exerted by public opinion, by the three representatives of the rubber-goods manufacturers, and by diplomatic pressure exercised by at least one of the important consuming countries.

LOCAL CONTROL ENFORCEMENT

In Article 3 of the agreement the signatory governments pledged themselves to undertake all measures necessary for the maintenance and enforcement of the regulation scheme. Except for the control of native-rubber production in the Netherlands Indies and Sarawak, all agreement countries adopted the procedure of the Stevenson plan for the distribution of their total permissible exports among the individual producers.[9]

In British Malaya, for example, an Assessment Committee appointed by the High Commissioner was charged with the assessment of estate-production capacity. Of the six members on the committee at least four were to be recruited from the ranks of estate producers. In principle, assessment rules were identical for all estates. Generally, output capacity was assessed on the basis of production records for the years from 1929 to 1932. Yet this rule often had to be departed from and supplemented in various ways. Sometimes reliable and comprehensive records were lacking. During the base period, when prices had been declining persistently, some estates had, more than others, suspended tapping on part of their plantations and had postponed the initial tapping of maturing Hevea stands. Again, the existence of partially mature and maturing plantations had to be taken into account. Because of their large number and the absence of reliable crop data, the capacities of small holdings were determined summarily by district officers in accordance with definite assessment rules.

The percentage of assessed standard capacity a producer was

---

[9] For details of administrative machinery and procedures see *Rubber News Letter,* June 4, 1934; *Bulletin* (Rubber Growers Association, London), July 1934, XVI, 414–19; Netherlands Indies, Departament van Economische Zaken, Afdeeling Onderneemingsland-bouw van den Dienst van den Landbouw, *Verslag over de Uitvoering en Werking der Rubber restrictie, Gedeerende de Erste Restrictieperiode* (Batavia, 1940), pp. 50–59 *et passim;* Gehlsen, *World Rubber Production and Trade 1935–1939,* pp. 37–41; and Lewis, *Rubber Regulation and the Malayan Plantation Industry,* pp. 1–6.

permitted to export in any one control period was in conformity with the exportable percentage fixed by the IRRC. To enforce this rule, a so-called Export Ledger System was employed for estates and export dealers. Each was given a ledger account at the customs office of the port of exit from which each one made shipments. In this account export rights acquired were credited and exports debited. Small holders, on the other hand, were provided with transferable export coupons that had the form of banknotes. With the rubber they sold, the native rubber growers passed these coupons on to local dealers who, in turn, delivered both to export dealers.

Export rights for estates were issued quarterly and ceased to be valid at the end of the current control year. The coupons given to small holders remained valid one additional month in order to allow for the longer period of time it takes native rubber to reach the ports of exit. Both export rights and coupons were made freely transferable to other producers within the country of issue. Without accompanying rubber they could not be transferred to dealers. But since most dealers were at the same time plantation owners, there was no limit to the number of rights and coupons that might be transferred to them.

The High Commissioner appointed a Chief Rubber Controller, to supervise the entire administration of the control scheme, and a Rubber Advisory Board, to advise the Controller on matters of administrative policy. The Controller exercised direct control in the Federated Malay States and on the mainland of the Straits Settlements. Separate officers on the islands of Singapore and Penang, and Deputy Controllers in the several Unfederated Malay States, wielded local authority on the advice of the Chief Controller. A "cess" of one Straits cent (about .6 U.S. cent) was levied on each pound of rubber exported from British Malaya. The accruing fund was devoted to defraying the local cost of administering rubber control, paying the country's share in the expenses of the IRRC, and financing research and propaganda work.

In other agreement countries exports were regulated in roughly the same manner. In the Netherlands Indies, however, this system of individual assessment and licensing was applied only to estates and about 10,000 small holders in Java. At the time it was not suited to the nearly 800,000 native growers in the Outer Provinces. Owing to their large number, the great distances involved, and limited administrative personnel, these holdings had never been surveyed and registered, and the task of doing so when the scheme was put into effect was altogether impracticable. The authorities therefore decided to regulate native rubber production in the Outer Provinces by means of a sliding scale of export duties. Since the great majority of these small holders tapped their trees only when prices appeared sufficiently remunerative, and varied the extent of tapping with the course of rubber prices, it was assumed that their output could be controlled easily by the raising or lowering of a special export tax. Sarawak was confronted with the same difficulty. There it was decided to regulate native production by the periodic suspension of tapping until all small holdings had been properly surveyed and registered, an undertaking that was not completed before the beginning of 1938.

The problem of assessing output capacity demonstrates the vexatious difficulties inherent in the administration of a tight restriction scheme. Administrative procedure requires rules that are definite and simple. However, the less complex the assessment rules are, the larger bulks the element of arbitrariness in their application. It has been pointed out that the selection of the base period, as selections of base periods usually are, was too arbitrary to be the sole determinant of the assessment formula. But all subsidiary determinants were necessarily applied in a mechanical manner. Thus, as far as maturing plantations were concerned, the formula usually considered the age of the trees, the number of acres, and whether unimproved or bud-grafted stock had been used. But, needless to stress, all acres of improved or bud-grafted Heveas of the same age were not equally productive. Ordinarily, no distinction was made between efficient and inefficient estates. As an exception, Burma in December 1935 introduced a subsidiary system of assessing capacity by broadly distinguishing between well-managed estates in fair condition and estates in poor condition.[10] Yet apparently

[10] *Bulletin* (Rubber Growers Association), February 1938, XX, 81.

no criteria were established by which estates could be classified in the suggested manner.

The official history of the IRRA maintains that in the division of the national quota of British Malaya between estates and small holdings, the assessing authorities were instructed to be generous to the native producer and that, where any doubt arose on this matter, it should be resolved in favor of the "little man."[11] However, there is considerable evidence and testimony that this directive was flaunted and that the division actually fixed markedly favored the estate industry. In 1936, McFadyean admitted that the small holders were relatively underassessed (see above, p. 167). This view is confirmed by many observers.[12] The small holders were fully aware of this partiality in assessment and vigorously pressed for revision.[13] A rough indication of the unequal treatment accorded to the two types of producers in British Malaya is shown in the following tabulations:[14]

	Exports			Standard Production	
Year	Small holders (*per cent*)	Estates (*per cent*)	Year	Small holders (*per cent*)	Estates (*per cent*)
1929	45.5	54.5	1934	40.9	59.1
1930	45.4	54.6	1935	36.8	63.2
1931	44.9	55.1	1936	34.8	64.2
1932	42.4	57.6			
1933	47.8	55.1			

While the production capacity of individual native planters in Sumatra and Borneo was not assessed, it nevertheless was necessary to fix their contribution to the total permissible exports of the Netherlands Indies. Representatives of the native interests agitated for a fifty-fifty division. But, fixing their shares on the basis of 1929 outputs, the government decided on a ratio of 100 : 71.5 in favor of estate industry. This was grossly unjust, since during the intervening years native productive capacity was known to have expanded enormously in con-

[11] McFadyean, *op. cit.*, p. 45.

[12] See the following issues of *Rubber News Letter:* Aug. 11, 1934, pp. 8–10; Aug. 5, 1935, p. 2; July 30, 1936, p. 5; Dec. 22, 1936, p. 4. See also Lewis, *op. cit.*, pp. 7–9; George, *Kautschuk*, p. 173; Schulz, *Der Plantagenkautschuk in Britisch-Malaya*, pp. 51–55.

[13] *Rubber News Letter*, July 30, 1935, p. 2.

[14] Data from *ibid.*, July 30, 1936, pp. 5–6.

sequence of new plantings which, undertaken by small holders in the boom years from 1924 to 1927, had trebled their previous Hevea acreage (see pp. 67–69). It is true that in 1934 nobody knew even approximately just how large native output capacity was. But early in 1934 small holders had produced rubber at an annual rate in excess of 250,000 tons, which indicated a capacity far larger than the official annual assessment of total native capacity. This assessment gradually increased from 146,752 tons in 1934 to 202,201 tons in 1938. As early as 1935, different observers estimated the current production capacity of the Netherlands Indies natives to be between 300,000 and 600,000 tons a year.[15]

The method of restricting native production in the Netherlands Indies by the imposition of a variable export tax was evidently the only practicable one at the time the IRRA was put into operation. In view of the price-responsiveness of this source of supply, the device adopted, if applied rigorously, could be expected to insure any desired degree of restriction. The striking underassessment of the total capacity of these native producers, however, made a very high degree of restriction unavoidable. As a result of this plan, the small holders not only labored under the disadvantage of sharply reduced outputs; they also received a much lower price for their produce than estate producers, for the native grower would have to bear the full amount of the tax. It is true that the government of the Netherlands Indies pledged itself to spend all the proceeds from the tax upon public improvements in the native-rubber-growing districts. But this could be considered no more than partial compensation at best. In fact, as large sums accumulated the government found it increasingly difficult to devise suitable projects for the spending of the funds.[16]

The working of the new regulation plan tended to discriminate against the small holders in still other ways. The prohibition of new planting had this effect. The authors of the scheme were obliged to forbid the extension of the Malaysian Hevea acreage because the remunerative price level they aspired to

---

[15] *Rubber News Letter*, Aug. 5, 1935, p. 1; Schulz, *op. cit.*, p. 52.
[16] McFadyean, *op. cit.*, p. 96.

maintain would most certainly have stimulated vigorous planting activity on the part of the small holders. However, the prohibition of new planting harmed the native interest also because of a peculiarity of native Hevea cultivation. Estates cultivate intensively in order to maintain the productive capacity of their plantations. Often, when Hevea stands are excessively thinned out, they are replanted. Small holders, on the other hand, bestow little care on their Hevea gardens, tap them fairly heavily and simply move on to new ground when the yield of the trees appears to be definitely on the wane. Natives, in other words, tend to preserve their productive capacity by new planting rather than by intensive maintenance work and replanting. The complete prohibition of new planting therefore confronted the small holder with an entirely new situation. As late as 1939 it was reported that the natives had been unable fully to adjust themselves to this change of conditions.[17]

[17] *Bulletin* (Rubber Growers Association), November–December 1939, XXI, 533–34.

CHAPTER VII

THE CONTROL SCHEME IN OPERATION

The IRRA originally provided for a duration of control from June 1, 1934, to the end of 1938. It was renewed in 1937, with only minor modifications of its provisions, for a five-year period ending with 1943. For a few months the agreement was extended to facilitate the postwar establishment of a non-regulatory organization embracing major importing countries as well as the producing countries. However, on April 30, 1944, the agreement was finally terminated. The following is a brief account of the history of rubber under the scheme.[1] Chart 21 (p. 126) conveniently summarizes the basic data on production, consumption, stocks, and prices during the entire restriction period.[2]

THE FIRST CONTROL PERIOD (1934-38)

The immediate effect of the announcement of the IRRA and the subsequent institution of control was to raise prices from 13 cents in May to over 15 cents a pound in the third quarter of 1934. The reasons for this price spurt were psychological and speculative, for shipments continued to exceed absorption and world stocks were still expanding at a marked rate. The IRRC, quite aware that this price level could not be maintained without reversing the prevailing trend of stocks, nevertheless introduced supply restriction only gradually. Permissible exports were fixed at 100 per cent of basic quotas for June and July, 90 per cent for August and September, 80 per cent for October and November, and 70 per cent for December 1934. The wish to gain the confidence of consumers' interests and to facilitate

---

[1] This account is based chiefly on successive issues of the following periodicals: *Bulletin* (Rubber Growers' Association); *Economist* (London); *Rubber News Letter; and Statistical Bulletin* (International Rubber Regulation Committee). The following books were also heavily drawn upon: Gehlsen, *World Rubber Production and Trade 1935-1939;* and McFadyean, *The History of Rubber Regulation 1934-1943.*

[2] Appendix Table VIII presents the exportable percentages fixed by the IRRC for each successive quarter.

the enforcement of control supplied the reasons for this initial moderation.

CHART 21.—ANNUAL WORLD RUBBER EXPORTS AND ABSORPTION, END-QUARTER STOCKS, AND QUARTERLY AVERAGE NEW YORK PRICES, 1934–40*

(Thousand tons; cents per pound)

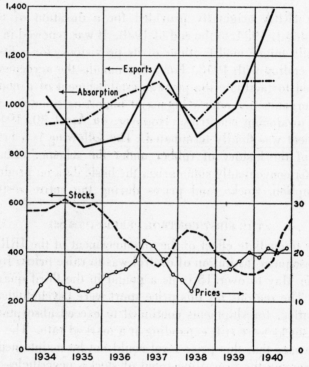

* Data from McFadyean, *op. cit.*, pp. 230, 236; *Survey of Current Business*, successive supplements.

By the end of 1934, world stocks amounted to 726,000 tons, equivalent to 9½ months' current absorption. Prices declined to around 13 cents a pound in December. At the end of October the IRRC met to decide the restriction rate for the first quarter of 1935. Determined to reduce world stocks, the British delegation advocated exports at 65 or 70 per cent of basic quotas. This demand for more rigorous curtailment clashed with the reluctance of the Netherlands Indies delegation to fix the percentage below 80. Still distrustful of the working of the control scheme, the Advisory Panel likewise favored a higher percentage. The British members, not controlling the required three-quarters majority of the votes, could not override the opposition of the Dutch delegation. Finally, a compromise was agreed upon that set the export quota for the first quarter of 1935 at 75 per cent of the basic quotas.

The Dutch refusal to accept a sharper restriction rate originated in the difficulty of controlling native production by the export-tax device. The device was technically well suited to the purpose. But because of the striking underassessment of native production capacity the tax had to be fixed at a very high level and increased with every reduction in the exportable percentage set by the IRRC. The accompanying tabulation[3] shows how severely this duty reduced the income of the native planter in the Netherlands Indies. The price of standard sheet in Batavia is compared with the estimated income received by the small holder

Year	Price of Java standard sheet at Batavia (Guilder cents per kg.)	Calculated income of Netherlands Indies natives	
		(Guilder cents per kg.)	(U.S. cents per pound)
1934	38.5	11.53	3.52
1935	36.7	12.24	3.76
1936	51.5	13.07	3.82

from 1934 to 1936.[4] At the beginning of restriction the duty was fixed at 10 guilder cents per kilogram of rubber. In the course of two control years the tax amounted to over 50 guilder cents. Over the first two years and seven months of the scheme, two-thirds of the value of all native rubber exported was absorbed by export duties. In the closing months of 1936, the duties accounted for as much as 85 per cent of the value.[5]

[3] Income data from Holt, *Pre-War Costs of Production for Plantation Rubber*, in U.S. War Production Board, Office of Rubber Director, *Special Report . . . . on the Synthetic Rubber Program* (Aug. 31, 1944), Appendix A, p. 17.

[4] The entire difference between price and income is not to be attributed to the incidence of the special export tax. Owing to the inferior quality of the native product, the middlemen and transportation cost involved, the native would in any case have received a price several guilder cents lower than the Batavia price quoted. In addition, the Netherlands Indies government levied a 5 per cent ad valorem duty on all rubber exports from the country.

[5] Holt, *op. cit.*, p. 17.

In view of this patently unjust effect of restriction, it is easy to understand the concern of the government of the Netherlands Indies over the further tax increases that each additional degree of over-all restriction would necessitate. On the other hand, the British members of the IRRC were evidently right in pointing out that the agreement objectives could not be attained without more rigorous curtailment of new supplies. Rubber prices kept on declining, and fluctuated around an average of 12 cents per pound in the second and third quarters of 1935. Though world stocks were now contracting, the rate of diminution was too small to impress itself on the rubber market.

Reluctantly the Netherlands Indies consented to a gradual tightening of the restriction screw. In February 1935, the IRRC announced that exports would be fixed provisionally at 75 per cent for the second and 70 per cent for the third quarter. Continuously low rubber prices, however, influenced the committee to revise this schedule and set the exportable percentages at 70, 65, and 60 for the three last quarters of the control year.

Although the Netherlands Indies government repeatedly raised the special restriction tax on native rubber exports, small holders continued to produce in excess of their quota. In October the government was obliged to buy up estate export rights covering 20,000 metric tons, destroy the licenses, and credit the amount to the native export quota. In December the IRRC increased the basic quota of the Netherlands Indies for 1936 from 443,000 to 500,000 tons. The increment was assigned to the natives' share in the country's total quota. The basic quotas of India and Burma were also slightly increased.

The tightening of restriction in the second half of 1935 had the desired effect. For the year as a whole, absorption exceeded world rubber shipments by about 100,000 tons. At the end of the year, stocks had fallen to 600,000 tons and prices had recovered slightly. With the full concurrence of the Advisory Panel, the IRRC decided to maintain shipments at the rate of 60 per cent of basic tonnages during the first half of 1936. It must be remembered, however, that aggregate basic quotas were fixed on an annually ascending scale. Sixty per cent of the basic quotas in 1936 was equivalent to 67.5 per cent in the preceding year.

World industrial production in 1936 was far above the depression level. World rubber absorption, at over one million tons, established a new record. At the same time, a severe degree of restriction remained clamped on the world's rubber supply. In April, the IRRC fixed the quota for the second half of the year at 65 per cent, only five per cent higher than in the first half. It was then estimated that this curtailment rate would insure a further diminution of world stocks by 125,000 tons at the year-end. Yet world rubber consumption turned out to be far larger than estimated. At the end of 1936 world stocks had shrunk by over 180,000 to 464,000 tons—only 5½ months' current requirements. American stocks were even lower in terms of current consumption. As a result prices rose vigorously from a monthly average of 13.2 cents a pound in December 1935 to 20.0 cents a year later.

World economic activity was evidently headed for a minor boom. In December the IRRC convened to reconsider an earlier decision to settle exports for the first half of 1937 at 70 per cent of the basic quotas. Misgivings over the world stocks position prompted the Advisory Panel to recommend an increase of supplies to 80 per cent. The committee decided on 75 per cent for the first and 80 per cent for the second quarter. However, with rubber stocks continuing to decline and prices to rise, the United States government exerted pressure toward an immediate upward revision of permissible exports. In view of increasingly scarce spot rubber, the market had turned extremely nervous and the policy of the IRRC was widely criticized. Until then the committee had enjoyed a reputation for moderation. Now the comment came forth that, confronted for the first time with a real challenge, it had taken action that jeopardized rather than insured stability. Profoundly apprehensive, some observers predicted a repetition of the 1925–26 boom the Stevenson scheme had encouraged.[6]

The IRRC met in January 1937 to re-examine the situation. Now the Advisory Panel advised lifting control percentages to 90 for the second and third quarters of the year, and proposed that the committee publicly reaffirm its intention to keep rubber stocks

[6] *Rubber News Letter*, Dec. 22, 1936, pp. 1–3.

at all times at a level sufficient for current requirements. The IRRC opposed the drastic relaxation of restriction it was asked to decree. It based this attitude on the ground that so steep a supply increase would hardly be feasible in view of the limited labor supply on hand in the chief producing areas. For the second quarter the exportable percentage was maintained at 80 as previously fixed, while an increase to 85 per cent was set for the third quarter.

The rubber market in the first quarter of 1937 seemed to substantiate earlier consumer apprehensions. Supplies did not expand speedily enough to satisfy the unprecedented volume of rubber demanded, and prices rose sharply to a high of 26.6 cents per pound in April. Shipments in January and February were well below the permissible level, since the upward revision of the quota in mid-December had come too late for a speedy adjustment of production schedules. The chief rubber-importing countries took a more and more alarmist view of the situation. On March 30, the United States Department of Commerce announced flatly: "The effect of . . . . International Rubber Regulation thus far is in the direction of a reduced volume of international trade at an unreasonable price, when the world needs increased volume at a reasonable price."[7]

Fortunately this sharp disequilibrium of supply and consumption was shortlived. Rubber exports increased in response to higher quotas. Above all, the prevalent high rate of absorption began to slacken and, in July, fell off markedly. The business boom collapsed and gave way to a slump. Since this cyclical change originated in the United States, it hit rubber consumption especially hard. In the latter half of the year, therefore, world stocks gradually expanded and prices receded from their high spring level.

In the meantime the Netherlands government was able to introduce a system of individual restriction of the native rubber growers in the Outer Provinces. In the course of 1935 and 1936, native Hevea holdings were gradually registered and their productive capacity summarily determined by sample tests. With questionable justification, the expenses of this huge under-

---

[7] *Rubber News Letter,* Mar. 31, 1937, p. 2.

taking were met from the proceeds of the special export tax by which native exports were then regulated. According to the survey, there were 790,000 native producers owning a total of 582 million rubber trees. The new system of individual assessment and variable "harvest" permits and export coupons was initiated on January 1, 1937. Even at that time the results of registration were generally considered to be on the low side. It was known that many native rubber planters, fearing that further taxation was the ulterior purpose of registration, had decided not to report their holdings or to under-represent them. Actually, native production capacity was far larger than was then assumed. In 1937, the Netherlands Indies authorities restricted the natives on the basis of an estimated 1,806,516 acres of small holdings. A resurvey, begun in 1938, necessitated an upward revision of this estimate to no less than 3,200,000 acres. However, this new estimate was not made public before 1944.

The recession of business activity in the United States continued unabated until the middle of 1938. In order to prevent an undue accumulation of world stocks and halt the progressive collapse of rubber prices, the IRRC reinstituted a more rigorous curtailment of rubber shipments. The percentage of permissible exports was reduced from 70 in the first, to 60 in the second, and to 45 in the remaining quarters of the year. With this unprecedentedly low supply rate, prices recovered from a monthly low of 11.6 cents per pound in May 1938 to over 16 cents from August through December.

RENEWAL OF CONTROL

The IRRA was scheduled to expire at the end of 1938. The IRRC announced as early as February that it had approved a subcommittee draft that provided for a slightly revised scheme. This new agreement would continue regulation until the end of 1943. The draft was submitted to the signatory governments with the request for their comments within three months. It soon transpired that none of the agreement countries was in principle opposed to continued control. Many of them, however, made renewed adherence contingent upon the allotment of an increased basic quota. These demands had to be conceded, at least par-

tially, since the defection of any of the countries concerned
would have weakened the monopoly power enjoyed by all the
parties to the agreement.

In fact, all other countries received a larger share of the
aggregate basic quota at the expense of British Malaya. This
is revealed in Table 9, which compares the amended basic
quotas for 1939 with those of the preceding year. The Nether-

TABLE 9.—AMENDED BASIC EXPORT QUOTAS OF AGREEMENT COUNTRIES,
ANNUALLY 1938–43*

Country	1938		1939		1940	1941	1942	1943
	Tons	Per cent	Tons	Per cent	Tons			
British Malaya	602,000	45.1	632,000	41.6	642,500	648,000	651,000	651,500
Netherlands Indies..	540,000	40.4	631,500	41.6	640,000	645,500	650,000	651,000
Ceylon	82,500	6.2	106,000	7.0	107,500	109,000	109,500	110,000
India	13,000	1.0	17,500	1.1	17,750	17,750	17,750	17,750
Burma	9,250	0.7	13,500	0.9	13,750	13,750	13,750	13,750
North Boreno.......	16,500	1.2	21,000	1.4	21,000	21,000	21,000	21,000
Sarawak	32,000	2.4	43,000	2.8	43,750	44,000	44,000	44,000
Thailand	40,000	3.0	54,500	3.6	55,300	55,700	56,000	60,000
Total	1,335,250	100.0	1,519,000	100.0	1,541,500	1,554,700	1,563,000	1,569,000

* Data from International Labour Office, *op. cit.*, p. 122.

lands Indies, Ceylon, Sarawak, and Thailand gained most.
French Indo-China and Thailand again were able to press for and
secure special concessions. The restriction rate fixed by the
IRRC would apply to Thailand only to the extent that it permitted the country to export a minimum of 41,000 tons of rubber
per annum. In effect, this meant that Thailand's exports would
not be restricted by more than 30 per cent of her output capacity. Up to a maximum of 60,000 tons, French Indo-China's
exports were to be free from any restrictions. This quantity
roughly corresponded to the country's production capacity and
the average consumption of France. Exports in excess of 60,000
tons would be subject to the penalties incorporated in the expir-
ing agreement.

The new agreement did not differ substantially from its pred-
ecessor. Control purposes, machinery, and methods remained
unchanged. The distribution of voting power in the IRRC was,
of course, altered in correspondence with the modified distribu-

tion of the aggregate basic quota. Exports of planting material to non-agreement countries remained forbidden, but were now allowed from one agreement country to another. The stocks which producers were allowed to hold on their plantations were increased to the equivalent of three months' permissible production during any control year. This change signified the intention of the agreement countries to facilitate quick upward adjustment of supplies in case of sharply increased export quotas.

The new agreement invited a second United States delegate to sit on the Advisory Panel. The intention of this invitation was to have the second American member appointed by the United States government. Such an innovation would have enhanced the prestige of the control scheme and facilitated co-operation with the world's leading consuming country. It also would have meant official sanction of the commodity control arrangement by the United States. It was probably for this reason that the United States government refused to nominate a representative to serve on the Advisory Panel.

The most important modification of the restriction scheme concerned the regulation of new planting and replanting. For purposes of control administration, Article 4 of the new agreement fixed the total acreage of each member country. During the two-year period from 1939 to 1940, each country was allowed new Hevea plantings up to five per cent of its total planted area. After 1940, the IRRC was to set up new rules for the control of new planting. Replanting was completely freed from restrictions, but the IRRC reserved the right to review the position and to limit replanting after the end of 1940 should this seem desirable.

By thus relaxing the limitations previously placed on new planting and replanting, the new agreement permitted the rejuvenation of the rubber-plantation industry. It also allowed expansion of existing production capacity not only through areal extension but also through replanting and new planting with material of superior yield. Since existing output capacity was then still markedly in excess of average world requirements, this departure from the less liberal provisions of the old agreement tended to retard the re-establishment of equilibrium by secular expansion of world rubber consumption. But at this stage, the controlling countries seem to have accepted regulation as the normal condition of the industry.

THE SECOND CONTROL PERIOD (1939–42)

Toward the end of 1938, the IRRC convened to fix the rate of release for the first quarter of 1939. It estimated that by the end of the year world stocks would be equivalent to about 6 months' current requirements. The Advisory Panel, foreseeing a large expansion of consumption as the depression gave way to a definite revival of industrial production, pressed for raising the release rate from 45 to 55 or 60 per cent of basic quotas. This request involved a considerable augmentation of supplies because aggregate basic quotas in 1939 were 183,750 tons larger than in 1938. Taking a less pessimistic view of the stocks position, the committee fixed the release rate for the first quarter of 1939 at 50 per cent.

While shipments expanded in response to the higher percentage of permissible exports, the increment was insufficient to keep pace with rising absorption. Indeed, during the first half of the year consumption exceeded exports by 79,000 tons. World stocks declined from 446,000 tons at the end of the previous year to about 375,000 tons at the end of June. United States stocks declined to 181,000 tons. Curiously enough, rubber prices did not rise in response to declining stocks. Because of the uncertainty inherent in the political situation, and probably also because of the confidence in the ability of the agreement countries to expand production quickly if necessary, industrial consumers and traders pursued a policy of holding only low stocks.

Forward-looking observers found a disquieting element in the precarious stocks position. They regarded the policy of the IRRC as an attempt to raise prices while stocks were at a hazardously low level. With stocks barely above necessary working amounts and still declining, any untoward event was, in their opinion, likely to upset the market.[8] Despite a recommendation for a higher release rate by the Advisory Panel and a special

[8] *Rubber News Letter*, Mar. 31, 1939, p. 69; *ibid.*, May 31, 1939, pp. 114–16.

message to the same effect from the United States government, the IRRC did not raise the permissible rate of supplies for the second quarter. Only for the third quarter was the rate increased to 55 per cent of basic quotas.

The outbreak of war therefore caught the non-Axis countries with extremely low rubber stocks. The London market was placed under government control. In New York, prices shot up from an average of 16.7 cents a pound in August to a high of 24 cents in September. Yet while the market registered apprehension, it was by no means panicky. The United States Department of Commerce appraised the rubber outlook by comparing it with that of August 1914. It emphasized that visible stocks were small but concluded "that there can be no expectation of lack of rubber except for transportation reasons."[9] The blockade of Germany was expected to cut European consumption by about 100,000 tons a year and world output capacity was estimated at 50 per cent in excess of requirements. The spreading of hostilities to the Pacific was not foreseen at the time.

In view of the complacent outlook which generally prevailed, the United States government deserves high credit for the foresighted negotiation of the Anglo-American agreement for the barter of crude rubber against cotton. The agreement was announced on June 23, 1939.[10] The two signatory governments arranged for the exchange of 600,000 bales of American cotton for an amount of crude rubber of equivalent value (about 85,000 tons). Article 4 of the agreement stated expressly that it was the intention of the two governments "to acquire reserves of cotton and rubber, respectively, against the contingency of a major war emergency."

Each government undertook not to dispose of its stock except in the event of such an emergency. If at any future date either government should decide that the time had come to liquidate its stock, it agreed to do so only after consulting the other government "as to the means employed for the disposal" and after "taking all steps to avoid disturbance of the markets." Except in a war emergency, neither government could dispose of its

[9] *Rubber News Letter*, Sept. 15, 1939, p. 179.
[10] This agreement is reprinted in McFadyean, *op. cit.*, pp. 206–9.

stocks before a date seven years after the agreement had come into force. Thus, the rubber stock acquired by the United States government was to be strictly a war reserve. Every precaution was taken in order that it could not be used to weaken the supply policy of the IRRC.

Article 5 of the agreement provided that the British government would "use their best endeavours" to secure from the IRRC release of the quantity of rubber involved in addition to the supply that "would under the normal operation of the scheme be released to meet current consumption needs." In July the IRRC accordingly increased the release rate for the current quarter from 55 to 60 per cent and fixed a rate of 70 per cent for the last quarter.

The American member on the Advisory Panel and also the United States government were anxious to have rubber-goods manufacturers build up their inventories. They requested that the quota for the first quarter of 1940 be set at 80 per cent. After prolonged deliberation the committee raised the rate to 75 per cent. With absorption expanding, American stocks were still contracting. In November, the United States government, seconded by the British Ministry of Supply, requested that the release rate for the first quarter of 1940 be set at 85 per cent. Again the committee weighed the pros and cons of the market and stocks position and finally decided on a rate of 80 per cent. In February, the committee agreed reluctantly to maintain this rate for the second quarter. From what is known of the deliberations of the IRRC it appears that it was ever prone to underestimate future absorption and was afraid of a sudden turn of the market that might cause a drop in price while stocks were high.

Thereafter, until Japan conquered the major rubber-growing areas of Malaysia, the rubber-supply situation was dominated by an unexampled increase in United States rubber consumption for civilian use and the endeavor of the United States government to build up a large stockpile of this strategic material in case the imminent war emergency materialized. As the consequence of an accelerating production boom, rubber consumption in the United States expanded enormously from an average of 524,000 tons in 1937–39 to annual rates of over 900,000 tons in the second quarter of 1941 and of over one million tons in June 1941. At the same time, the sense of urgency over the threat of war in the Pacific became intensified and the United States government, acting through the Rubber Reserve Company, established as a subsidiary of the Reconstruction Finance Corporation in June 1940, launched a vigorous stockpiling policy. The sights of this program were repeatedly raised until in October 1941 the accumulation of 800,000 tons of reserve rubber was fixed as its goal.

To implement this ambitious program, the Rubber Reserve Company entered into contracts with the IRRC by which the latter agreed to effect supply releases sufficient to meet these stock-pile purchases in addition to other rubber requirements. The United States government, on the other hand, pledged itself to an ultimate disposal of emergency stocks that would not unduly disturb the rubber market to the detriment of the producing industry. Throughout 1940 and 1941, and especially until the middle of 1941, the accumulation of reserve rubber in the United States lagged far behind its projected rate. When World War II actually spread to the Pacific and the United States was cut off from the Malaysian source of supply, this delay in stock accumulation was widely attributed to the procrastinating tactics and greediness of the IRRC and, according to inveterate Anglophobes, of Great Britain.

There is no need here to give a full account of the rubber market during the two years preceding the assault on Pearl Harbor. All the important facts have been assembled with fairness in the official history of the IRRA.[11] Following are the chief reasons the United States stockpiling program fell seriously into arrears. (1) The Malaysian rubber-producing industry did not operate at full capacity until the fourth quarter of 1941. (2) Again and again, shortages of shipping space delayed the transportation of rubber from the East to American ports. (3) The huge expansion of rubber absorption in the United States diverted increasing supplies to private channels. (4) Until the middle of 1941, the Rubber Reserve Company was reluctant to purchase forward rubber. (5) The company faced the compe-

[11] McFadyean, *op. cit.*, chap. xi.

tition of many other bidders in the Eastern markets, and competitive bidding frequently drove local prices above the company's fixed buying price of 18.5 cents f.o.b. Asiatic ports.

This situation improved only late in 1941 when all British and American rubber imports were placed under a government monopoly. The single buying agency scheme established did away with competitive bidding and allowed an augmented flow of rubber into the reserve stocks. Even then the Rubber Reserve Company had to feed a large portion of its purchases to rubber-goods manufacturers who clamored for ever larger supplies.

If the IRRC must shoulder any responsibility for the delay in the American stockpiling program, it is decidedly a minor one. It must be clearly understood that the agreements between the Rubber Reserve Company and the IRRC were not contracts for the purchase and delivery of rubber. It is true that the scramble for supplies in 1940–41 might have been somewhat less disorderly if world stocks in 1939 had been at a higher level and if the committee had been less reluctant to increase supply releases in 1940. But such reluctance, always sustained by underestimation of expanding United States absorption, must reasonably be expected from a control body whose purpose it is to look after the interests of producers and producing countries. The committee was charged with the maintenance of a certain desirable price level, and it naturally hesitated to jeopardize this aim by augmenting supplies and stocks to such an extent that a sudden slackening of demand would bring about a collapse of prices.

It is ludicrous, on the other hand, to accuse the IRRC of having exploited the supply shortage for the purpose of deliberately engineering exorbitantly high prices. If prices advanced to over 22 cents a pound in 1942, this was not excessive in view of competitive bidding and the marked rise of labor, shipping, and insurance costs. Owing to a stiff excess-profits tax, moreover, British producers stood to gain little from sharply mounting prices. Shorn of spurious arguments, the widespread criticism of the IRRC, as well as of United States government officials in charge of the stockpiling program, usually boils down to the implicit accusation that they did not foresee the Japanese conquest of the chief Malaysian producing countries. Can the critics prove that *they* did?

One fact that contributed to the relative scarcity of supplies in 1941 requires discussion because it is relevant to the subsequent appraisal of rubber regulation. This is the failure of the agreement countries to produce and export rubber to the full extent of the permitted quantities. The rate of release determined by the IRRC was 100 per cent of basic quotas during the first three quarters of 1941 and 120 per cent during the fourth quarter. Actual shipments were 206,000 tons below the permitted level. All control countries shared in the deficit.

This export deficit in 1941 is of interest because performance under a release rate of 100 per cent of basic quotas was a test of the accuracy or justice with which the productive capacity of different producer groups and individual producers had been assessed. Unfortunately, several circumstances combined to render the result of this test rather unclear, if not inconclusive. No one denies that the native producers were generally able to produce up to their permits while the estate industry as a whole fell into arrears. However, shortages of labor and coagulants, and the encroachment of military training on the time of European estate personnel, hindered the production performance of estates more than that of the small holdings. Lack of detailed statistical information makes it impossible to determine the full difference in the performance of these two producers' groups. Such data as are available show that after the first five months of 1941, shipments of estate rubber from the Netherlands Indies showed a deficit of nearly 28,000 tons while native producers overexported to the extent of more than 3,000 tons.[12] Yet even if comparable figures were available for other countries and for the entire year, the effect of malassessment on production performance could not be satisfactorily measured. For many estates, unable to produce up to their permitted quota and apprehensive of a future reassessment of quotas, bought up native rubber in order to narrow down or wipe out the margin between their actual and their permitted production volume.

[12] U.S. Dept. Comm., Bur. Foreign and Domestic Comm., *Rubber and Its Products* (Industrial Reference Service 10, September 1941), p. 3.

CHAPTER VIII

THE SUCCESS OF REGULATION

The following analysis of the working of the IRRA is divided into two parts. First, the success or failure of the control scheme is appraised in terms of its own objectives. Second, in chapter ix, the all-round effects of the scheme are examined in order to arrive at a judgment of its value from the general social point of view.

As expressly avowed in its preamble, the primary objective of the IRRA was to bring about and maintain a desirable price level by eliminating surplus stocks and adjusting supplies to current demand. To have this adjustment proceed "in an orderly manner," that is, to subdue excessive short-term price fluctuations, was another acknowledged aim of the agreement. How successful was the IRRC in approximating these goals?

It must be admitted at the outset that success or failure in these two respects cannot be precisely measured, for the objectives of the agreement were not stated with any degree of precision. There could be as many interpretations of what constitutes a "fair and equitable" and "reasonably remunerative" price as there are interpreters. Similarly, there are many conceivable degrees of market "orderliness" in the adjustment of supply and demand.

The official history of the agreement frankly concedes[1] that the directive of manipulating supplies so as to achieve a price "reasonably remunerative to the efficient producers" presented an insoluble dilemma. According to accepted meaning, an efficient producer is one who in the long run is able to sell his output profitably in a free market. Obviously, this concept was inapplicable to the artificial conditions which the scheme imposed on the rubber-growing industry. As stated in chapter vi (pp. 30,

---

[1] McFadyean, *The History of Rubber Regulation, 1934–1943*, pp. 143–46.

104), the IRRC had recourse to an elaborate costing formula by which individual estate companies reported their costs. This formula was rather arbitrary. It did not correspond to the accounting practice of rubber companies. The presumption is that the resulting cost survey tended to overstate costs. But under the circumstances the procedure adopted was perhaps the only practicable one.

The official history of the scheme declares that

returns received from 1935 onwards indicated a price round about 6*d.* to 6½*d.* as the average cost of estate producers in Malaya; costs in Ceylon were somewhat higher, and in the Netherlands Indies and French Indo-China after devaluation of the guilder and the franc somewhat lower. Assuming a modest return for tropical enterprises of 7½ per cent on invested capital, a price level of over 8*d.* was indicated as the lowest reasonably remunerative level for the average estate.....[2]

The "average" estate is here substituted for the "efficient" estate. The average cost level of from 12 to 13 cents, here mentioned, was of course bound to vary with the degree of restriction imposed upon production at any one time. Because of the relative invariability of overhead costs, a release rate low in terms of standard quotas tended to augment unit costs, a high release rate to reduce them. To remain equally remunerative, therefore, prices needed to vary directly with the rate of output curtailment in force.

The average estate costs stated in the above quotation include ample allowances for amortization and depreciation. The postulated return of 7½ per cent is strictly the investor's profit derived in the form of dividends. It might be doubted that the rate mentioned is strikingly "modest." Control policy was to maintain such an average rate regularly from year to year and thus reduce the risk factor which under free-market conditions would require compensation. Finally, it must be clearly understood that the average-cost basis that was to guide the IRRC referred only to estate companies, not to all types of producers. The average-cost level of the entire rubber-producing industry in the late 1930's must be presumed to have been quite different, and most certainly lower, than the range indicated by a survey of estate-output costs.

[2] *Ibid.*, p. 112.

The ideas of rubber planters as to the "fairness" of rubber prices tended to change directly with changes in actual prices.[3] Prior to the inauguration of the scheme, the majority of estate planters agreed that a price of 6*d*. (12 U.S. cents) would be a godsend. When the introduction of restriction stimulated a sharp price rise, the majority of estate producers looked askance at a "fair" price of 7*d*. and began to talk hopefully of shilling rubber. When prices dropped in 1935, the majority opinion again settled on 6*d*. or 6½*d*. as an "equitable" price. With the subsequent and sustained rise of rubber prices, expectations were gradually raised to 10*d*. and 1*s*. per pound of rubber. Demands of British investors usually aimed at a "fair" price several pence above that postulated by local rubber planters.

This is one basic trouble with an inexact criterion that invites subjective interpretation. The meaning of a "fair" price is likely to change the instant it is actually achieved. As long as its interpretation is left to producers' and investors' interests, the change is bound to involve an upward revision. By giving due consideration to the cost data returned by estate companies, the IRRC introduced as much of an objective element into its interpretation of a "fair" price as could reasonably be expected under the control frame erected by the IRRA. The committee also deserves commendation for having resisted extreme price demands, an attitude not shared by the International Tin Committee. The moderation it displayed was motivated by the desire not to offend the United States government; yet this desire in itself was laudable.

Nevertheless, when faced with the alternative of either jeopardizing its "fair"-price level or the availability of sufficient world rubber stocks, the IRRC again and again decided to base its release policy on considerations of price (see above, pp. 125–38). Nor does the praise of the committee's relative restraint in affecting price through supply manipulation imply that rubber prices under the scheme averaged low in relation to the costs of efficient producers or "fair" to the consumer (see above,

[3] *Rubber News Letter*, Sept. 16, 1935, pp. 1–2; *ibid.*, Feb. 29, 1936, p. 2; *ibid.*, May 26, 1936, p. 2; *ibid.*, Sept. 15, 1936, pp. 1–2; F. J. Tompsett, "Should International Rubber Regulation Be Renewed?", *Rubber Age* (London, 1937–38), XVIII, 183–84; "Fair Price for Rubber," *Rubber Age* (New York, June 1939), XLV, 166.

p. 144). All that this review can concede at this point is that, given the kind of control scheme set up by the IRRA, the "controllers" did not willfully abuse their powers.

That the IRRC did not exploit its monopoly power to maximize profits is demonstrated by Chart 22. It shows the aggregate net profits or losses of 87 British rubber companies from

CHART 22.—PROFITS OF SELECTED RUBBER COMPANIES, AND RUBBER
PRICES IN LONDON, ANNUALLY, 1920–39*

(Thousand pounds; shillings per pound)

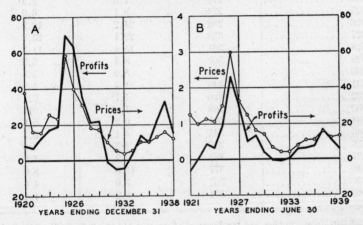

* Data from *Economist* (London), successive issues; *Board of Trade Journal* (London), various issues.

1919–20 to 1938–39. The fiscal year of 64 companies in the upper section ends on December 31, that of the 23 remaining companies in the lower section on June 30. While this presentation furnishes only a rough indication (no allowance is made for changes in capitalization), the conclusion seems warranted that, on the whole, profits were not strikingly high under regulation. Owing to the existence of large surplus stocks and the difficulty of curbing native rubber production in the Netherlands Indies, the scheme was unable during the first two control years to bring about a rise of rubber prices to the suggested remunerative level of 8*d*. per pound. The sudden and steep price advance in 1936–37 was the cumulative result of a business boom, lack of foresight, and perhaps negligence on the part of the IRRC, rather than of deliberate price-rigging. The high profitability of rubber production in that short period, moreover, must be attributed to a high output level as well as to high prices.

TABLE 10.—BRITISH RUBBER COMPANY EARNINGS AND DIVIDENDS, ANNUALLY 1924–40*

Twelve months to June 30	Number of companies analyzed	Average earned per ordinary share (*per cent*)	Average paid per ordinary share (*per cent*)
1924	275	7.8	5.9
1925	274	8.1	6.9
1926	280	24.2	19.9
1927	333	29.1	23.8
1928	361	15.4	11.2
1929	360	8.4	6.2
1930	336	8.0	5.8
1931	340	1.4	1.2
1932	326	1.7ᵃ	0.1
1933	298	1.4ᵃ	0.1
1934	301	0.4	0.8
1935	345	4.1	3.3
1936	346	4.3	3.6
1937	388	6.2	4.8
1938	377	11.8	8.0
1939	362	7.0	4.6
1940	331	5.2	4.4

* Data from "Rubber and the Investor," *Economist* (London), Sept. 21, 1940, p. 373. These data relate to companies whose fiscal year ends in the twelve months preceding June 30.

ᵃ Loss.

Table 10 indicates how the investor fared under regulation. The dividend record of a large number of rubber companies is given for the period from 1924 to 1940. The average dividend on common shares paid out in 1937–38 was not excessively high. Unfortunately, the period on which a summary judgment can be based is very brief. It seems safe to conclude, however, that international rubber regulation in the late 1930's was successful in making estate rubber production profitable. Without control, average profits would most certainly have been much lower.

How successful was rubber regulation in moderating the violent price fluctuations characteristic of the free rubber market? The official history of the scheme declares: "The steadiness of the price is illustrated by the fact that the average price throughout the pre-war period of regulation was 7.35*d.* per lb.; this is to a decimal point the price which prevailed when the agreement was signed in May, 1934."[4] Whatever this statement proves, it does not prove that rubber prices were steady.

It is exceedingly difficult to answer the question by reference to empirical evidence, for there is no readily available basis for comparison. We do not know how the price of rubber in the late 1930's would have behaved in the absence of regulation. The nature of the demand for and supply of the non-ferrous metals is perhaps most similar to that of crude rubber among all industrial raw materials. But the supply of these metals was subject to artificial interference during the greater part of the 1930's. A comparison between the price behavior of the rubber market under the IRRA with its behavior during any preceding period can yield only imperfect results. There simply is no satisfactorily comparable period. Before the end of World War I, crude rubber had not attained the dominant position in the rubber market which it commanded thereafter. The short period from the end of the war to November 1922 was characterized by the effects of wartime dislocations and, especially, the post-war business boom and slump. For seven years after October 1922 the Stevenson scheme held sway over the market, causing it to be more erratic than during any other part of the inter-war period. From the end of 1928 to the end of 1932, the market participated in the 1929 boom and the subsequent depression, which was one of the severest in economic history.

These facts must be taken into account when the price behavior of the rubber market under the IRRA is scrutinized. It is especially noteworthy that the fluctuations in industrial activity during the boom and recession of 1937–38 were mild in striking comparison with the changes of 1929–31. Chart 23 shows the monthly and quarterly ranges of crude-rubber prices, e.g., the differences between the highest and the lowest quotations. Comparison with the free-rubber market of 1929–33 does not suggest that the IRRC was successful in preventing undue price oscillation. The real test of success lies in the price be-

[4] McFadyean, *op. cit.*, p. 155.

havior during a period of fluctuating industrial activity such as 1937–38. The failure of the committee to subdue the volatility of rubber prices in this period is fair testimony of its incapacity to meet the test.

CHART 23.—MONTHLY AND QUARTERLY RANGES OF RUBBER PRICES, NEW YORK, 1920–39*

(Cents per pound)

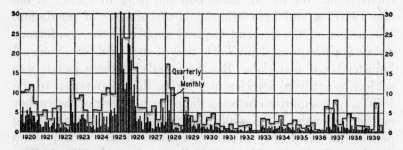

* Data from E. G. Holt, *Marketing of Crude Rubber* . . . . (U.S. Dept. Comm., Bur. Foreign and Domestic Comm., Trade Promotion Series 55, 1927), pp. 14–15; J. S. Bache and Company, *Commodities 1944* (New York), p. 180. Some years provided by J. S. Bache and Company on request.

It is easy to perceive why the scheme failed in confining price fluctuations to a moderate range whenever the total volume of rubber demanded underwent a sudden change. Owing to the time lag incident to the preparation of rubber and its transportation to the chief consuming countries, alterations in output schedules do not immediately become reflected in altered supplies of spot rubber. This period of rigidity lasts normally from two to three months. If a required increase in output volume is so large that migrant estate labor must be either imported or repatriated, an additional delay may ensue before the flow of supply is completely adapted to a changed market situation. Owing to the distribution of the "wintering" period, furthermore, supplies can be increased less quickly in the first than in the second half of a calendar year.

Indeed, throughout the control period, the flow of exports from the producing areas was far more irregular than is indicated by the supply releases fixed for quarterly periods by the IRRC. The official history of the scheme proudly points to the fact that actual exports in any one control year, excepting 1941, did not exceed or fall below permissible exports by more than 2.9 per cent.[5] Yet it is rather arbitrary to infer from annual data that market supplies within the year corresponded faithfully to the supply rates determined by the "controllers." Chart 24 (p. 148) compares the level of permissible exports with actual shipments during each month from January 1936 to October 1941. The irregularity of exports from month to month is quite evident. Although alterations in release rates were usually announced several weeks in advance, actual exports at the beginning of a new control quarter were often sharply at variance with the supply curve envisaged by the IRRC.

Export control by necessity introduced new elements of rigidity. Practical reasons of control and business administration do not permit too frequent and irregular alterations in the rate of permissible shipments fixed by the IRRC (see p. 117). At times of unexpected market developments the committee often met to revise a quota previously fixed for a certain control quarter. Nevertheless, precious days and weeks were bound to elapse before such revisions were decided upon.

Under these circumstances, the success of the control arrangement in combating undue price oscillation depended obviously on the ability of the IRRC to forecast requirements at least three or four months ahead. The official history of the agreement admits that the IRRC again and again underestimated future increases. But it is inclined to exonerate the committee from any charges of lack of foresight, on the ground that a release decision, subsequently found faulty, was fully justified by the information available at the time the decision was taken.

The underestimation of future rubber consumption in 1936–37, according to one student of control, suggests that "human control of supplies, stocks, and export quotas sometimes calls for super-human foresight."[6] Indeed, in the absence of any reliable method of forecasting the trend of a commodity market so subject to erratic changes in the volume demanded as is the

---

[5] McFadyean, *op. cit.*, p. 154.

[6] Alfred Plummer, *International Combines in Modern Industry* (2d ed., London, 1938), p. 181.

rubber market, faulty control decisions must be expected, and this expectation must be put down to the debit side of control schemes.

CHART 24.—MONTHLY RUBBER EXPORTS, EXPORT QUOTAS, AND STANDARD TONNAGES FOR ALL AGREEMENT COUNTRIES AND NETHERLANDS INDIES ESTATE AND NATIVE PRODUCERS, 1936–41*

(*Thousand tons*)

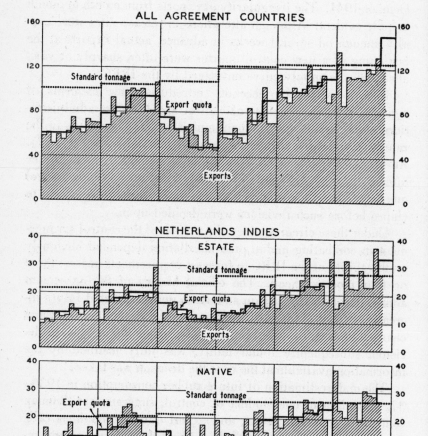

* Data from *Statistical Bulletin* (International Rubber Regulation Committee, London), various issues. Included in the total are Ceylon, India, Burma, British Malaya, Brunei, Labuan, North Borneo, Sarawak, and the Netherlands Indies.

However, the history of rubber regulation suggests that mistaken decisions on supply releases were not exclusively the result of the difficulty of forecasting impending changes in the total volume of rubber demanded. Whenever such changes seemed imminent—notably in the years from 1936 to 1941—the decision of the IRRC usually conflicted with the recommendation of the Advisory Panel of industrial consumers. Preoccupied with the need for sufficient supplies, the Panel was ever inclined to overestimate future requirements. Preoccupied with the policy of maintaining a "remunerative" price, the IRRC was ever inclined to underestimate future requirements.

On balance, the predictions of the committee proved incorrect more often than the forecasts of members of the Advisory Panel. Yet this was inevitable in view of the generally rising trend of requirements from the bottom of the depression to the wartime-inflated expansion in 1940–41, notably interrupted only by the short depression of 1937–38. When United States rubber consumption forged ahead from 1939 onward, the IRRC continuously set its sights too low. The official history of the scheme declares: "It was no fault of the committee that consumption in America constantly outstripped all forecasts."[7]

On the two occasions when crude-rubber prices rose spectacularly—stimulated first by an accelerating business boom from December 1936 to April 1937 and again by the outbreak of war in September 1939—a sudden expansion of the total volume of rubber demanded hit the market when rubber stocks were very low. As the history of the International Tin Control Scheme confirms,[8] this tendency to let world stocks fall to a relatively low level is implicit in most, if not all, producer-operated restriction plans. The primary concern of such schemes is evidently to prevent prices from dropping below a level insuring "fair" remuneration to producers. Low world stocks minimize the risk of price falls as a result of suddenly contracting consumption. It is true that they also magnify the risk of upward price spurts should requirements suddenly expand. But the latter

---

[7] McFadyean, *op. cit.*, p. 144.

[8] K. E. Knorr, *Tin Under Control* (Food Research Institute Commodity Policy Studies 5, Stanford University, Calif., January 1945), pp. 204–13.

"risk" actually means a "windfall" profit to producers, and hence is easily borne.

No one can blame the IRRC for its inability, demonstrated on several occasions, to make a correct forecast of future requirements. Yet the tendency to underestimate future consumption again reflects the primary concern over the danger of a possible price fall. Lest they overestimate future requirements and thereby permit a price-depressing augmentation of world stocks, the controllers are prone to err on the "safe" side, though such caution may involve a temporary upspurt of prices.

In theory, both the unsettling effects of the diverse elements of supply rigidity and the risks inherent in letting world stocks recede to a low level could be counteracted by the holding of some kind of "buffer" stocks. As a useful auxiliary to the manipulation of export rates, the availability of such stocks would impart to a control scheme additional flexibility for the purpose of ironing out short-run price fluctuations. By releasing supplies from a buffer stock to a suddenly expanding market, invaluable time would be gained for the adaptation of exports to a higher level of consumption. At the same time, the operation of a reserve pool would tend to diminish the necessity for frequent and sometimes abrupt alterations in export rates which, in turn, would encourage more stable employment of estate labor.

From time to time, while the IRRA was in operation, proposals for the formation of buffer stocks were indeed advanced.[9] As early as September 1934, the idea was tentatively broached by the Netherlands delegation to the IRRC. The object, however, was to avoid a further tightening of restriction at a time when the curtailment of native production seemed impossible. The committee decided not to act on the proposal "at a time when stocks were excessive and required reducing. . . . ."

The next proposal, submitted in January 1935, came from the Rubber Manufacturers Association of America, which suggested that "there should be established a reserve stock of crude rubber under the control of the International Rubber Regulation Committee, to be used for the purpose of preventing a speculative market. . . . ." Although in February the American representa-

[9] McFadyean, op. cit., pp. 89–93.

tive on the Advisory Panel withdrew the proposal because the time for such a scheme was not "opportune," discussion of the idea did not immediately subside. Strong opposition was voiced both in London and British Malaya. According to the London correspondent of the *Times of Malaya,* producers' interests apprehended that the formation of such a stock would eventually hinder any further price advances. "The trade would know what stock would be on offer and at what price, and its buying policy would be conducted accordingly. The function of a Pool of this type might result in control passing, to all intents and purposes, out of the hands of the industry."[10] The previous collapse of the pepper and shellac pools and the ensuing depression of the prices of these commodities were still vividly in the minds of Malayan business men.

The violent price fluctuations experienced during the period from 1936 to 1937 revived interest in the buffer-stock idea. At the beginning of 1938, Otto Friedrich, German representative on the Advisory Panel, again suggested the formation of such a stock as a means of enhancing the elasticity of the regulation scheme. The United States government likewise advocated the buffer-stock device, and A. L. Viles, American representative on the Advisory Panel, submitted a rough project of such a scheme. This plan envisaged that buying and selling limits of the stock should be definitely agreed upon by the IRRC and industrial consumers. A possible range of from 6*d*. to 8*d*. per pound was mentioned. The stock would consist of not less than 100,000 tons of crude rubber, of which half was to be held in the United States and the rest in the United Kingdom and on the European continent. Control over the stock would be in the hands of the IRRC. At the same time, J. Fairbairn and P. J. Burgess, both former chairmen of the RGA and chairmen of large rubber companies, supported the buffer-stock idea.

Yet again the proposal came to naught. The discussion of the American plan by the IRRC was repeatedly delayed until, in January 1939, Mr. Viles withdrew it and suggested that the discussion on buffer stocks be postponed until such time as his association could present a project that would be "more definite

[10] *Rubber News Letter,* July 30, 1935, pp. 3–4

and designed to operate in a more normal economic world than exists at the present time." It should be pointed out, however, that in producers' circles opposition to the establishment of a buffer stock was exceedingly strong, and that this opposition was backed by the rubber traders who feared that excessively stabilized prices would make dealers' operations difficult."[11]

Whether buffer stocks of rubber would have assisted in the stabilization of prices is a question. As stated before, an adequate buffer stock, properly guided, could well have served this function. But since its existence would lead rubber-goods manufacturers and dealers to reduce their rubber stocks, a successful buffer pool would have to contain large quantities of rubber. Moreover, experiences with the tin buffer stocks under the International Tin Control Scheme make it doubtful that any stock, similarly controlled, would insure limitation on upward price movements. The existence of tin buffer stocks only encouraged the tin "controllers" to let world stocks fall to even lower levels than they would have dared to in their absence. When the market suddenly expanded, the buffer stocks proved far too small and were released too late to prevent prices from soaring.[12]

Instead of giving serious consideration to the buffer-stock idea, the agreement countries, at the suggestion of the IRRC, provided for larger producers' stocks inside the producing areas. Under the second IRRA, estate producers were allowed to maintain stocks equivalent to 25 per cent of their standard quota for the preceding control year, while small holders' stocks were limited to a quantity equivalent to their permitted exports during the preceding quarter. The purpose of this amendment was plainly to create some kind of buffer stock. The official history of the scheme states:

This alteration was due to the lesson learned at the beginning of 1937, when, in spite of the Committee's action in raising the rate of release, supplies did not come out rapidly enough to prevent a sharp rise in price. The Committee felt that if larger stocks could be built up inside the regulated areas, they could be quickly utilised if supplies were needed urgently, and rapid increases in the rate of release could then be followed by equivalent exports from the regulated areas.[13]

[11] *Rubber News Letter*, May 31, 1938, p. 2; *ibid.*, June 15, 1938, p. 2.
[12] Knorr, *op. cit.*, pp. 207–12.   [13] McFadyean, *op. cit.*, p. 86.

This statement unambiguously acknowledges the practical impossibility of confining price fluctuations to a reasonable range by a system of export restriction alone. Yet the particular substitute for a buffer stock here projected was not able to enhance control flexibility materially. The IRRC permitted application of these new stock rules toward the end of 1938. Then the rate of permissible exports was as low as 45 per cent of standard quotas, and it was raised to only 50 per cent for the first half of the following year. Total stocks inside the regulating countries did increase over their 1938 level; yet the increment was no more than about 20 per cent, while the new rule allowed an increase of about 140 per cent.

For reasons pointed out previously (p. 82), native rubber growers are not in the habit of keeping stocks, and estate producers do not command adequate financial and storage facilities for the maintenance of much more than necessary working stocks. Whatever expansion of estate stocks did take place in 1939 was for the most part offset by simultaneous reductions in dealers' stocks. Dealers were happy to transfer to producers part of the expense and risk of holding the necessary working stocks of the industry. Under the circumstances, the merely negative action of permitting the accumulation of larger producers' stocks could at best no more than slightly improve control flexibility in adopting supply rates to the market.

The success of the IRRA in terms of its own explicit objectives is soberly and, on the whole, correctly appraised in an official document published by the Netherlands Indies authorities:

Viewing the statistical position as a whole, there is reason for satisfaction. The stocks that accumulated during the depression have been markedly diminished; the temporary setback at the end of 1937 and at the beginning of 1938 was not of serious proportions. The primary aim of restriction, i.e., the reduction of world stocks to a normal level, has been accomplished. As for prices, the hoped-for stabilization was not realized. The IRRC could prevent neither a vigorous price rise at the end of 1936 and the beginning of 1937 nor a marked decline in the fall of 1937 and the ensuing months. The unavoidable fixing of export percentages some time before they became applicable and the relatively slow adjustment of the production apparatus to these percentages were the reasons for this failure.[14]

[14] Netherlands Indies, Departament van Economische Zaken, Afdeeling Onderneemingslandbouw van den Dienst van den Landbouw, *Verslag over de Uitvoering en Werking der Rubber restrictie, Gedeerende de Erste Restrictieperiode* (Batavia, 1940), pp. 34–35.

Since the achievement of a relatively stable price level was secondary to the accomplishment of a "fair"-price level, it may be inferred that in terms of its avowed objectives the IRRA was, on balance, successful.

This impression of success is fortified if the frame of reference is extended to the tacit goals of the restriction arrangement (see pp. 109–10). The scheme did not attempt an internal reorganization of the estate industry. By not relieving the industry of its surplus capacity, and by restricting high-cost and low-cost producers on an equal basis, the financial structure of the estate industry was effectively protected. In particular, the estate industry was also spared further competitive encroachment on the part of the native small holders.

However, the frame of reference must be still further extended in order to arrive at a full appraisal of the IRRA. The operation of the scheme had many effects that were neither avowedly nor unavowedly aimed at by its authors. A comprehensive survey of these variegated effects and concomitants, undertaken in the following chapter, will contrast the benefits of regulation with an impressive array of disadvantages and harmful consequences.

CHAPTER IX

THE COSTS OF CONTROL

In the preceding chapter we examined the benefits which the authors of the IRRA sought to confer and those which they actually conferred upon the ailing rubber-growing industry. In the present chapter, our attention will be focused on the costs of operating the rubber-regulation scheme. The term "costs" of course does not refer simply to the administrative expenditure, which was relatively moderate. Rather, it refers to the drawbacks, disadvantages, and harmful effects inherent in the operation of the scheme. These were borne partly by the industry and the producing countries themselves, but predominantly by the consumers and consuming countries.

Despite the immediate benefits which accrued from the IRRA to producers and investors, it was clear to some representatives of these interest groups that such advantages were reaped at a price. In May 1936, H. J. Welch, chairman of the Rubber Plantations Investment Trust, Ltd., discussed the merits of regulation schemes, with particular reference to rubber and tea. He granted that such arrangements produce certain benefits, but went on to say:

> Such interferences with the working of the laws of supply and demand bring certain temporary advantages, but are generally accompanied by disadvantages of a more permanent kind. The difference of opinion between the supporters and opponents of such schemes may largely be explained as differences between "short period" and "long period" views applied to the industries in question . . . . such schemes have the disadvantage of keeping production and strengthening the organization of weak or high-cost producers—they increase the cost of production by reduction of outputs and by the costs of administration of the scheme—they discourage consumption by increasing the price of the commodity. . . . . Further, whatever efforts are made to secure equitable treatment of all producers, grave inequities in the administration of such schemes are inevitable. . . . . Having regard to the above considerations, regulation schemes should never be prolonged for a greater period than is absolutely necessary. . . . . Schemes for restriction and regulation of such industries as ours only become nec-

essary because the conditions of the industries are economically unhealthy, and consequently the same return upon capital should not be expected of them while working under such schemes as could reasonably be expected if the industries were in an economically healthy condition.[1]

In August 1938, when the renewal of the IRRC was announced, the *Straits Times* of Singapore printed a special "Rubber Regulation Supplement." The anonymous author of the lead article, apparently a shareholder, agreed with the writers of the other articles that the continuation of restriction was necessary. He said in part:

> The structure of the industry is still such that no thoughtful critic would venture to suggest that . . . . the absence or collapse of control would not entail ruin; or, at least, the gravest financial embarrassment for all save the few most fortunate or efficient of estate producers.

But this writer went on to remark that the estate industry had done nothing to "rationalize" itself, that is, to improve productive efficiency and lower costs by the amalgamation of small estates and the application of the best high-yielding stock in the gradual replacement of existing Hevea stands. Only by such "self-organization" could the industry hope to assure its future "health" without reference to the "palliative of restriction," and compete profitably with the Asiatic small holder. He concluded:

> But if it continues to muddle along as in recent years its doom as a field for capital and the employment of European directorial and managerial initiative may be sealed within no great space of time—even though further doses of regulation prolong its dissolution to an indeterminable extent.[2]

It should be noted that both animadversions agree on the fundamentally "unhealthy" condition of the rubber-growing industry at the time the restriction scheme was launched. They also agree that the operation of the agreement—while keeping the patient alive—did not cure him. The chief ill of the industry was that it could produce much more rubber than the world was prepared to use, and, because it was slow to respond to changing prices, tended to supply the market excessively. A secondary ill was the inability of a great many estates to operate profitably at a level of rubber prices that did not attract huge supplies from native producers.

[1] *Rubber News Letter*, June 15, 1936, pp. 3–4.
[2] *Ibid.*, Oct. 29, 1938, p. 5.

To cure the first ill it was obviously necessary to lower output capacity by the elimination of relatively high-cost producing units. This could be achieved either by the tortuously slow and harsh process of continued free competition, or by a planned operation. To cure the second ill it was necessary to lower the average cost level of the estate industry through reorganization. Cost reduction through the utilization of superior planting stock would work too slowly to give early results. The reform of the directorial and agency system, the employment of native personnel in some managerial positions, the merging of estates below optimum size, and the reduction of the capital burden by financial reorganization were probably the only effective means toward this end.

All these operations, while ultimately beneficial, would have been exceedingly painful in the short run. The IRRA chose none of them. Continuation of unbounded competition was unacceptable to the governments of the producing countries as well as to the majority of vocal producers and investors. The planned elimination of redundant output capacity, though not impossible (see pp. 110–11), posed so many legal, political, and financial problems that it was not seriously considered. Drastic reorganization of the estate industry likewise seemed impracticable, since it would have been staunchly opposed by the powerful vested interests that would suffer from such a bold step.

The easiest way out, the remedy chosen by the authors of the IRRA and regarded as a palliative by the critics quoted above, was to prevent the flow of excess supplies by export restriction and adapt the release of exports to the manipulation of a price level profitable to the majority of estate producers. The estate industry was protected against native competition by the restriction of individual producing units on the basis of a largely historical status quo. This design left the existing productive capacity and financial structure of the industry untouched. As will be seen below, it had the great advantage, at least in the shorter run, of sparing producers and investors any financial sacrifices by transferring the cost of operating the scheme to the consumers of rubber.

In several ways, the adopted arrangement necessarily raised

the average cost level of the industry over what it would have been had any of the other remedies been chosen. Under continued conditions of a free rubber market, all producing units would have been forced to adapt their costs to a continued low-price level. If the margin of excess output capacity had been eliminated by planned intervention, both the disappearance of high-cost producing units and the ability of the remaining producers to operate near capacity would have lowered the level of average costs.[3] By protecting investments in obsolete producing units, by keeping them in production on the same basis as efficient producers, and by necessitating a sharp average rate of output restriction, the cost level was artificially raised.

A rough indication of the cost-raising effect is presented in Table 11. It should be noted that only very tentative inferences can be drawn from these data. "All-in costs" were derived from returns received by estate producers on the basis of a rather arbitrary costing formula (see p. 104). They include allowances for depreciation and amortization on a generally very liberal scale. According to the table, less than half of the output in 1937 came from estates which could have announced profits because their all-in production costs did not exceed London prices. Chart 20 (p. 105) and Table 10 (p. 144) patently contradict this conclusion. On the whole, the operation of estate companies was profitable in that year. The average amount earned by 345 companies per ordinary share was over 4 per cent.

While the absolute figures given for plantation costs must, therefore, be taken with a grain of salt, the distribution of output over relative-cost groups remains relevant to our discussion. In all three years concerned, about three-fourths of the Malayan estate output was contributed by companies whose all-in costs did not exceed 6.5d. per pound. Had those high-cost companies producing the remainder been eliminated, the average cost level of Malayan estates would have been lowered not only through

---

[3] This cost-raising effect of restriction was bluntly stated by J. L. Milne, the chairman of the RGA in 1939. Exhorting the members of the association to reduce costs in every possible way, he continued: "This is all the more necessary in view of the fact that we have to maintain one hundred per cent of our areas and endeavor to pay dividends on one hundred per cent of our capital out of revenue from working, perhaps, only 50 per cent or 60 per cent of our areas." *Bulletin* (Rubber Growers Association), April 1939, XXI, 225.

their exclusion, but also because the remaining companies could have produced at a higher percentage of their capacity.

TABLE 11.—ESTATE OUTPUTS IN BRITISH MALAYA AT VARIOUS ALL-IN COSTS, 1935–37*

Production costs (*Pence per lb.*)	Cumulative percentages of total output		
	1935	1936	1937
Under			
5.00	2.5	1.4	....
5.25	12.1	1.4	15.9
5.50	12.1	12.2	15.9
5.75	31.6	26.9	27.1
6.00	47.0	53.7	43.5
6.25	71.4	74.7	61.2
6.50	88.2	74.7	78.4
6.75	88.2	92.2	84.4
7.00	92.6	92.2	84.4
7.25	96.2	95.8	88.4
7.50	97.6	96.6	94.3
7.75	97.6	96.6	94.3
8.00	99.0	96.6	97.3
8.25	99.0	98.5	98.1
8.50	99.0	98.5	98.1
8.75	100.0	98.5	98.1
9.00	100.0	98.5	100.0
9.25	100.0	100.0	100.0
Average London price (*pence per lb.*)	6.00	7.75	9.50

* Data from E. G. Holt, *Pre-war Costs of Production for Plantation Rubber*, U.S. War Production Board, Office of Rubber Director, *Special Report . . . . on the Synthetic Rubber Program, Investment and Production Costs* (Aug. 31, 1944), Appendix A, p. 20.

The "unhealthy" protection of obsolete surplus capacity and its effects on the cost level were not, of course, confined to the estate industry in British Malaya. Exactly the same conditions characterized other sections of the Eastern rubber plantation industry and, furthermore, operated as between these various sections. Not only were there relatively high-cost and low-cost units within the different classes of producers, but also average cost levels differed among the several sections of the entire Malaysian industry. Following a keen analysis of production costs during the period 1935–38, Holt arranged the most important of these sections in their order of group efficiency, from highest-cost to lowest-cost, as follows:[4]

> Ceylon sterling companies
> Malayan sterling companies
> Netherlands Indies estates
> Malayan dollar companies
> Ceylon rupee companies
> French Indo-China estates
> Ceylon small holders
> Malayan small holders
> Netherlands Indies small holders

In principle, all producing units in all producing areas were supposed to be restricted on an equal basis. In practice, the distribution of the aggregate recognized production capacity over the different agreement countries was also affected by bargaining (see pp. 113–14). The important deviation from the principle of equal treatment, however, occurred in the assessment of native productive capacity. As has been pointed out, the large native rubber-producing industries in the Netherlands Indies and in British Malaya were underassessed in relation to their estate competitors. This meant that groups of relatively less efficient producers were favored over groups of relatively more efficient ones.

To summarize, the introduction of the IRRA raised the average cost level of the Malaysian rubber-growing industry (1) by protecting obsolete producing units that represented the industry's surplus output capacity; (2) by generally restricting relatively low-cost producers more rigorously than high-cost producers; and (3) by enforcing the operation of all producing units markedly below their capacity, which again was necessitated by the protection of investments in obsolete units.

The official history of the scheme takes great pains to belittle the extent to which rubber regulation impaired average efficiency by the protection of obsolete producing units.[5] The following

---

[4] E. G. Holt, *Pre-war Costs of Production for Plantation Rubber*, in *Special Report* (cited above under Table 11), Appendix A, p. 25.

[5] McFadyean, *The History of Rubber Regulation 1934–1943*, pp. 149–50.

are the arguments—mostly subterfuges—employed to this end, and the rebuttals:

1. "Judged by one test, general efficiency was not impaired; ample supplies of rubber were available at prices which were not out of line with prices in general." This test is irrelevant. Price is a dubious indicator of efficiency under conditions of restrictive control. Furthermore, the expression "not out of line with prices in general" is ambiguous. The comparison of price levels of different commodities may be made only through indexes based on a common period, and the choice of this base is necessarily arbitrary. A comparison of relative fluctuations shows that rubber prices were more volatile than "prices in general." It is, of course, natural that the price fluctuations of a single commodity should be wider in range than those of a group of commodities. Yet the comparison also shows that short-term trends in rubber prices were independent of the trend of general prices. Whatever the comparative levels, it cannot be said that rubber prices were in line with "prices in general."

2. Regulation "did not, in any degree which was important to consumers, protect territories which were inefficient rubber producers; there is no reason to suppose that costs in the two important producing centres, Malaya and the N.E.I., differed so appreciably that the consumer would have gained substantially if a new price level had been established as a result of full competitive production." Average estate production costs in the Netherlands Indies were admittedly not substantially lower than those in British Malaya. But, in the first place, under free competition the large and vigorously growing capacity of native producers in the Netherlands Indies would have made for an appreciably lower cost level in that country as compared with British Malaya. In the second place, the important differences in average efficiency did not lie between different producing *territories* but between different *types* of producers.

3. ". . . . there is a very real check on the protection of inefficiency within a territory, since marked inefficiency would impair the ability of a territory to provide its quota, which would sooner or later be lowered. . . . . " At best, this argument proposes a grotesque test of efficiency—the possible bankruptcy of

"inefficient" producing units under an artificially supported price level, although such bankruptcies were not forthcoming under conditions of sharply depressed prices in 1930–32.

4. "Some, if not all, producing territories weight efficiency as well as straight productive capacity in assessing individual estates." This is a good point. Yet such consideration of efficiency, based on the physical appearance of plantations, was not allowed to enter the assessment formula except to a very minor extent.

5. ". . . . profits were, as always, a continuing incentive to individual efficiency." Obviously, even under restriction, the low-cost producers found the same price more profitable than the high-cost producers, and, to this extent, the profit motive continued to work toward efficiency. This incentive was not permitted, however, to affect the distribution of production over different producing units.[6] Under a free market the more efficient producer can lower his price and, eventually, force his inefficient competitor to accept this price or discontinue production. Under the IRRA, this effect of the profit system was suspended. Individual efficiency meant solely higher profits to individual investors.

6. Since, under regulation, rubber producers were enabled to earn profits, they could devote "large sums to the improvement of their plantations," i.e., through replanting and new planting with superior Hevea stock. To the limited extent that such planting could and did take place under the agreement, it would only improve *future* efficiency, from seven to ten years after planting. It could not affect current efficiency. Continuation of free-market conditions would have forced increased efficiency of *current* production. Planned elimination of obsolete surplus capacity likewise would have raised the average *current* efficiency of the industry.

7. ". . . . efficient production should create an improvement in the standard of living of the labour force engaged upon

---

[6] The transferability of output and export certificates allowed low-cost producers to produce above the level determined by restriction. But trading in such certificates was ordinarily light and the profitability of purchasing them was diminished by their price, which varied directly with the degree of restriction. Purchasing transactions were profitable only as long as certificate prices were less than the cost economies that could be achieved by increasing the output.

it. There was a general rise in the rate of wages payable to estate tappers and other labourers, and most estates took advantage of returning prosperity to accelerate the provision of better housing and medical attention . . . ." This reasoning is rather oblique. A general rise in wage rates did take place under the agreement. As far as the prosperity of the rubber industry contributed to the increase, it was obviously not the result of enhanced efficiency but of higher prices arising from restriction. Wage increases are made possible by scarcity profits as well as by efficiency profits.

We may conclude that these counter-arguments are, for the most part, spurious and do not invalidate the observations made above on the cost-raising effects of the IRRA. Such slight discrimination in favor of more efficient producers which some local control administrations permitted to influence the assessment of individual output capacity were excellent in principle but, unfortunately, minor in total effect. The authors of the scheme might, by the elaboration and progressive extension of this principle of unequal treatment, have encouraged a gradual reorganization of the estate industry on a sounder basis.

A full evaluation of the IRRA requires that these two central facts of rubber regulation—the preservation of economically and technically obsolete capacity and the cost-raising tendencies of restriction—be appraised from the viewpoints of both the producing industry and producing countries on the one hand, and the consumers and consuming countries on the other.

Every cent by which the "controllers" managed to raise prices in order to compensate for the cost-raising effects of restriction was paid by the consumer. He also paid for the expense of administering the scheme, for the defrayment of which a special tax was imposed on rubber exports from the agreement countries.[7] Specifically, the cost and price increment involved was primarily borne by the ultimate consumer of crude rubber. The demand for rubber contained in rubber goods being markedly price-unresponsive, industrial consumers could usually pass on the extra costs of their raw material to the final consumer.

[7] Only the cost of surveying and assessing native output capacity in the Netherlands Indies was met from the huge fund accumulated by the restrictive taxes levied on native shipments through 1936.

The regulated industry was able to shift the costs of operating its restriction scheme to the consumers because of the price unresponsiveness of the demand for rubber and the high degree of monopoly power commanded by the agreement countries. No major rubber-producing areas remained outside the agreement, nor was there any danger that an important outside rubber-plantation industry could be developed in the foreseeable future. As regards substitute materials, increased prices of crude rubber probably entailed a somewhat enhanced use of reclaimed rubber but, since prices were not maintained at an exceedingly high level, there were definite limits to the extension of reclaim production and consumption (see pp. 14–15). The synthetic-rubber manufacturing industry was generally still in its incubatory stage. Where it was more advanced, as in the USSR and in Germany, its development was not stimulated by high crude-rubber prices, but was planned and protected by the government for reasons of high policy.

Thus, restriction enabled the regulating countries to shift to other people's shoulders the losses which would have befallen the industry under continuing free competition. Consumers bore the cost of artificially prolonging the life of a redundant and obsolete production capacity, the extra costs inherent in restricted output operations, and the expense of administering the scheme. Since we do not know how much lower the price of rubber would have ranged in the absence of the IRRA, these costs cannot be even approximately estimated. Yet they certainly were not trifling. With annual average rubber consumption ranging around 900,000 tons, every additional cent per pound paid by the consumer involved a sum in the neighborhood of 20 million dollars a year. From 1934 to 1939, the aggregate loss borne by consumers probably amounted to several hundred million dollars.

The interests of rubber-goods manufacturers differ from those of the ultimate consumer of rubber. As long as prices are not excessively high—and generally they were not under the IRRA —their dominant concern is over stability of price. Stable prices minimize, unstable prices maximize inventory losses. How did the industrial consumer then fare under restriction?

It is the considered conjecture of this writer that the IRRA was not successful in preventing undue price gyrations. Yet, since we cannot know how violently prices would have fluctuated in the absence of the scheme, no more than conjecture can be offered. At various times under the agreement spot rubber was scarce and, as the repeated discrepancy between the supply policy of the IRRC and the advice of the American representative on the Advisory Panel indicates, less cautious release decisions on the part of the "controllers" could have prevented such scarcities. In so far as the rise in average rubber prices necessitated by restriction militated against extension of rubber use, the rubber-goods manufacturing industry was liable to suffer a long-run disadvantage. Yet, on the whole, it seems justifiable to conclude that any beneficial or adverse control effects on industrial consumers were slight.

The "costs" of the IRRA to the ultimate consumers were, of course, the "costs" of the agreement to the consuming countries which received no comparable compensatory benefits from the scheme. More than five-sixths of all crude rubber absorbed was consumed outside the producing countries, the United Kingdom, and the Netherlands. Higher prices of rubber articles, necessitated by higher costs of the raw material, absorb a correspondingly larger share of money incomes, which fact may have a depressional effect on other industries or slow up accumulation of investment capital on savings account. However, such indirect deleterious effects are admittedly of minor importance, and negligible in the leading importing countries. More telling is the adverse influence of higher rubber prices on countries that, in a period of disintegrating multilateral trade, labored under a difficult foreign-exchange position. Indeed, owing to differences in the foreign-exchange situation and per capita real income, a rubber price raised by means of restriction places a burden of unequal magnitude on different countries and peoples. It creates differences in access to raw materials.

The question might be posed whether there are any compensatory advantages which international rubber regulation conferred upon consumers and net-importing countries. The official history of the scheme suggests two:

It may be conjectured that the continuance for several years of unregulated production in a depressed or shrinking world would have resulted in such a fall in productive capacity as to threaten a shortage if depression and restriction in trade generally were succeeded by boom and expansion. Some estates would have been liquidated and many more would have been neglected; some would have been tapped to death in an effort to hold out for better days. There is no evidence to suggest that native production would have served to fill the gap; it fell off more steeply than plantation production in the depth of the depression and would certainly not have been extended. And incidentally the excess capacity of the early thirties proved to be rather less than adequate for the requirements of a world at war less than ten years later.[8]

Neither of these ostensible benefits to consumers can be accepted without rebuttal. It is quite unlikely that continuation of a free rubber market would have resulted in an excessive amputation of productive capacity. First, regulation was not initiated at a time of depressed and shrinking consumption. On the contrary, in 1934 the world was definitely recovering from the Great Depression and absorption was expanding above the 1929 level. Second, while some plantations under continued low prices might have been liquidated, neglected, or tapped to death, the majority of those representing current surplus capacity simply would have changed ownership and, at greatly reduced capitalization, have been held in reserve as long as rubber prices did not cover prime costs of production. Mature Hevea plantations can be neglected for many years before their output capacity deteriorates appreciably. Third, native production fell off more steeply than estate production in the depth of depression because it was more price-elastic, not because its output capacity somehow disappeared.

The fortuitous benefit of having a surplus production capacity when the United States and other countries decided, after the outbreak of World War II, to build a strategic stockpile of crude rubber is totally unrelated to the merits of international rubber regulation. With a material like rubber, stockpiles, not preservation of large reserve capacity, are the economical and safe insurance against wartime shortages. Besides, it was not foreknowledge of the events of 1939–41 that deterred the authors of the IRRA from attacking the problem of surplus capacity.

[8] McFadyean, *op. cit.*, Introduction.

As Mr. Welch stated, from the viewpoint of the producing interests and producing countries, the evaluation of the control scheme depended on whether one focused on its immediate or its lasting effects. From the perspective of immediate or short-run benefits, international rubber regulation undoubtedly seemed a boon. While it did not moderate price swings, surplus stocks were gradually reduced, a profitable price level was maintained, investors were saved from painful losses, and the consumer paid for it.

In the short run, the plantation laborer also may be assumed to have reaped modest gains from the artificially created prosperity of the rubber industry. Because of lack of statistics and for many other reasons, the exact proportion of this gain cannot be calculated. The general rise of Malaysian wage rates in the middle and late 1930's was due to several factors. In part it was simply a recovery from the depression level; in part it was the result of several recovering industries competing for the labor supply, and of increasing unionization.

In no respect, even in the short run, was the control scheme as favorable to the native small holders as to the estate companies. While the former profited from the higher price level maintained by restriction, their interests were seriously injured by the iniquitous system of differential assessment. The fact of mal-assessment has been admitted by many observers representative of the estate industry (see p. 122). In 1935 a Malayan rubber planter stated in a pamphlet on "Asiatic Production" that it "is generally admitted now that European estates, both in Malaya and Netherlands India, have been collectively over-assessed. . . . ."[9] In 1937, even the *Straits Times* conceded in an editorial that "it is by no means an uncommon opinion that Malayan small-holders could produce 100 pounds per acre above their assessments . . . ."[10] In view of their generally lower output costs there can be no doubt that, in the absence of restriction, the native planters would have captured a gradually increasing share of the world's rubber market.

The authors of the IRRA set hopes on accelerating the secular

[9] *Rubber News Letter*, Jan. 15, 1936, p. 2.
[10] *Ibid.*, Apr. 28, 1937, p. 5.

increase of crude-rubber consumption by the encouragement of new uses of the material. Yet the effects of mere propaganda and scientific research were vitiated by the relatively high average rubber prices necessitated by restriction and by the undue price fluctuations the scheme failed to subdue. Indeed, instead of encouraging extension of crude-rubber uses, these conditions were bound to stimulate efforts to develop substitutes. While the synthetic rubber industry was not a serious competitor of the plantations in the late 1930's, experimentation with artificial rubbers was gradually multiplying. Even in the absence of World War II, relatively high and unstable prices of crude rubber would have provided a constant incentive in that direction.

From the longer-run point of view, the "success" of regulation appears in an even less satisfactory light. The basically "unhealthy" condition of the industry remained. Had the agreement not been renewed in 1938, the industry's distress in the following years would have been no less than that which it would have suffered in the absence of the IRRA from 1934 to 1938. The artificial prosperity of the industry thus remained contingent upon the indefinite continuation of restrictive regulation.

Provisions for replanting and new planting necessarily postponed the time when secular consumption growth could be expected to catch up with productive capacity. Even replanting, it must be understood, involved more than preservation of existing capacity because the rules took into account only acreage and the number of trees, while the planting of superior stock made for an automatic extension of capacity.

In view of these considerations it is not surprising that the authors of the IRRA did not think the scheme ideal. "Some at least of those responsible for the institution and administration of rubber regulation have never regarded any form of restriction as better than a *pis aller*."[11] But they contend that "as things were what seemed good to those interested in protecting the producers of coffee, cotton, sugar, wheat, copper, tin and tea could not seem a nefarious practice when adopted by those inter-

[11] McFadyean, *op. cit.*, Introduction.

ested in protecting one of the chief industries of Malaya, the Dutch East Indies and Ceylon."[12]

But few critics would insist on calling the IRRA nefarious either in conception or application. The crucial question is whether the agreement solved an admittedly urgent problem in such a manner that short-run and long-run disadvantages did not grossly outweigh short-run benefits. The authors of the IRRA patently did not evolve such a solution. Rubber regulation did not simply transfer to the consumers the losses that producers and producing countries would have suffered under continued conditions of free competition. Since restriction deflected production from the most economical channels and, hence, raised the cost level of the industry, the producers and producing countries gained only part of the increment in price which consumers were made to pay. Necessitated by an uneconomic organization of production, the balance represented a total loss to society.

In the long run, the interest of wage earners also was not promoted by restriction. Over a period of time, they stood to benefit from a thriving industry whose prosperity rested on a healthy basis of increasing efficiency and a rising level of consumption made possible by low rubber prices.

Could the producing industry and countries have framed a control plan that would have eliminated the evils of continued free competition without resulting in others quantitatively greater, though more diffused? In other words, could there have been a more "economic" regulation scheme? Once the Great Depression had passed, the principal source of distress to the rubber plantation industry was the existence of surplus output capacity represented by technically obsolete units. Any intelligent solution of the problem, therefore, required the amputation of that margin of capacity. The disadvantage of the free rubber market was not that its pricing mechanism tended to bring about this desirable result, but that it operated with agonizing slowness because the owners of marginal capacity resisted elimination *à outrance*. The defect of the free pricing system lay not in the loss to imprudent investors, but in temporary losses to all investors,

[12] *Ibid.*

and in the prolonged depression it might bring to the entire industry until equilibrium was restored.

To hasten the elimination of relatively inefficient capacity, and thereby to obviate prolonged suffering for efficient producers, workers, and producing countries seems a highly rational object of planned intervention in the rubber market. Such a solution would have been in the interest both of consumers and of the efficient majority of producers. A temporary control plan would have constituted an appropriately specific remedy for a specific ill.

It is easier, however, to demonstrate the theoretical advantages of the principle than to cite practicable ways of implementing it. Obviously, superfluous and obsolete marginal capacity cannot be simply dictated out of existence where the rights of private ownership are constitutionally protected. Under such circumstances, the only effective way of accelerating the process of selective disinvestment is to bolster the appropriate positive or negative incentives. The method of providing positive incentive employed by certain private cartels that aimed at effecting "internal economies" was to shut down redundant and technically obsolete producing units. These units were, in effect, bought up by the cartel and then disposed of. Yet, apart from its economically objectionable implications,[13] this approach would hardly have been feasible under the conditions ruling in the plantation-rubber industry. With a number of different producing countries and various types of producers involved, the identification of the redundant units, the determination of compensation for the owners, and the acquisition of the requisite funds would have posed formidable if not insuperable difficulties.

The negative incentives might have been provided by amending the IRRA along the following lines:

1. Provide for the effective assessment of native and estate capacity on an equal basis.

---

[13] The compensation of the owners of retired units places a burden on the remaining "rationalized" industry which increases its capitalization and tends to raise its cost level. If in possession of a sufficiently high degree of monopoly power, the cartellized industry can, of course, make consumers pay the compensation given to the stockholders of the eliminated enterprises.

2. Extend the principle of differential assessment of estate capacity in accordance with a few broad classes of "efficiency" determined by the age of the trees, plantation upkeep, and yields per acre on the basis of a suitable tapping schedule.

3. Maintain through regulation a low price level that might not be considered "fair" by the majority of producers but would be higher than prices would have averaged in the absence of control. (In concrete terms, during the middle and late 1930's control policy should have prevented prices from rising above 10 cents a pound until a sufficient margin of surplus capacity had been eliminated.)

4. Maintain an adequate buffer stock for the purpose of enhancing control flexibility to an extent that undue price fluctuations could have been dependably prevented.

5. Liquidate the scheme, retaining perhaps the buffer stock, as soon as a rough balance between output and absorption capacity had been re-established.

A control plan along these or similar lines would doubtless have contained serious flaws and drawbacks. The industry and producing countries would not have been as prosperous, in the short run, as they were under the IRRA. The selection of relatively inefficient plantations on the basis of the criteria mentioned would have disregarded other causes of high-cost production such as overcapitalization and uneconomic estate size. The consumers of rubber would still have had to pay prices higher than would have evolved under laissez-faire conditions. But, on the other hand, the combination of relatively unattractive prices and sharp output curtailment would have squeezed out the majority of technically obsolete plantations with relative speed. Within a few years the industry would have recovered its "health" and returned to prosperous conditions on a sound basis. The selective favoring of the low-cost against the high-cost producers would have furthered efficiency as much as is compatible with any tight control plan. Finally, the sacrifices imposed on consumers would have been smaller in amount than under the IRRA and, furthermore, limited in time.

If one compares the implications to producers and producing countries of such a "surgical" scheme, designed to go to the root of the trouble, with those of the IRRA, it is by no means surprising that the latter type was adopted in preference to the former. With a persistency that borders on invariability, business men as well as governments tend to orient policies toward the short-run approach. From that perspective, the plan accepted was strikingly attractive. That is as obviously true for the governments concerned as for investors in inefficient producing units. It is even true for the majority of efficient producers. It is not true for consumers and consuming countries, but their participation in the scheme was unnecessary.

Under these circumstances it may appear doubtful that agreement on a scheme so fundamentally different from the IRRA could have been reached. Indeed, it would have been possible only if the governments of the United Kingdom and the Netherlands Indies, desiring a remedy effective in the long run, had made their indispensable support of a control arrangement conditional on the industry's acceptance of unpalatable control features. Faced with the alternative of a "tough" control plan or none at all, the majority of estate producers might have accepted the former, for from their short-term point of view continuation of laissez-faire conditions would have been more disadvantageous than the type of plan suggested.

But while prompted by the certain distress accompanying a continued free rubber market, the major governments concerned were not disposed to give weighty consideration to the long-run prospects of the industry. They, too, followed the line of least resistance. Thus they supported a scheme, devised by the producing interests themselves, that abated competition for the sake of stabilizing things as they were, protected the inefficient instead of weeding them out, and thus encouraged the economic ossification of one of the world's most important industries.

Under free competition, the consumers, in the end, exercise sovereignty over the market. Their interests are automatically safeguarded. But where competition is imperfect or is abated in favor of monopolistic control, the individual consumer is dethroned and, in the absence of effective counter-organization, his interests are disregarded. It is for this reason that the formation of commodity control schemes in restraint of the free market raises the question of consumer representation.

As shown in a preceding section of this chapter, the "costs" of operating the rubber restriction scheme were shifted to the consumers. But the consumers or consuming countries were not as such invited to join in the formulation of the IRRA. In a very real sense, that agreement provided for self-rule by interests directly or indirectly vested in the production of crude rubber. Although such procedure puts a premium on group pressures from directly interested parties and lessens the consideration extended to consumers, the participating countries acted well within their rights when they signed and ratified the agreement. There is no international law that prohibits such quasi-unilateral action. Nor is there any law against the utilization of such international arrangements for the purpose of manipulating high, and if so chosen, extortionate prices.

Where control schemes were arrived at and administered by a combination of net-exporting and net-importing countries, as in the ill-starred cases of sugar and wheat, the net-importing countries were also producing countries and were capable of expanding the production of the commodity concerned. Without participation on their part, an exclusive combination of net-exporting countries could not have possessed an adequate degree of monopoly power. Where such a high degree of monopoly power could be marshaled, as by the exporters of crude rubber and tin, the importing countries were not asked to participate, and their only guaranty against abuses of monopoly power lay in the good faith, foresight, and wisdom of the controlling authorities.

The IRRC did not share its power with representatives of the large importing countries, for the three members of the Advisory Panel were not accorded voting rights. Yet the committee did not purposely abuse its powers and there is, in fact, considerable evidence that the recommendations of the Advisory Panel, and particularly of its United States member, were heeded and seriously considered, though not always acted upon. On several occasions, the United States government itself interceded on behalf of the country's vital interests, and its advice was not disregarded. To a considerable extent the consideration accorded by the IRRC to such advice rested undoubtedly on the recognition that it contained valuable information on the trend of rubber consumption. To an indeterminable extent it may have rested on the unwillingness of the United Kingdom and the Netherlands, in a period of growing international crisis, to antagonize the United States government and its people. Whether it rested at all on genuine concern over the consumers' interests must remain a question.

The nature of the advice tendered depends, of course, on the specific interest that the adviser is authorized to represent. The American representative on the Advisory Panel represented the American rubber-goods manufacturing industry. After 1939, when the United States government intervened directly, it did so because of the urgency of the stockpiling program. The ultimate consumer of rubber was not represented, for his interest does not coincide with that of the rubber-goods manufacturer and, in actual fact, may diverge considerably from it.

Stable prices are the primary concern of the industrial consumer. Because the IRRA held out the hope of leveling out abrupt and violent fluctuations of price, many industrial consumers were disposed to approve of the establishment of the scheme.[14] If relative stability of price can be effected only at the expense of somewhat raising the price level, the industrial consumer still benefits, for he can avoid inventory losses and pass the extra costs of his material on to the final consumer. Inventory losses, caused by an abrupt price fall, are borne chiefly by the investor in rubber-goods-manufacturing companies, not by the consumer of rubber articles. The ultimate consumer of rubber, on the other hand, could not expect to derive any benefit from the establishment of the agreement. His primary concern is *low* rubber prices and the effect of the scheme was to make rubber dearer.

Indeed, to place a representative of this interest in an advisory capacity would be rather superfluous. His interest is known and is unambiguous. The highly problematic question of how to

[14] Rubber Manufacturers Association, Inc., *Crude Rubber*, p. 35.

represent this interest and render this representation effective, therefore, arises only if its representative is given the opportunity to share decision-making power with other interests. The IRRA did not provide for this opportunity.

If we weigh the various consequences of the International Rubber Regulation Agreement in the light of the principles laid down in the Preface, the net effect appears to have been conspicuously negative. The investors in obsolete and redundant processing units were the chief beneficiaries; but on the basis of considerations of public policy no valid reasons exist for their being favored. All advantages accruing to other beneficiaries were of a precarious short-run nature. Over a length of time, the prosperity of the industry (and of the producing countries) required that it be stripped of all dead weight in order to achieve optimum efficiency. The disadvantages of the control scheme to consumers and consuming countries are incontestable. The bald fact is that a restriction plan, especially one organized on an equalitarian basis, involves interference with economic processes that is entirely out of line with the requirements of an expanding world economy.

CHAPTER X

THE RISE OF SYNTHETIC RUBBERS

Shortly after the spread of World War II to the Pacific and southeastern Asia, Japan seized control of the entire Malaysian producing region, with the exception of Ceylon and India. The United States and the United Kingdom were thus denied access to sources of crude rubber that, in 1940–41, had supplied about nine-tenths of the world's exports.

Lack of information forbids extensive discussion of the position of Continental Europe and the USSR. Developing large-scale cultivation of *kok-saghyz* (a latex-yielding species of dandelion) as well as a big synthetic-rubber industry, Soviet Russia had made rapid strides toward self-sufficiency in prewar years. A total *kok-saghyz* acreage of 300,000 hectares was planned for 1941. Assuming an average yield of 350 pounds of rubber per hectare of 2-year-old plants, annual crude-rubber production can be estimated at around 30,000 tons. Capacity for the manufacture of a Buna-type of synthetic—with butadiene derived from ethyl alcohol—has been estimated at between 90,000 and 100,000 tons. How large the country's stockpile of Malaysian rubber and her imports from Japan were, we do not know at this time, nor the extent to which the destruction or capture of her domestic capacity by the German armies was offset by rubber and rubber-goods shipments from the United Nations.

The Allied naval blockade cut Germany off almost completely from the Malaysian producing areas. That country, too, had established a substantial synthetic-rubber industry prior to the war. It had also laid in stocks of crude rubber and rubber scrap, and accumulated more of both in the wake of her conquests. Rigorously limiting consumption to strictly essential military and civilian requirements, Germany was able to manage so well as to make some quantities of artificial rubbers available to other European countries. By 1943, the country produced as many as ten types of Buna rubber, and her total capacity was estimated at least at 75,000 tons. Production of crude rubber, mostly from *kok-saghyz*, was also directed or encouraged in most European countries, notably in the conquered Ukraine and Poland, and in Rumania, Bulgaria, and Hungary. The total acreages involved were too small to have yielded more than a small quantity of crude rubber.[1] Experiments with rubber-yielding plants were undertaken also in neutral Sweden, Switzerland, Spain, and Turkey, and small synthetic-rubber manufacturing plants were established in Sweden.[2]

Japan's intervention in World War II found the United Kingdom with crude-rubber stocks estimated at between 100,000 and 200,000 tons, equivalent to one to two years' peacetime absorption. Great Britain controlled the plantation industry of Ceylon and India, but was obliged to share their output with the other members of the British Commonwealth of Nations and with the United States. Her position was relatively unfavorable because the country's capacity for reclaiming rubber was very small and her synthetic manufacturing industry negligible. Indeed, controlling the major portion of the world's rubber-plantation capacity, Great Britain was reluctant to build a synthetic-rubber manufacturing industry of substantial size. It was not until late in 1943 that British Celanese, Ltd., a large rayon manufacturing concern, was licensed to build plants of 36,000 tons capacity for the production of a Buna synthetic. Actual manufacture was scheduled to begin in the latter part of 1944. In the meantime, the country depended to a considerable extent upon imports of synthetics from the United States.[3]

THE AMERICAN RUBBER PROBLEM

It was in North America that the sudden wartime isolation of the Malaysian rubber-producing areas was most stimulating

[1] Hugo Ahlfeld, "Pflanzenkautschuk aus europäischem Boden," *Südost-Echo*, Jan. 14, 1944, pp. 5–6; Hugo Ahlfeld, "Rund um die Weltkautschukwirtschaft," *Südost-Echo*, Sept. 22, 1944, pp. 3–4; Arno Sölter, "Rationalisierung in der chemischen Industrie," *Die Deutsche Volkswirtschaft*, August 1943, XII, 674.

[2] *Neue Zürcher Zeitung*, Aug. 12, 1943, p. 5.

[3] *Economist*, Jan. 3, 1942, p. 35; and *ibid.*, Nov. 20, 1943, p. 686; *Bulletin* (Institute of Statistics, Oxford), Jan. 31, 1942, IV, 55.

to the creation of a gigantic synthetic industry. At the end of 1941 the United States industrial and government stocks of crude rubber were 538,000 tons. But shipments from the Far East were still coming in, and by July 1, 1942, the total stockpile amounted to 578,000 tons.[4] In view of the huge anticipated requirements and the smallness of the prospective supplies, this was not a large stock. As the report of the Baruch Committee pointed out:

Of all critical and strategic materials, rubber is the one which presents the greatest threat to the safety of our Nation and the success of the Allied cause. Production of steel, copper, aluminum, alloys, or aviation gasoline may be inadequate to prosecute the war as rapidly and effectively as we could wish, but at the worst we still are assured of sufficient supplies of these items to operate our armed forces on a very powerful scale. But if we fail to secure quickly a large new rubber supply our war effort and our domestic economy both will collapse.[5]

Thanks to the remarkable resources of this country, especially to its unexampled fund of scientific, engineering, and managerial skills, this challenging crisis was weathered. Although repeatedly beset by production "bottlenecks" and although crude-rubber stocks ran dangerously low, the domestic transportation system did not collapse, and the conduct of the war was not materially impeded. Escape from the apparent impasse was made possible by rigorous regimentation of rubber consumption, on the one hand, and persevering efforts at increasing supplies of all kinds of rubber on the other.

Drastic restriction of crude rubber uses was instituted promptly. Indeed, some curtailment was effected prior to the attack on Pearl Harbor. After July 1, 1941, each rubber-goods manufacturer was allotted only a certain percentage of his monthly consumption during the base period from April 1, 1940, through March 31, 1941. Following the declarations of war in

---

[4] The following survey of the United States effort to cope with the wartime rubber shortage is based chiefly on the following official sources of information: S. Rept. 480, Pt. 7, 77th Cong., 2d Sess. (Rubber. Additional Report of the Special Committee Investigating the National Defense Program, S. Res. 71.); H. Doc. 836, 77th Cong., 2d Sess., *The Rubber Situation*. Message from the President of the United States (Sept. 10, 1942), hereafter cited as *Baruch Report*; the following reports of the U.S. War Production Board, Office of Rubber Director: *Progress Reports 1–6* (1942–44); *1944 Year End Report*; *Special Report, Recommending Termination of Special Powers (July 25, 1944)*; and *Special Report . . . . on the Synthetic Rubber Program: Investment and Production Costs* (Aug. 31, 1944), hereafter cited as *Special Report*.

[5] *Baruch Report*, p. 17.

December 1941, the Office of Production Management and, subsequently, the War Production Board, issued a series of orders by which crude rubber was increasingly limited to the most essential uses. In most civilian items utilization of crude rubber was prohibited and the use of a high percentage of reclaim was enforced in many others. On June 1, 1943, the Office of Rubber Director of the WPB made available limited quantities of artificial rubbers for experimental use in rubber-goods manufacture. As synthetic materials became available in larger quantities, subsequent orders compelled the use of synthetics in almost every product. The use of crude rubber was limited more and more to the manufacture of products such as truck tires, whose serviceability required an admixture of the natural material.

Until the supply of synthetic materials became substantial, the problem of economizing crude rubber in the tire-and-tube field for civilian automobiles was chiefly one of conservation. At the outbreak of war there were about one million tons of crude rubber on the wheels of motor vehicles. This was a huge stockpile. A conservation program was implemented by the regulation of maximum speeds, the curtailment of nonessential driving through gasoline rationing, and the encouragement of "car pools." Tires in stock at the beginning of the war were carefully rationed. Allotment of a small and only gradually increasing amount of reclaim and synthetic rubber provided for a tire replacement and recapping program. By 1945 the production of synthetic rubbers had been expanded to an extent that the rationing of tires made of artificial materials could be gradually relaxed.

On the supply side, various measures were adopted to increase the availability of reclaim, natural, and synthetic rubbers. The role initially played by reclaim was vital. It saved the day while the synthetic industry was in the process of construction. Yet the obligatory substitution of reclaimed for crude rubber on a vast scale inevitably engendered a temporary scarcity of reclaim. With an annual capacity of 350,000 tons, the country's reclaiming plant was ample. The reclaim scarcity of 1942 was caused by the failure of ordinary commercial channels to supply an adequate flow of rubber scrap to the reclaiming mills. A quickly organized scrap drive overcame this obstacle. About 1,148,000 short tons were collected. By the end of 1944, all but 170,571 tons had been fed to the reclaiming industry. Yet the plants still possessed substantial inventories and additional rubber carcasses became available as more new tires were distributed. In 1945, moreover, synthetic rubber displaced reclaim in many uses which, in turn, confronted the reclaiming industry with the necessity of processing scrap containing synthetic materials. While entirely satisfactory methods for reclaiming such mixtures had not been developed, the industry was making rapid strides in that direction.

WARTIME CRUDE-RUBBER SUPPLIES

Allied efforts to expand crude rubber supplies from the areas under their control proved only moderately rewarding. Stimulated by high prices, bonus payments and a "slaughter tapping" plan that compensated owners for the destruction of trees in consequence of overtapping, Ceylonese exports rose markedly over the 1941 level of about 90,000 tons. Exports expanded to nearly 125,000 tons in 1942 and 150,000 tons in the following year. Labor shortages and the effects of previous overtapping, combined with adverse weather conditions, reduced the country's output to less than 100,000 tons in 1944. In Liberia, the production on the Firestone plantations was stepped up to about 10,000 tons a year. The organization of intensive collecting campaigns in tropical Africa, especially in the Belgian Congo, resulted in greatly increased shipments of wild rubber, but the aggregate amount did not exceed 20,000 tons a year in 1942–44.

By far the greatest efforts were made in Latin America, and there the results were sorely disappointing. Alarmed over the prospect of war in the Pacific, the United States embarked in the summer of 1940 on a long-range program of developing a sizable rubber-plantation industry in Central and South America. It was realized that 10 to 20 years must elapse before substantial quantities of rubber could be expected to materialize from this project. Nevertheless, the plan was not abandoned after hostilities commenced in the Far East. Pending the successful construction of a synthetic-rubber industry, the creation of a Latin-American plantation industry appeared desirable as a long-range insurance policy. It was also supported as an implementation of the hemispheric "Good Neighbor Policy" in the economic sphere. Surveys of potential producing areas, construction of experiment stations and nurseries, and actual establishment of plantations on a large scale were undertaken. Most of the projected plantations were of Hevea. But other rubber trees were also experimented with, and *cryptostegia* plantations were organized in Haiti.

However, after the Japanese conquest of the Malaysian producing region, the main interest centered upon means of immediately increasing supplies of Latin-American wild rubber. In 1942–43 the United States entered into separate agreements with all the countries concerned and bound itself to accept, until the end of 1946, any amounts of wild rubber offered at stipulated prices.[6] These prices varied with different types and grades of rubber, but were generally set at an extremely attractive level. In addition the United States agreed to extend ample financial and technical assistance and to provide supplies and equipment for the collecting expeditions. Yet the optimistic expectations, nursed in some quarters, were not realized. Wild-rubber exports did not increase, when every increment was welcome; and total shipments stayed below 30,000 tons a year. Brazilian exports, indeed, declined from their 1941 level of 16,500 tons. Only 12,100 and 14,600 tons were exported in 1942 and 1943. The difficulties of mobilizing suitable labor forces and overcoming transportation obstacles, and expanding Latin-American rubber absorption, were chiefly responsible for the failure to get larger supplies for export to the United States.

The sharp reduction in wartime imports of crude rubber is brought out in Table 12. These small acquisitions were greatly exceeded by the amounts of crude rubber concurrently absorbed. Even when the supply of synthetic materials became relatively abundant, the necessary inclusion of natural rubber in heavy-duty tires and other essential items set narrow limits to the

[6] E. G. Holt, "The Inter-American Rubber Agreements," *Arbitration in Action*, April–May, 1943, I, 17–18.

reduction of crude-rubber requirements. In 1944 the average ratio between crude- and synthetic-rubber consumption was about one to four, and no substantial change in this ratio is expected for 1945. As a result the United States stockpile of natural rubber shrank rapidly and eventually dwindled to a mere 93,000 tons at the end of 1944. Not counting upon the imminent defeat of Japan, 1945 requirements were estimated at 157,000 tons,

TABLE 12.—UNITED STATES RUBBER POSITION, 1941–44*
(*Tons*)

Year	Net imports of crude rubber	Consumption of crude rubber	Year-end stocks of crude rubber	Production of synthetic rubbers
1941	1,023,000	775,000	533,000	.......ᵃ
1942	271,000	376,000	422,000	24,000
1943	34,000	317,000	139,000	234,000
1944	98,000	144,000	93,000	763,000

* Data from *New York Times*, Mar. 12, 1945, p. 21; released by the Rubber Reserve Company.
ᵃ Data not available, but probably not much over 5,000 tons.

as compared with imports forecast at about 123,000 tons, and further inroads upon these critically depleted stocks were anticipated. Japan's surrender in August 1945 is likely to permit somewhat larger imports, but contraction of war rubber needs will be offset by increasing civilian requirements.

Endeavors to create an indigenous source of crude rubber in continental United States added but little to the scarce wartime supplies. Indeed, in terms of the resources bestowed on the projects, they had probably a negative effect on the total war production effort. Experiments with *kok-saghyz*, the Russian dandelion, and *cryptostegia* were soon abandoned as impractical or uneconomic. Extensive cultivation of *guayule* was the core of the program.[7] In March 1942, Congress passed a law providing for the planting and growing of, and the recovery of rubber from *guayule* to make available a source of crude rubber for emergency and defense uses. It authorized plantings up to 75,000 acres. In October 1942 an amendment increased the

[7] For the history of this program, see H. Rept. 2098, 78th Cong., 2d Sess., House of Representatives, *Study of Rubber in United States, Mexico, and Haiti* (Jan. 2, 1945).

authorization to 500,000 acres. The Department of Agriculture was made responsible for the project.

Surveys, research, leasing of suitable land, construction of housing facilities and mills, the establishment of nurseries and plantations were immediately started, mostly in California. In March 1943, however, the Rubber Director of the WPB requested that the program be drastically curtailed. Besides conflicting with the food-production effort, it could not be expected to yield substantial quantities before 1946 or 1947. The project was immediately retrenched. Altogether, 31,356 acres had been planted—70 per cent on irrigated, the rest on unirrigated land. Provided harvesting were deferred until the shrubs reached an age allowing maximum yields, this acreage plus the nurseries could have produced about 26,000 tons of crude rubber over the period from December 1944 to June 1950. In view of the dwindling stock of crude rubber, however, the War Production Board was forced to request the harvesting of all guayule by April 1947, expecting a total yield of about 12,000 tons of rubber.[8]

THE SYNTHETIC-RUBBER PROGRAM

In view of the impossibility of creating quickly new sources of substantial crude-rubber supplies, the United States government built a huge synthetic-rubber industry. Since all production resources of the country were committed to the total war-production effort, this was no mean undertaking. In contrast to Germany and the USSR, the United States possessed only an embryonic synthetic-rubber industry before the war. With crude rubber readily obtainable from the Far East, there was no large commercial market for general-purpose synthetic substitutes. The manufacture of special-purpose synthetics—Neoprene, Thiokol, Koroseal, Vistanex, and others—was growing in volume, and some manufacturers were experimenting with general-purpose types. In the summer of 1940 the B. F. Goodrich Company placed small numbers of Ameripol tires on the market, and the Standard Oil Company of New Jersey was developing butyl rubber. Development of a Buna type of synthetic was

[8] U.S. War Production Board, *Report of the Special Director of Rubber Programs to the War Production Board* (June 25, 1945), p. 5.

retarded because of patent agreements between Standard Oil and I. G. Farben, the German chemical concern. Annual synthetic output capacity was expanding, but the aggregate was still small—about 10,000 tons at the end of 1940.

The same uneasiness over the international situation that led the United States government to accumulate a stockpile of crude rubber prompted explorations as early as the middle of 1940 toward the building of a government-sponsored synthetic-rubber industry. The rubber committee of the National Defense Advisory Council in April 1940 recommended to the Reconstruction Finance Corporation (RFC) the construction of 100,-000 tons of annual capacity. In September the Army and Navy Munitions Board approved this proposal, and in October President Roosevelt put the entire rubber program in the hands of Jesse Jones of the RFC. Apparently less impressed than other agencies by the critical nature of the country's rubber position, Mr. Jones unfortunately did not act with sufficient dispatch. Following lengthy discussions and negotiations with representatives of the rubber industry, the RFC in May 1941 concluded contracts with four major rubber-goods manufacturers for the erection and equipment of four synthetic-rubber plants with an initial capacity of 2,500 and an ultimate capacity of 10,000 tons each. No provisions were made for the production of the requisite raw materials before November. Privately financed plants in the meantime had been expanded to about 30,000 tons annual capacity at the end of the year.

This was the state of the synthetic-rubber industry when the country was plunged into World War II. An imminent emergency suddenly had become an acute one. Now the government program was speedily adapted to the prospective rubber crisis. Within less than half a year the building of 872,000 tons annual capacity was authorized. In September 1942 the Baruch Committee recommended a construction program of 1,074,000 tons rated capacity, including Canadian plants of 37,000 tons capacity. Since it was subsequently found that many plants were able to operate markedly in excess of their planned capacity, the Baruch program was retrenched in terms of rated, though not of actual, capacity. As Table 13 shows, the final construction program was for 873,000 tons of rated capacity, but about 1,-145,000 tons of actual output capacity per year. In order to make full use of the actual capacities, the War Production Board directed the elimination of certain "bottlenecks" in the summer of 1945. This order was expected to raise operational capacity to about 1,200,000 tons by 1946.[9]

TABLE 13.—COMPARISON OF UNITED STATES SYNTHETIC RUBBER PROGRAM WITH BARUCH COMMITTEE RECOMMENDATIONS*

(Tons)

Type of rubber	Rated annual capacity			Estimated actual capacity after completion of program (U.S. and Canada)
	Baruch report (U.S. only)	U.S. program only	U.S. and Canadian program	
Buna-S	845,000	705,000	735,000	1,000,000
Butyl	132,000	68,000	75,000	75,000
Neoprene	69,000	63,000	63,000	70,000
Thiokol-N	60,000	......	......	......
Total	1,106,000	836,000	873,000	1,145,000

* From U.S. War Production Board, Office of Rubber Director, *Special Report . . . . on the Synthetic Rubber Program: Plant Investment and Production Costs* (Aug. 31, 1944), p. 3.

In 1942–43 the bulk of the planned capacity, including facilities for the production of the necessary raw materials, was under construction. With all resources of the country absorbed in war production, it is only natural that particular "bottlenecks" at times retarded construction, and that finished plants were sometimes prevented, by materials shortages, from immediately producing at full capacity. Nevertheless, the overall record was admirable and increasing supplies became rapidly available. Total production in 1944 amounted to 763,000 short tons, of which 85,000 tons were placed at the disposal of the United Kingdom. This output met total essential requirements to the full, and was expected to be considerably exceeded in 1945. If this remarkable accomplishment did not immediately relieve the shortage of rubber goods, the reasons lay outside the field of synthetic manufacture.

Conversion from crude to synthetic rubber confronted the

[9] *Special Report*, p. 3.

rubber-goods industry with complex problems of adjustment that were superimposed upon the general conversion from peace-time to wartime manufacture. Satisfactory techniques of fabri-cating articles from synthetic materials had to be developed, and their application called for speedy adaptation of equipment and labor skills. Besides, utilization of synthetics in place of natural rubber lengthened the processing time so much that the maintenance of a given monthly output of tires, for instance, required additions to existing plants. Capacity expansion, furthermore, was necessitated by enlarged demands for new types of heavy tires and other rubber articles for the Armed Forces. At various times shortages of component materials, in addition to the perennial crude-rubber shortage, slowed up pro-duction schedules. Thus beadwire and carbon black became scarce in 1944; and when the making of satisfactory heavy-duty tires from Buna-S required the substitution of rayon for cotton fabrics, existing facilities for producing rayon cord proved in-adequate. All these adjustment and expansion problems had to be solved in an economy in which every resource, including man-power, was strained to the utmost.

THE MANUFACTURE OF SYNTHETIC RUBBERS

The present study is concerned with economic and policy questions. It cannot deal with the scientific and technical aspects of synthetics-rubber production beyond pointing to the type of processes and raw materials required.

The principle of chemical synthesis involved may be illus-trated by the example of Buna-S production. The chief raw materials are about three-fourths butadiene and one-fourth styrene. To obtain Buna-S, these materials must be co-polymer-ized. Polymerization is the technical term for the chemical linkage of two or more molecules of a compound to form a new compound of higher molecular weight. Co-polymerization unites two or more molecules of different compounds to form a new compound of higher molecular weight. Crude rubber is a polymer of isoprene. Buna-S is a co-polymer of butadiene and styrene. The synthetic industries of the USSR, Germany, and the United States have thus far been unable to discover a cheap process for making isoprene and polymerizing a substance chemically closer to natural rubber than Buna-S.

To produce Buna-S industrially, butadiene and styrene are fed into a soap-water solution for purposes of emulsification. Emulsified, the mixture is placed into large reactors where catalysts are added and the temperature is raised to speed the reaction. The resulting latex is transferred to coagulation tanks and mixed with salt, sulphuric acid, and anti-oxidants. The coagulating latex rises to the surface of the tank and is skimmed off, washed, dried, and pressed into blocks for shipment. The entire manufacturing process demands the utmost care in control of timing, temperatures, pressures, and the proportionate quantities of the various ingredients. Improper control is likely to result in a vastly inferior product lacking uniformity.

Butadiene can be produced abundantly from such petroleum fractions as ethyl alcohol, butane, and acetylene, or from distilled coal, or from alcohol derived from such vegetable products as potatoes, soybeans, grain, molasses, turpentine, and wood sugar. Styrene can be made from petroleum or coal. Yet, like the polymerization process itself, the production of butadiene and styrene constitutes separate industries requiring a great deal of intricate and expensive machinery and equipment.

Neoprene is a polymer of chloroprene, which has a chlorine atom in place of the methyl atom of isoprene. It is produced by reacting calcium carbide with water to obtain acetylene gas. This is polymerized in the presence of a catalyst to produce vinyl acetylene which, in turn, is combined with hydrogen chloride to form chloroprene. This substance is finally polymerized to Neoprene. In the manufacture of Butyl, isobutylene is collected from petroleum-refinery gases and then co-polymerized with either butadiene or isoprene. Buna-N, or Perbunan, is a co-polymer of butadiene and acrylonitrile, which is gained from ethylene and hydrocyanic acid. A great many rubberlike products are manufactured without polymerization. Thus, Thiokol is produced by the reaction between ethylene dichloride and alkali polysulphide, and Koroseal is a plasticized polyvinyl chloride. There are literally dozens of other rubber plastics thus far produced in small quantities for specialty purposes.

COMPOSITION AND STRUCTURE OF THE SYNTHETIC INDUSTRY

The choice of the types of synthetic materials to be included in the government program, as well as their proportion, depended first upon the specific needs of the country and second upon expediency. The imperative need was the mass production of a general-purpose rubber that could largely replace the natural material. Increased production of an oil-resistant special-purpose synthetic was a subsidiary need. Expediency focused attention on the relative state of development of production processes, the time and critical dearth of materials required for the building of output facilities, and the resources needed for the production of raw materials. On the basis of these considerations Buna-S was selected as the general-purpose synthetic and made the backbone of the entire program, and Neoprene was chosen as the safest special-purpose type. While butyl rubber had shown definite promise as a general-purpose synthetic, experience with its manufacture and use was so limited that it was deemed unwise to accord it a major share in the total program.

The butadiene plants of the program were planned to have a rated capacity of 690,400 short tons, of which one-third were to be based on alcohol and two-thirds on petroleum processes. Initially, 69 per cent of the butadiene-from-alcohol plants were given priority while only 40 per cent of the butadiene-from-petroleum plants were accorded an equivalent advantage. This preference was motivated by conflicting requirements of high-octane gasoline production and by differences in the time and availability of materials required for construction. The main process for the production of butadiene in the petroleum field was based on the dehydrogenation of normal butylene (250,000 short tons capacity). Most of the remaining capacity was built for the butane dehydrogenation process (75,000 short tons), the naphtha cracking process (37,600 short tons), and a combination of the butylene and naphtha processes (55,000 short tons).

The synthetic-rubber industry of the United States comprises about 60 plants, varying greatly in size, each operated by a private company and nearly all built with government funds.

The bulk of the industry is, of course, geared to the manufacture of Buna-S. Twenty-two butadiene plants were built during the war with a combined projected capacity of 687,600 short tons per year. These plants range in size from 5,000 to 100,000 short tons of rated annual capacity. The three large butadiene-from-alcohol plants are operated by chemical companies and are located in West Virginia, Kentucky, and Pennsylvania. The plants based on petroleum fractions are operated by oil companies and are located chiefly in Texas, Louisiana, and southern California. There are six styrene plants, ranging in size from 4,200 to 50,000 short tons annual productive capacity, operated by chemical concerns.

The 15 large co-polymer plants with designed productive capacities of 30,000 to 90,000 tons a year are operated by rubber-goods manufacturing companies and are located chiefly near the butadiene or rubber-goods manufacturing plants. Two Neoprene plants, one with 54,000 tons rated capacity in Kentucky, and the other with 9,000 tons capacity in New Jersey, are operated by E. I. Du Pont de Nemours and Company. The smaller plant is also owned by the company. One Butyl plant of 38,000 tons rated capacity is located in Louisiana, the other of 30,000 tons in Texas. Both are operated by oil companies.

It has been estimated that all plants, operating at full rated capacity, will require a total staff of about 20,000 employees of whom about three-fourths will be wage earners.[10] Co-polymer and butadiene plants will require some 7,860 and 6,680 employees respectively. According to recent estimates, Buna-S production will require an average of 22.7 employees per 1,000 tons of output with plants operating at full designed capacity, and Butyl and Neoprene an average of 30.8. Naturally, there is a marked increase in the number of workers required per unit of output as plant size or output decreases. Unit labor requirements for the smallest plants are about three times those for the largest.

Table 14 shows the aggregate government investment in the synthetic-rubber program classified by sections of the industry.

[10] U.S. Dept. Labor, Bur. Labor Statistics, "Labor Requirements for Manufacture of Synthetic Rubber," *Monthly Labor Review*, May 1945, LX, 990.

There is a considerable variation from plant to plant in the amount of capital invested per capacity unit. Thus, average investment per 1,000 tons of estimated actual capacity varies from $139 to $286 for co-polymer facilities; from $207 to $396 for the styrene plants; from $294 to $1,310 for the butadiene plants based on petroleum fractions, and from $273 to $330 for the

TABLE 14.—CAPACITY OF, AND GOVERNMENT INVESTMENT IN, THE
UNITED STATES SYNTHETIC-RUBBER INDUSTRY*

Product	Total rated capacity per year (*Tons*)ᵃ	Estimated actual capacity (*Per cent of rated capacity*)	Estimated total investment (*Million dollars*)	Investment per annual ton	
				Rated capacity (*Dollars*)	Estimated actual capacity (*Dollars*)
Grand total ..	827,000	125	700	845	675
Buna-S	705,000	129	604ᵇ	857	663
Co-polymer	(705,000)	(129)	162	230	178
Butadiene ..	626,000	139	347	553	398
Styrene	188,500	154	83	439	285
Butyl	68,000	100	53	779	779
Neoprene	54,000	111	43	786	717

* Data from *Special Report*, pp. 4–5.

ᵃ Long tons of Buna-S, Butyl, and Neoprene; short tons of butadiene and styrene.

ᵇ Including investments in facilities making miscellaneous chemicals used in the co-polymer process.

butadiene-from-alcohol plants. The magnitude of these ranges is worth noting, since unit investment costs affect over-all production costs. The average investment outlay per 1,000 tons of actual capacity for butadiene production is $294 for the alcohol process, $422 for the butylene process, $553 for the naphtha-cracking process, $398 for the butane process, and $576 for the combined naphtha-and-butylene process.

The Buna-S program absorbed about 86 per cent of the total funds invested, but average unit outlays for the three types of synthetics included in the program are not far apart. Data on investments in privately-owned synthetic-rubber facilities are not publicly available. Also, investments in private plants producing such raw materials as alcohol, butylene, naphtha, butane, ethylene, calcium carbide, soap, and other necessary ingredients are excluded from the above table.

PROPERTIES OF SYNTHETIC RUBBERS

In its combined properties no synthetic rubber is identical with crude rubber. Each has some quality that makes it in some respects distinctly superior to the natural material. Thus far, all of them have certain characteristics that render them in other respects inferior to crude rubber. Such artificial materials as Neoprene, Buna-N, Thiokol, Koroseal, and Vistanex excel the plantation product in all or some of the following qualities: resistance to gas diffusion, oil, water, light, and certain chemicals. They are excelled by crude rubber in such properties as tensile strength, abrasion resistance, and adhesion to fabrics and metals. In applications where their superior qualities are essential, they command a premium over the natural material. As special-purpose synthetics they are not crude-rubber substitutes, but indispensable engineering materials. Indeed, owing to these very superior qualities, they are serving and will serve uses that, because of its deficiencies, natural rubber cannot. Moreover, there appear no limits to the diversity in the synthesis of such rubberlike substances. Especially recent experiments with the technique of cross-linking rubber plastics are likely to make available a large variety of "tailor-made" industrial materials.

Some of the special-purpose synthetics may find new bulk uses. Their possible utilization as an upholstery material is an example. Others, if further improved, may eventually invade the field of tire-and-tube manufacture. During the war emergency, Buna-S and Butyl have been substituted for crude rubber in this predominant bulk use. While still greatly inferior to natural rubber in workability and not its equal in tensile strength, excellent inner tubes have been made from Butyl. In impermeability to air and in age resistance, Butyl tubes are superior to crude-rubber tubes. As a result of the relative scarcity of Butyl in 1944, inner tubes were also produced with Buna-S, but their over-all performance has not equaled that of Butyl or natural-rubber tubes.

Buna-S became the chief tire material. It greatly excels crude rubber in resistance to age, oil, and abrasion. It is roughly its equal in tensile strength. Yet it compares unfavorably with the natural material in workability, adhesion, tear resistance, and elasticity. In improving the workability of Buna-S, marked progress has been·made and further progress is confidently expected. It must be remembered that the workability of crude rubber was vastly enhanced over the decades by the development of superior compounding ingredients and formulas, while the corresponding development of compounding and vulcanizing techniques adapted to Buna-S has only begun.

Buna-S tires are less resilient than those made from crude rubber, and because of inferior tackiness, tire plies have to be specially cemented. Thus far they have also proven less uniform in performance. Their most striking deficiency is excessive heat generation under conditions of high temperatures, especially when heavily loaded and driven at high speeds. This heat generation adversely affects tensile strength and tear resistance. As a result, passenger-car tires made from Buna-S must be given greater care than crude-rubber tires. To insure satisfactory service, they must be kept properly inflated, and high speeds, especially on poor roads, need to be avoided. This particular deficiency shows up even more disadvantageously in heavy truck and bus tires. Admixture of crude rubber and the replacement of cotton fabrics by rayon or nylon cords markedly reduce this deficiency.

It is quite possible that, as many rubber chemists have promised, some or all of these shortcomings will be eventually removed by the discovery of suitable vulcanizing agents and accelerators. As far as their various properties are concerned, the simple fact is that the development of synthetic rubbers is only in its initial stage. Continuous research may bring conspicuous changes, the degree and directions of which cannot yet be foreseen. But even at this stage, Buna-S treads are notable for wear and skid resistance that is definitely superior to that of crude-rubber tires. At the beginning of 1945, rubber-goods manufacturers were willing to pay a premium for the use of crude rubber as the bulk material in tire manufacture. What will be the situation by 1946 or 1948 it is impossible now to predict.

PRODUCTION COSTS

Our present knowledge of the cost of producing synthetic rubbers is necessarily fragmentary and provisional. The industry is largely a wartime creation. Construction speed was imperative. The facilities were built and are operated at inflated levels of wage and materials costs. Many plants have been worked at full capacity, but some have not. With the government an insatiable customer, there are no selling expenses. Management is on a cost-plus-fee basis. Customary provisions for amortization and interest as well as profit considerations are absent. Cost analyses for synthetics produced outside the government program are not on public record. Most fabricating processes are technically in more or less constant flux and technological changes are likely to affect the cost structure. "Know-how" of labor and management is only gradually accumulating and maturing. Thus, no more than tentative generalizations can be hazarded on this complex subject.

Little information is available on the cost of producing such special-purpose materials as Perbunan, Thiokol, and Koroseal. Their prices are all over 30 cents a pound. Further technical advancement, diminishing raw-materials costs, and economies of large-scale manufacture may well bring cost reductions and encourage extended applications. As yet there is no indication, however, that they will compete with general-purpose rubbers for bulk consumption in tire-and-tube manufacture.

Representatives of the producing and consuming industries have made numerous and conflicting cost forecasts for Buna-S, Butyl, and Neoprene. Fortunately, relatively detailed cost analyses on the production of these materials have been published by the WPB.[11] These official data are based on out-of-pocket operating charges. They do not contain provisions for amortization, sales expenditure, and interest or profit on investment. They do include plant insurance, taxes, nominal royalties, and small management charges covering general expenses.

Table 15 presents approximate operating costs for Neoprene

[11] *Special Report . . . . on the Synthetic Rubber Program: Plant Investment and Production Costs*, pp. 6–12.

and Butyl during the first half of 1944. Aggregate out-of-pocket expense in the Neoprene plants is based on an acetylene price of 11.67 cents a pound. The WPB estimates that acetylene may sell for around 7 cents after the war. With anticipated minor reductions in labor and salary costs, total postwar operating costs may fall to about 19 cents a pound. One cent will have to be added for storage and distribution costs. Amortization charges unfortunately constitute a cost item that defies present appraisal.

TABLE 15.—NEOPRENE AND BUTYL OPERATIONS COSTS, 1944*
(Cents per pound)

Cost Items	Neoprene	Butyl
Feedstocks	11.10	2.51
Other chemicals	4.19	4.12
Utilities	1.33	1.71
Operating labor	1.50	3.51
Other costs[a]	4.51	8.16
Royalties and management fee	1.89	1.50
By-product credits	(.48)	(....)
Total out-of-pocket costs	24.04	21.51

* Data from *Special Report*, p. 6.
[a] Other costs include supervision, repairs and maintenance, operating supplies, laboratory expense, shipping costs, and plant overhead.

For the type of plant and equipment in question, amortization on a ten- or twelve-year average is the ordinary assumption. Yet there are vast differences in the efficiency of different synthetic plants. Undoubtedly with inefficient facilities in mind, some cautious appraisers have suggested allowances on a five-year basis.[12] But patently high-cost units may not find a buyer. The capital investment per ton of estimated actual capacity of Neoprene plants is $717. Amortized over 10 years, charges at full-capacity operation would run to about 3 cents a pound. There is no way of predicting, however, on what terms government-owned plants will be released to private industry and hence the capital investment to which amortization rates must be applied. Production facilities were established at wartime-inflated costs, and the plants will have operated for several years

[12] U.S. Tariff Commission, *Rubber*, pp. 78–82.

by the time they change ownership. In addition to allowing for these factors, the government may choose to charge only a fraction of the capital investment in order to give, openly or unavowedly, an initial subsidy to the industry. In that event, the residual investment can be amortized by a small charge per output unit. J. L. Collyer suggests that it might be one cent a pound for Buna-S.[13] In the absence of any knowledge permitting a more precise estimate, we may assume arbitrarily a nominal charge of around one cent per pound for all synthetic rubbers produced in government-built plants. Charges are bound to be higher, however, for subsequent private investments.

The postwar cost of producing Neoprene, then, may amount to about 21 cents a pound. To allow for a reasonable profit, it has been suggested a selling price of from 23 to 25 cents seems indicated. As will be shown below, such a price would range markedly above the prices of crude rubber, Buna-S, and Butyl. Owing to its special properties, Neoprene should, nonetheless, play an important role as a special-purpose material. Yet it is not likely to compete for bulk uses.

Compared with Neoprene production, the feedstock—that is, the primary raw material—represents a small cost item in the manufacture of Butyl. On the other hand, labor, maintenance and repair charges, as well as plant overhead, run much higher. However, the cost data released by the WPB are not likely to be representative of ultimate output costs. Only one plant was in operation at the time and it then produced only at 41 per cent of rated capacity. Besides, major operation difficulties were encountered which necessitated an extensive research and development program as well as substantial alterations to all installed units. The analysts of the WPB believe that Butyl may be ultimately produced at an operating cost of from 10 to 14 cents a pound. Making allowances for marketing costs, amortization charges and profits, a postwar price of from 13 to 17 cents can be expected. This compares favorably with Neoprene. Yet whether Butyl will be applied to bulk uses on a large scale depends not only on the realization of the low price range stated, but also on the improvement of its qualities, particularly its workability. In any case, Butyl should find extensive use as a cheap special-purpose synthetic, and probably as a rubber for inner-tube manufacture.

Future cost estimates for Buna-S, the chief general-purpose synthetic, are difficult because the appraisal must include the cost of producing butadiene and styrene in addition to the co-

TABLE 16.—BUTADIENE, STYRENE, AND CO-POLYMER PLANT
OPERATIONS COSTS*

(Cents per pound)

Cost items	Butadiene				Styrene		Co-polymer	
	From alcohol		From butylene					
	1944	Postwar	1944	Postwar	1944	Postwar	1944	Postwar
Chemicals (excluding feedstocks)	0.18	0.13	0.57	0.50	0.42	0.42	2.10	1.90
Utilities	.95	.75	1.20	1.20	.46	.46	.26	.26
Operating labor	.14	.12	.48	.44	.27	.25	.52	.45
Other costs*..	.66	.70	1.73	1.71	.83	.89	1.43	1.32
Royalties and management fee	.51	.63	.65	.63	.68	.63	.52	.51
By-product credit	(.23)	.14	(...)	(...)	(.14)	(.14)	(...)	(...)
Total out-of-pocket costs.	2.21	2.19	4.63	4.48	2.52	2.51	4.83	4.44

* Data from *Special Report*, p. 7.

ᵃ Other costs include supervision, repairs and maintenance, operating supplies, laboratory expense, shipping cost, and plant overhead.

polymerization process, excluding feedstocks. Table 16 compares out-of-pocket costs for these three operations during the first half of 1944 with probable postwar costs. Butadiene cost is the major constituent of Buna-S costs. Plant-operating costs for the alcohol process are only half that for the butylene-hydrogenation process. Charges for chemicals, utilities, labor, and most other cost items are much lower in the alcohol plants. In addition, investments per annual ton of estimated actual capacity average $422 for the butylene in contrast with only $294 for the alcohol plants.

However, the introduction of feedstock costs substantially alters the picture. With 1944 prices in the vicinity of 90 cents a gallon of 190-proof alcohol, and a maximum yield of 2.25 pounds of butadiene per gallon, the cost of alcohol employed per pound of Buna-S amounted to no less than 35 cents. On the other hand, with butylene averaging 9.5 cents a gallon and an average utilization rate of .65, butadiene made from this material cost only about 7.6 cents a pound. The difference is prodigious. Unless scientific discoveries will permit an increase in butadiene yield per unit of feedstock, the postwar cost of making butadiene from industrial alcohol will depend on the postwar price of that liquid.

Owing to the wartime shortage of molasses, industrial alcohol for the butadiene plants was produced first from corn, and when that became scarce, from wheat. In the early months of 1944, corn sold for $1.15 and wheat for $1.65 per bushel. The high cost of these primary materials accounts for the soaring wartime price of alcohol. In normal times the butadiene plants could obtain much cheaper alcohol from blackstrap molasses. During the ten-year period from 1931 to 1940, molasses averaged about 6.5 cents a gallon, and corn 61 cents a bushel. The cost of producing alcohol from these materials averaged 19.5 and 27 cents a gallon respectively. With a return to cheaper basic materials, estimates of the postwar costs of alcohol range from 12 to 20 cents a gallon. Assuming a rather low price of 15 cents a gallon, butadiene should cost about 8.75 cents a pound.

Petroleum prices, on the other hand, have not advanced far above their prewar level. The postwar price of butylene, therefore, cannot be expected to decline far below the wartime level. The WPB analysts estimate that with a petroleum price of 6 cents a gallon, butadiene could be produced for approximately 6.4 cents a pound. No reliable data are available on the cost of making butadiene by the butane-hydrogenation and the naphtha-cracking processes. Preliminary indications are, however, that the butane process will be able to compete with the butylene and alcohol processes, while the naphtha process will not. Barring the unpredictable effects of possible technical improvements of the alcohol process, the WPB assumes that the butylene and butane-hydrogenation plants will be the low-cost butadiene producers.

With wartime prices of ethylene and benzene at 6 and 16 cents a gallon respectively, the out-of-pocket costs of producing styrene came to about 6.6 cents a pound. Estimated peacetime reductions in the cost of ethylene and benzene would bring operating cost down to from 4 to 5 cents per pound of styrene. Moderate decreases in co-polymerizing costs can also be expected. The WPB analysts conclude that, considering only the low-cost producers of styrene and butadiene, Buna-S was produced in the first half of 1944 for an out-of-pocket cost of about 12.2 cents a pound. With decreased postwar operating cost of 7 cents and 5 cents per pound of butadiene and styrene, Buna-S might be manufactured at an out-of-pocket cost of as little as 10.7 cents a pound. Adding selling expenses, uncertain amortization allowances, and a reasonable profit margin, the postwar price of Buna-S may range as low as 14 to 16 cents a pound.

Several qualifications, however, must be appended to this estimate. First, this low-price estimate is based on the performance of the low-cost plants only. According to reliable estimates, no more than one-third to one-half of Buna-S production can be expected to be produced at this price level. Second, the allowances for amortization charges are rather arbitrary. While initially these charges may be lower than assumed, eventually they may have to be set at a higher rate. Third, all estimates imply full-capacity operation. In the long run, the synthetic industry cannot expect to run their plants at capacity level and—with overhead costs bulking exceedingly large in total cost—below-capacity output will mean sharply higher unit costs. Fourth, changes in the general price level are not considered in these estimates. The cost and price figures mentioned are based on roughly the prewar price level.

These qualifications should make it clear that, even disregarding monetary factors, the low-price forecast for Buna-S may prove unduly optimistic. Actually, prices may run as high as 18 or 20 cents a pound. Nothing more definite can be inferred at this time.

CHAPTER XI

POSTWAR CONSUMPTION, SUPPLIES, AND COMPETITION

We turn now to the postwar prospects of the international rubber market. What kind of equilibrium can be expected between the various sources of crude rubber and synthetic materials, on the one hand, and total supply and world consumption on the other? What will be the outcome if the equilibrating process is left to unhampered competition? What if it is in some or all respects controlled? No complete answers can be given to these important questions, but certain possibilities or probabilities can be explored and tentative conclusions reached. Particularly the inherent tendency of certain types of intervention can be broadly discussed and certain principles advanced that, for the sake of all parties interested in the rubber market, should not be flouted.

PROSPECTIVE POSTWAR CONSUMPTION

This war's rubber famine and the insatiable production requirements of modern warfare sharply altered the trend of rubber consumption. Following the reconversion of the world's productive resources to the manufacture of peacetime goods, the demand for rubber will not immediately settle down to the prewar "normal" or any other. As a result of greatly expanded individual savings, on the one hand, and the accumulation of a deferred demand for many rubber goods on the other, the rubber market in many countries is expected to experience an exceptionally heavy transitional demand.

Demand for rubber in tires and tubes will figure most heavily in this development. Market analysts of the large rubber-goods manufacturers in the United States have estimated[1] that

[1] For estimates of rubber consumption during the transition period, see "Rubber on the Rebound," *Fortune*, July 1944, p. 197; *India Rubber World*, November 1943, CIX, 167; *New York Times*, Dec. 5, 1943, Sec. 5, p. 6; R. P. Dinsmore, *Future Prospects in Rubber* (Goodyear Tire and Rubber Company, Dec. 20, 1944, mimeographed).

during the first five postwar years over five million passenger automobiles will be annually produced in this country, and that an average of at least 75 million tires of all kinds will be required every year. Two-fifths of these casings will be for original equipment on new motor vehicles, the other three-fifths for the replacement market. At the same time the demand for tires on tractors and farm vehicles is expected to increase to about three times its prewar magnitude. A large pent-up demand for non-tire products is also assumed to lead to abnormally heavy transitional consumption.

Finally, new uses will make their appearance, and some uses insignificant before the war will be expanded. Thus the cushioning and energy-absorbing qualities of rubber will be utilized in latex sponge to be used in automobiles, trucks, and railway coaches, made into mattresses for Pullman cars, hospitals, hotels, and homes, and used generally for furniture upholstering. Enhancing driving comfort and easing engine strain, rubber-spring suspensions for motor vehicles are reportedly on the way to replace steel springs. Similarly, vibration dampeners for all kinds of industrial machinery have demonstrated their value during the war. They reduce noise and wear. Another important new use of rubber is as a starting material for chemical reactions. Rubber derivatives suitable for lacquers, plastics, and adhesives can be made from both natural and synthetic rubbers. According to Dr. Dinsmore, such new applications promise a postwar market for 63,000 to 191,000 tons of rubber.[2]

Rubber-goods manufacturers estimate that for five years there will be a transitionally heavy rubber consumption averaging about 870,000 tons a year in the United States and 1,500,000 tons in the entire world. This is perhaps as good a forecast as can be made at this time.[3] There are reasons to anticipate, however, that the period of abnormally heavy demand will be briefer than is assumed, perhaps only two years during which absorption may be well above 1,500,000 tons a year. In most of Conti-

---

[2] R. P. Dinsmore, *op. cit.*, pp. 8–9, Table V.

[3] Meeting in January 1945, the Rubber Study Group of the Netherlands, the United Kingdom, and the United States assumed that, in spite of a large banked-up demand all over the world, average consumption is not likely to reach more than 1.5 million tons a year. *Bulletin* (U.S. State Dept.), Feb. 4, 1945, XII, 161.

nental Europe, on the other hand, the transition period may be more protracted, while in the vanquished Axis countries it will be long before their prewar level of rubber consumption is regained.

Following the period of abnormal demand, the development of rubber consumption can be expected to resume a more normal trend, though it will not necessarily return to its prewar level. Despite the probability of temporary setbacks due to cyclical influences, this trend can be assumed to be firmly upward. It is impossible to foresee the rate of its rise at this time, but a range of probable magnitude can be suggested.

Prior to World War II, the sales of tires and inner tubes accounted for roughly two-thirds of the world's absorption of rubber. Including the numerous other rubber articles contained in motor vehicles, more than 70 per cent of the world's rubber consumption was tied up with automobile usage. There is no reason to expect an abrupt change in this proportion in the near future. It is true that, before the war, United States rubber consumption in products other than tires and tubes was increasing in relation to total consumption. The discovery of new uses may accelerate this trend,[4] but some of these new uses, such as car seats, cushions, and rubber-spring suspensions, involving considerable quantities of rubber, will be constituents of automobile usage. Outside the United States, furthermore, the prewar trend indicated proportionally increasing rubber consumption in motor-vehicle production and use.

Under favorable conditions, automobile usage and concomitant rubber consumption are capable of vast expansion. We have seen (p. 56) that, whereas there was one motor car for about every four persons in the United States, prior to the war 17 Frenchmen, 88 Italians, 1,283 Bulgars, and 6,782 Chinese averaged only one automobile. Similarly, in the middle 1930's United States per capita consumption of rubber in tires and tubes amounted to about 5.5 pounds per year compared with only about 0.6 pound for all uses in the rest of the world. If the latter figure were raised by a mere half-pound, rubber con-

---

[4] The following paragraphs should be read against the background presented in chapter iii, pp. 47–57.

sumption would mount by nearly half a million tons a year. Is it realistic to anticipate increases of such or even greater magnitude?

The exceedingly complex factors determining the demand for automobile usage have been discussed in chapter iv (pp. 73–81). Taking the world as a whole, the passenger automobile is a durable consumers' commodity belonging in the class of luxuries. The primary condition determining the level of automobile usage is the development of supernumerary income—what is left of real income after the payment of subsistence living expenses, taxes, etc.—available for the purchase of this type of commodity. Supernumerary income changes with the size of national incomes and, to a lesser extent, with their distribution. It is particularly affected by changes in subsistence living costs and taxes.

Despite a great deal of sanguine talk about unprecedented economic expansion, a spectacular advance of consumers' supernumerary income above the prewar level is not indicated for the foreseeable future. To be sure, some advance can be safely expected. There is no sign that the secular trend toward increasing productive power will come to a stop. On the contrary, the tremendous industrial achievements of the war economies of the United States, the United Kingdom, Soviet Russia, and Germany bear convincing testimony to a healthy capacity for technological advancement and growing productive efficiency.

However, extensive technological exploitation of enlarged scientific knowledge depends on the maintenance of a maximum area of vigorous competition and the willingness of business men and governments to invest. In this respect, recent and current tendencies toward the growth of monopolistic practices augur ill. So do wage rigidities and labor practices which, in the form of heavy prior charges, increase investment risks while the profit incentive is curbed by certain features of present-day taxation. Some contracyclical methods of striving for maintained maximum employment are likely to insure greater stability of real income only at the expense of thwarting secular trends toward its continued rise. Moreover, spreading patterns of uneconomic resource use, inspired by economic nationalism, desire for military preparedness, and group selfishness, threaten to retard the forces driving toward augmented productivity.

Even marked increases in gross national incomes may net only a relatively moderate augmentation of supernumerary incomes. Contracyclical policies and the necessity of rehabilitating the damaged or destroyed production apparatus in the former theaters of war all over the globe postulate high rates of investment. Compared with prewar conditions, considerable increases in tax burdens are necessitated by huge war debts, reparations, the maintenance of relatively large armed forces, and increases in per capita expenditure resulting from increased social security benefits. All these will cut into the share of total incomes available for the purchase of durable consumers' goods. Some of the defeated countries, notably Germany and Japan, are likely to remain economically blighted areas for a considerable time to come, and their level of automobile usage and rubber consumption must be expected to fall much below prewar levels. On the other hand, the development of new and greatly enlarged markets in the economically backward regions of the world presupposes a prodigious and necessarily slow increase in the productive efficiency of their inhabitants. Greatly enhanced productivity in agriculture, a large measure of industrialization, and the development of relatively dense highway systems must be achieved before hopes for the motorization of China, Latin America, and countries of comparable economic structure can be fulfilled.

Certain technological trends operate toward a reduction of the rubber volume consumed in automobile usage. If predictions of a new tire with a synthetic tread and sidewalls increasing its longevity by 50 or 100 per cent should come true, this would diminish the replacement demands for tires in striking degree. Similarly, construction of lighter automobiles would exert an influence tending to decrease rubber consumption. The greater familiarity of many automobile owners with tire repair, and the large increase in repair facilities, must also be mentioned in this respect. Rubber-saving inventions and practices of this kind may be numerous and hence have to be reckoned with in estimating future consumption. We know that the increasing durability of casings and tubes exerted a strong negative effect on the replacement market in the 1930's (p. 52).

A considerably increased quantity of rubber will surely find application after the war, as compared with prewar years, in the construction and operation of airplanes, tractors, and farm vehicles. But in terms of total rubber consumption, these uses will continue to account for only a minor proportion. If, for example, rubber consumption in airplane tires and tubes should increase twenty times over the 1939–40 volume, the annual amount of rubber so involved in the United States would be about 10,000 tons. Optimistic forecasters anticipate a doubling or trebling of rubber consumption in tractor usage. But such consumption in the United States was only about 10,000 tons in 1940. Some extension of rubber use can be expected in nearly all non-tire items, and new uses will absorb considerable quantities of rubber as spring, cushioning, insulating, and coating materials. The possibilities of increasing rubber absorption in the textile, clothing, furniture, medical, and other trades and professions are certainly very great. Even experiments with rubber as a roofing and paving material may be resumed.

Yet while numerous new applications of rubber will certainly cause consumption to expand, the development of specialty into new bulk uses, in some instances technically quite feasible, will depend largely upon the availability of cheap rubbers. Only if the prices of both synthetic and natural products are low and reasonably stable can these markets be expected to expand vigorously. In all specialty uses, a little rubber goes a long way. The mentioning of figures is hazardous. It should be repeated, however, that Dr. Dinsmore anticipates additional rubber consumption in the United States of from 63,000 to 191,000 tons a year as a result of new rubber uses.

While the future expansion of rubber consumption is potentially enormous, it would be rash to anticipate a too rapid realization of these potentialities. On balance, it seems unsafe, during the immediate post-transition period, to count on much more than a firm resumption of the upward secular trend of the prewar decade. For purposes of the present discussion, we shall assume that, following abnormally heavy consumption during the transition period, world consumption of natural and artificial rubbers will average 1,600,000 tons annually for a period of from five to ten years. This is a very generous assumption. If borne out in fact, it would mean that the demand of the transition period is abnormally heavy only in comparison with the prewar consumption level, and that the transition period will pass over into a more normal period of greatly expanded rubber absorption. The figure mentioned compares with 1,100,000 tons in 1936–39, 840,000 tons in 1932–35, 700,000 tons in 1927–31, and 480,000 tons in 1922–26. Some estimates are as high as 2 million tons a year.[5] However, this projected rate of increase is likely to prove overstated. What will be the picture on the supply side?

PROSPECTIVE POSTWAR SUPPLIES

When Japan conquered the chief rubber-growing areas of the Far East, the production capacity of the Malaysian Hevea plantations was estimated at about 1,500,000 tons a year, and under normal conditions would have grown to at least 1,600,000 tons by 1944. The British and Dutch did not apply the scorched-earth policy to their rubber estates. Such a plan would have been senseless as well as impracticable. The suddenness of Japan's military collapse in August 1945 precluded land warfare in the chief producing areas.

Mature Hevea trees are capable of prodigious passive resistance when left to themselves. Immature trees in existence when the Nipponese overran these countries represented only a trifling percentage of the total acreage under rubber cultivation. Though jungle growth may have moved in on the fairly young trees, neglect of cultivation and general maintenance work does not materially harm the mature stands. In fact, a prolonged period of nontapping rests the trees and will result in temporary flush production once tapping is resumed. In some areas, such as Java, rubber plantations may have been cleared to make room for food production. However, the losses from all possible sources will be largely if not entirely offset by the growth of large

[5] John L. Collyer, president of the B. F. Goodrich Company, in *New York Times*, Dec. 5, 1943, Sec. 5, p. 6.

acreages to increased maturity with increased productivity. It seems safe to assume that probably no more than 10 per cent of the Malaysian rubber-plantation capacity will have been lost beyond redemption upon the liberation of the producing countries.

This does not mean, however, that the surviving capacity can be exploited instantaneously. Smokehouses, milling machinery, and other implements essential to the operation of rubber estates will doubtless have sustained extensive damage. Although these facilities constitute a very small fraction of estate assets, their replacement will take time. In addition, the repairing of the means of transportation, the reorganization of labor and food markets, the recruiting of adequate managerial staffs, and the re-establishment of trading facilities will present obstacles to full production at an early date. Crude rubber may remain scarce for a year or more beyond the fall of 1945. Chances of relatively speedy revival are better for the native industry, but here too, lack of implements, destruction of milling facilities, and disorganized transportation systems will slow down all-out production and exports. Fortunately, the British and Dutch authorities have made careful preparations for rapidly overcoming these impediments. Nevertheless, a considerable transition period will have to elapse before the world will be provided with abundant crude-rubber supplies.

In the longer run, somewhat increased quantities of crude rubber may be forthcoming from the Latin-American and especially the African producing areas. While the output of wild rubber will surely decline as a result of heavy overtapping of easily accessible trees during wartime, and probably lower rubber prices, production of plantation rubber will be expanding as recently planted trees attain tappable age.

As to synthetic rubbers, the plant capacity of countries outside the United States must be taken into account. Canada and Great Britain together will possess about 80,000 tons of annual capacity. Soviet Russia will certainly rebuild such factories as were destroyed during the war. The greater part of Germany's capacity, in Saxony, escaped unscathed from aerial warfare. The Saxonian plant is in the Soviet zone of occupation, and

Russia will find uses for its facilities. Smaller plants are located in several European countries. Following the postwar transition period, the world's total production capacity may be forecast roughly as follows:

Types and sources	Long tons
Natural rubber	
Malaysia	1,450,000–1,500,000
Latin America, Africa	70,000– 100,000
USSR, Eastern Europe	40,000– 50,000
Total	1,560,000–1,650,000
Synthetic rubbers	
United States	1,050,000–1,200,000
Canada, Great Britain	80,000– 90,000
USSR	90,000– 120,000
Other countries	70,000– 120,000
Total	1,290,000–1,530,000
Grand total	2,850,000–3,180,000

This tabulation does not include rubber-reclaiming facilities totaling at least 300,000 tons' annual capacity.

Total output facilities approximating 3 million tons of rubbers a year, faced with an average prospective demand of hardly more than 1.6 million tons and perhaps less, mean a surplus production capacity of between 80 and 90 per cent. Needless to stress, some of these figures on which this rough calculation is based may prove erroneous, but at least some of the errors may well be compensatory. The prospect of a huge excess of production capacity is certain. How to deal with the problem is an inevitable question that must be faced and answered in the not too remote future.

FUTURE COMPETITION OF NATURAL AND SYNTHETIC RUBBERS

In view of the large prospective surplus capacity to produce rubbers that will confront the world in the late 1940's and early 1950's, the question of the competitiveness of natural rubber and the synthetic materials has particular significance. Some American businessmen, rubber chemists, and government officials have expressed convictions that the price of the artificial products will shortly be as low as that of natural rubber. In that case, it is assumed, the war-born industry will be able to stand on its own feet and will need no protection in the postwar world. The prospect deserves analysis.

Disregarding for the moment the possibility of protection, the competitiveness of crude and artificial rubbers will be decided on the joint basis of qualities and prices. Both factors are variables subject to considerable changes within the next five or ten years. At this time, no more can be done than to indicate possible lines and limits of development.

Thus far there have been no claims that the special-purpose rubbers, including Neoprene, will be able to compete with crude rubber on a price basis. Their use depends on special properties that make them superior to the natural material for certain applications. This does not mean, however, that the price of these synthetic products is immaterial. There are undoubtedly many specialty uses in which the price differential may offset the quality differential. What happens to relative prices and improvement of over-all properties will, therefore, affect the proportional consumption of different rubbers in these uses.

On the basis of present expectations, Butyl may sell for 13 to 17 and Buna-S for 14 to 16 cents a pound, including a nominal charge for amortization, marketing expenses, and a moderate profit margin (see p. 195). Such low prices, however, are claimed only for full-capacity production of low-cost plants that comprise no more than one-third to one-half of the total industry. A few plants, it is claimed by some observers,[6] might be able to turn out Buna-S for an even lower price, perhaps 11 or 12 cents a pound. On the other hand, continued profitable production by all plants would require a markedly higher price. Besides, unless subsidies are received, amortization charges may run higher in the long run. On the other hand, manufacturing improvements may lead to further economies in the production of both raw materials and finished products.

Let us assume that the United States will discard half of the war-built capacity, that the remaining lower-cost plants will be able to run at an average of 80 per cent of capacity, and that

[6] *New York Times*, June 17, 1945, p. 26.

under these circumstances Buna-S and Butyl can be marketed for around 16 cents a pound. Actual prices may be either somewhat lower or somewhat higher, but the figures serve as a useful starting point for analysis. How would this price compare with the price of crude rubber?

Some experts who predict that the price of Buna-S and Butyl will not exceed that of the natural material fallaciously assume that the natural-rubber price of 1941 can be regarded as normal for postwar years. This is far from true. Owing to an abnormally heavy demand, local labor shortages, sharply rising shipping and insurance rates, and the restraining effects of the control scheme, the price of crude rubber averaged over 22 cents a pound in 1941. Yet from 1931 to 1939 the average annual price ranged all the way from 3.4 to 19.4 cents, and over the entire period the average was only 12.1 cents. It is true that the extremely low price in 1932 was the result of unprecedented depression. But the higher prices since 1935 in part reflected the raising of the cost level necessitated by the working of the IRRA (see pp. 158–60). For this reason, a comparison of rubber prices and the dividend records of rubber companies during the prewar decade gives no reliable clue to a rubber price reasonably profitable to the majority of small holders and low-cost estate producers. However, the estimate may be ventured that in the absence of restriction, and under conditions of production near full capacity, a price of from 8 to 10 cents a pound would have elicited the profitable production of about 800,000 tons a year from native producers and efficient estate companies.

Concerning the future price of crude rubber, it must be realized that the reorganization of the plantation industry after the eviction of the Japanese will offer it a chance to start with a clean slate except for the trees. Although individual British and Dutch spokesmen have called attention to this fact, there is yet no sign that the industry and governments involved will utilize this opportunity to the best long-run advantage. In a very real sense, the natural rubber-growing industry shares one dilemma with the United States synthetic-rubber industry: a large portion of total capacity is high-cost compared with the remaining part, and to maintain profitable operation for the entire industry therefore necessitates a price much higher than would be found remunerative by the efficient producers. Unlike the American industry, the plantation industry is privately owned, not government-owned, and the matter of abandoning inefficient units is therefore incomparably more complicated. As will be pointed out in the final chapter, there are also more opportunistic remedies that promise the prevention of disaster in the shorter run.

The industry's cost level is susceptible to considerable cuts by means other than structural invigoration through eliminating obsolete and redundant capacity. Smaller estates could be amalgamated, and huge estates broken up in order to remove numerous units of uneconomic size. The extravagant agency and directorial system could be reformed. A greater share of managerial positions could be filled by native personnel. Such readaptation of the Malaysian estate industry to vastly altered prospects would tend notably to diminish average output costs. In addition, the milling industry, with facilities largely damaged or destroyed, could be rebuilt on a centralized rather than the former excessively decentralized basis.[7] Just as the individual wheat grower does not produce his own flour or the beet-sugar grower his own sugar, there is no compelling reason why the individual rubber planter should prepare his own rubber. Large modern mills in central locations, perhaps run co-operatively, would promise greater uniformity of product and hence a better price for the average ton of rubber.

During the rehabilitation period, costs will undoubtedly move above their prewar levels. But after three or four years the economies of the past can be recaptured and new ones added, despite the possibility of permanently higher labor costs. Except under conditions of the large-scale preservation of obsolete capacity by a restriction scheme patterned on the IRRA, the industry should be capable of supplying adequate quantities of crude rubber at a price of around 10 cents a pound (prewar value), and still yield a modest profit.

[7] F. D. Ascoli, "A Post-War Reconstruction Problem," *India-Rubber Journal* (London) Jan. 22, 1944, pp. 2–3. See also the statement by Mr. Cremer, a Dutch rubber grower, in *India Rubber World*, December 1944, CXI, 230.

While such a price compares favorably with the possible price ranges projected for Buna-S and Butyl, it represents by no means the long-run limit to cost and price reduction. Provided the prospects of a soundly reorganized industry are promising and sufficient venture capital is forthcoming, it is fallacious to assume that further scientific progress with cost-decreasing effect is open only to the synthetic industry. By consistently utilizing only high-grade planting material, and ascertaining and applying optimum tapping schedules, both yields per acre and per tapping operation are capable of marked improvement. If at the same time native growers are generously supplied with technical assistance, it is by no means impossible that, in the not too remote future, adequate quantities of rubber can be produced profitably at prices ranging—perhaps markedly—below 8 cents a pound.

The prospective price differential has to be reappraised, of course, in the light of the comparative properties of the different materials. It is possible that the deficiencies that make synthetic rubbers at present inferior to crude rubber in many uses will eventually be overcome by improvements in the artificial materials and in processing techniques. Such deficiencies are as yet many, and some of them serious (pp. 191–92). How rapidly they will be eliminated cannot be foreseen now. As long as they persist, crude rubber will fetch a premium over its synthetic competitors for all applications in which the specific qualities concerned are vitally important. The spread of the premium will vary with the relative importance of the characteristic involved.

Where synthetic products are superior to crude rubber, and wherever these properties are important, synthetic rubber will command a premium price in direct proportion to its qualitative superiority, no more and no less. Wherever these qualities are of lesser or no importance, or whenever a low-priced product is to be manufactured, cheaper natural rubber will tend to command the field on a price basis. In these cases, the price differential will exceed the premium that can be justified for the more expensive material on a quality basis.

Substitution of synthetic materials for the plantation product, finally, may be somewhat furthered by differences in price instability. In the past, the extreme price fluctuations of crude rubber militated against its use in some potential applications. If the price of synthetics should be more stable, as it is likely to be, their use may be encouraged even though, on the basis of costs and/or qualities, crude rubber should enjoy a slight advantage over its rivals.

Even if, in the late 1940's and early 1950's, general-purpose synthetics should be cheaper and their prices more stable compared with the plantation product, crude rubber, on account of its qualitative superiority in certain applications, might fetch a premium for some uses and insure strong representation for the material in total rubber consumption. Despite marked differences in individual and over-all properties, price will not fail to remain a determining factor in the competition of the different rubbers. Owing to the unpredictable but certain changes that will occur in the qualities of different synthetic materials as well as in the costs of producing both crude and artificial rubbers, competition between the two groups will probably remain in a state of flux for an unforeseeable period of time.

Should it come to "cut-throat" competition between crude rubber on the one hand and synthetic products on the other, plantation production may continue for a considerable period of time at exceedingly low prices. Certainly, the astounding compressibility of output costs exhibited during the Great Depression suggests this possibility. Then production did not materially decline, although monthly rubber prices averaged less than 5 cents a pound from October 1931 to May 1933. In the 1950's, the industry may not be able to repeat this performance to the same extent, but, under pressure, it must be expected to show striking staying power.

CHAPTER XII

MAJOR PROBLEMS OF UNITED STATES POLICY

Instead of leaving to the forces of competition the eventual establishment of equilibrium between rubber supply and consumption capacity, some or all of the governments primarily interested in rubber production and trade may embark upon diverse policies of intervening in the free market. Motives for such action will be numerous—some simple, some complex, and some even conflicting. The necessity of demobilizing war industries and rehabilitating destroyed or damaged production facilities, the expediency of satisfying the demands of producers' groups, concern over the prosperity of depressed areas and populations, considerations of preparedness in a period of uncertain peace, the protection of consumer interests, and the need to husband scarce supplies of foreign exchange—such considerations will produce an impressive array of control motives.

Possible forms of intervention and control are likewise varied. The purpose of insuring for a certain rubber-producing industry a larger market than could be expected under laissez-faire conditions may lead to such control devices as tariff duties, import quotas, government bulk trading, compulsory use of certain rubbers for certain products, direct subsidies, and international marketing agreements. Attempts to prevent the price-depressing effects of excessive supplies may result in measures designed to amputate surplus output capacity or to restrict production and exports by international agreement. The aim of moderating undue price oscillations may call for the adoption of a buffer-stock plan or other expedients affecting or regulating prices.

These are only salient examples. Some policies would require intervention on a national, others on an international scale. Some controls might be of short duration, while others might be intended for long-run application. Various degrees of haphazard co-existence or integrated co-ordination among different types of

213

intervention can be imagined. Owing to such multiplicity of plans, only those possible types of control can here be discussed that are certain to attract interest groups and policy makers and, if adopted, to exert decisive influence on the world rubber industry and market. Because of the uncertain future status of different rubbers as regards comparative qualities and production costs, our discussion will be largely confined to questions of principle.

Following a brief survey of the chief problems of the transition period, this chapter will deal primarily with the issue of protection for the American synthetic-rubber industry. The final chapter will examine the possibility of international agreements intended to solve the problems of surplus output capacity and violent price fluctuations.

TRANSITIONAL CONTROLS

Synthetic materials are not in all uses satisfactory substitutes for crude rubber. Because of long-deferred consumers' demand and restocking requirements, the war-peace transition period will witness an abnormally large demand for rubber. It will be some time after their liberation before the Malaysian producing countries will be able to ship sizable supplies of crude rubber. For these reasons, rubbers in general, and natural rubber in particular, are likely to remain relatively scarce for perhaps a year or more after the fall of 1945.

It is essential, therefore, that the rubber market shall not at once be freed of governmental controls. Without the retention of ceiling prices and control of the international trade in as well as the internal distribution of rubber, prices would surely soar. Such a development would not only harm rubber consumers but, by encouraging excessive investments in new rubber-producing facilities, it might also work to the detriment of producers and producing countries. Fortunately, co-operation between the United States, the United Kingdom, and the Netherlands Indies since the outbreak of World War II warrants the hope that adequate if diminishing controls can be maintained during the transition period.

ARGUMENTS FOR PROTECTION OF THE SYNTHETIC-RUBBER INDUSTRY

Prior to World War II, the synthetic-rubber industries of Soviet Russia and Germany were protected from the competition of cheap crude rubber. There can be no doubt that the Soviet industry will remain so sheltered. Other countries may follow suit, although with different protectionist devices. However, the policy of the United States, which possesses nearly four-fifths of the world's facilities for manufacturing synthetic rubbers, will be of primary importance to the world rubber trade.[1]

The shocking experience of the wartime rubber shortage, combined with pride of achievement in building so vast an industry in so short a time, produces practically universal agreement in the United States to maintain a substantial synthetic-rubber industry. Few people acquainted with the rubber situation assume that the entire industry will survive either by virtue of the quality and cheapness of its products or by all-out protection, but there is a remarkable consensus that a sizable section of it will so survive.

The tremendous strides made by the industry between 1942 and 1945 and the constant technical progress convince some observers that general-purpose synthetics will be fully competitive with natural rubber by the time the plantation product becomes available in large quantities. Thus, Colonel Bradley Dewey, former Rubber Director of the WPB, believes that low-cost output facilities with from 400,000 to 600,000 tons annual capacity will remain in production without "duties or subsidies or international agreements."[2] Others, more doubtful, demand that the most efficient portion of the industry be protected if it cannot survive in a free market. Thus, John L. Collyer, president of B. F. Goodrich Company, recently stated: "Regardless of questions of cost or superiority, the nation should keep up a minimum production of 200,000 tons of synthetic rubber for

[1] In the preparation of this chapter the author has drawn on his *Rubber After the War* (Food Research Institute, War-Peace Pamphlets 4, Stanford University, Calif., February 1944).

[2] U.S. War Production Board, Office of Rubber Director, *Special Report . . . . on the Synthetic Rubber Program: Plant Investment and Production Costs* (Aug. 31, 1944), p. 2.

reasons of national security."[3] Similarly, the *India Rubber World* of New York editorialized: "No matter what happens there must be maintained in this country and in production according to the best scientific and technical knowledge at the time sufficient capacity for synthetic rubber to provide for military requirements, whether this production is at a cost higher than rubber could be obtained from outside sources or not."[4] Likewise in an editorial, the *New York Times* has advocated a temporary tariff as a means of preserving an "adequate" synthetic industry.[5]

If the optimists should prove correct—if by 1948–50 general-purpose synthetics from efficient plants can assert themselves against the competition of the plantation product—then no important problem of public policy arises for the time being and, as the United States Tariff Commission points out, the only question deserving consideration will be the easing of the strain on the Malaysian economies by some kind of transitional measure.[6]

This would not mean, however, that the question of protection is necessarily settled forever. We know that, when under relentless pressure, the Malaysian rubber industry is capable of a prolonged struggle at far less than profitable prices. Moreover, the plantation industry is capable of greatly reducing its costs in the longer run. Technical progress made by the synthetic-rubber industry may be so continuous and substantial that its products will remain competitive in any case. Yet there can be no certainty of this. The question of protection, therefore, may become acute at a later stage if it does not arise by the late 1940's.

On the other hand, should general-purpose synthetics be unable to compete with crude rubber on a combined price-quality basis, then the question of protection will have to be faced as soon as the Malaysian producers are rehabilitated. For what reasons should the United States retain ample facilities for producing synthetic rubbers of general-purpose types? Are these reasons

[3] John L. Collyer, "Raw Material Outlook in the Rubber Industry," *India Rubber World*, February 1945, CXI, 560.

[4] *India Rubber World*, November 1944, CXI, 191.

[5] *New York Times*, Oct. 18, 1943, p. 14.

[6] U.S. Tariff Commission, *Rubber*, p. 16.

valid? If so, how much annual capacity must be protected and what form should protection take?

Thus far, five principal arguments have been advanced in support of a protected synthetic-rubber industry. (1) Rubber is a critical, strategic material both in civilian economy and in the implements of war. An insured supply in wartime is therefore indispensable. (2) It would be foolish to "junk" the huge plants built at public cost. (3) Full employment is the cardinal postwar aim of social planners, and the domestic production of rubber will furnish employment for American labor. (4) The supply of plantation rubber is subject to foreign monopolistic control which lends itself to the exploitation of the American consumer. (5) A large supply of domestically produced artificial rubbers promises stable rubber prices, a development that would be greatly in the interest of rubber-goods manufacturers.

The military-security argument is generally conceded and fully deserves first place in protectionist considerations. Complete dependence upon a rubber supply accessible only over thousands of miles of vulnerable shipping lanes indeed spells danger in a world of intermittent strife. This is true of rubber as of many other essential raw stuffs. The postwar evolution of the international situation undoubtedly will influence the solution of the rubber problem. It can be taken for granted that the United States and Great Britain will be the two foremost naval powers of the world and will be able to maintain this supremacy, especially in Far Eastern waters, for more than a decade. To that extent, the defeat and disarmament of Japan means a prodigious change from the prewar situation. No overly hasty steps seem required to lessen dependence upon trans-Pacific sources of supply. Despite the advent of the atomic bomb, there is ample time to plan and to prepare.

On the other hand, it must be argued that the United States will not be omnipotent after this war. Vigilance may be relaxed in the future and faulty policies adopted. Unpredictable political changes may occur on the Asiatic mainland, and novel technological developments may radically alter methods of warfare as well as the global distribution of power. Finally, the new world Charter, evolved by the United Nations Conference

at San Francisco, does not provide for an international organization so basically different from the former League of Nations
as to render the prevention of wars a matter of course. Indeed,
no illusions of permanent security are widely entertained, and
all the great powers contemplate peacetime military establish-
ments much larger than before World War II. Nations that
pursue such policies will also seek to be prepared against wartime shortages of essential raw materials.

But this train of thought does not necessarily imply that the
United States must achieve self-sufficiency in even so vital a
material as rubber. A large measure of security can be easily
and cheaply attained by government acquisition and maintenance
of stocks comprising one or more years' normal requirements of
rubber.[7] The storability of rubber, perhaps in conjunction with
a regular turning over of stocks, makes such an arrangement
perfectly practicable. Maintenance of stockpiles, moreover,
permits flexibility. The size of rubber security stocks could be
cautiously reduced if the growth of the synthetic-rubber industry warrants, or augmented if a critical turn of international
relations recommends increasing prudence.

In addition to a large rubber stockpile, a potent reclaiming
industry, and a small but fairly secure source of crude rubber
in near-by Latin America, the United States will possess under
any circumstance a synthetic-rubber industry incomparably
larger than before the war. How large a portion of the synthetic
industry would be able, in the 1950's, to withstand, unassisted,
the competition of rubber plantations cannot be foreseen now.
If considerably less than one-third, there would be excellent
reasons for correcting the results of laissez-faire conditions by
government intervention. It seems to the writer that security
demands the preservation of a synthetic-rubber industry possessing about one-quarter of the capacity erected during World
War II.

Various synthetic materials of the special-purpose type are
bound to find dependable postwar markets. It is unlikely that

---

[7] Such government reserves might well be acquired in such ways as to moderate price
fluctuations and be subject to be drawn upon, under certain conditions. if rubber prices
soared and security was not in question.

less than 50,000 tons annual capacity will be thus maintained for the production of this type of product and no protectionist devices are needed. In addition, about 200,000 tons annual output capacity for general-purpose synthetics should be maintained for security reasons. A peacetime industry of that size is large enough to sustain all research essential to further technical progress and to constitute a potent nucleus capable of relatively speedy expansion.

In case of emergency, then, the United States would have a large government stockpile, rubber inventories carried by the rubber-goods manufacturing industry, rubber shipments from accessible Latin-American countries, and a substantial synthetic-rubber industry. At the outbreak of World War II, the task of expanding facilities—which produced a mere 1,900 tons in 1939 —to their spectacular magnitude in 1945 was truly gigantic. To expand, in a future emergency, an industry of about 250,000 tons capacity for all types would obviously be much easier and far less time-consuming, particularly with the necessary "know-how."

Such a program should satisfy any reasonable demands for security. If anything, it errs on the safe side. The proposal, furthermore, is based on rather pessimistic premises. If, as some expert observers expect, the present and future trend of development should favor the synthetic materials more than here assumed, the American rubber position will be even stronger from the viewpoint of military preparedness than we have suggested.

Whether it is foolish or wise to "junk" a large war industry built at public expense, once the security problem is solved, is obviously an economic question. If it should be less costly to the public than to "protect" or subsidize, then "junking" is undoubtedly wise. Nobody will advocate full postwar utilization of war-inflated shipyards and airplane factories just because they were expanded at the expense of the taxpayer. To be sure, the proposition to continue operation of the entire synthetic-rubber industry appears to many to make more sense because its product would replace an imported material. But upon closer analysis the issue appears in a different light.

Even if such a policy were to be found sound in principle,

however, a considerable measure of contraction would be unavoidable because a capacity of over a million tons would exceed the country's normal postwar demand for rubber. Since the United States could not for quality reasons do without crude rubber, perhaps not much less than half of the wartime-built capacity would have to be abandoned in any case. These would be the high-cost units which, in Colonel Dewey's words, "will be in the same boat with a laid-up battleship that might eventually go to the scrap heap."[8] Since the preservation of perhaps up to one-fourth of the total production capacity may be considered vital for reasons of military security, the question of abandoning existing plants is likely to be controversial only for from one-fourth to one-third of the facilities constructed during the war.

The direct government investments in Neoprene, Butyl, butadiene, styrene, and co-polymer facilities have been estimated at approximately 700 million dollars.[9] While investments per ton of capacity vary from plant to plant, we may assume that the controversial one-fourth or one-third of the industry to be scrapped represents roughly 200 million dollars. That is the original investment. But the plants will have been operated for 5 or 6 years and, with amortization on an 8-year basis, the investments would have been depreciated by about two-thirds. Nor would the abandonment of the plants in question be equivalent to a total loss. Land, buildings, and part of the equipment could be diverted to other uses. On the other hand, if the maintenance of this capacity should require a subsidy of several cents per pound of United States–produced rubber, it can be easily seen that the cost of protection to the American taxpayer or consumer of rubber goods would soon exceed the value of the abandoned facilities. The decision, if necessary, to protect only that portion of the industry which is indispensable for security reasons would have the additional advantage of eliminating or minimizing the deleterious effects of protection discussed below (pp. 223–24).

The notion that the domestic production of all rubber consumed in this country will furnish American labor with additional employment—a stock argument resorted to by every

[8] *New York Times*, Dec. 9, 1943, p. 39.   [9] See Table 14, p. 190.

industry desirous of protection—has been proved fallacious by generations of economists. To insure the highest possible degree of employment after the war is beyond doubt a most desirable social objective, although to accomplish it at any price would be economically retrogressive and politically dangerous. However, economically satisfactory solution of this problem is possible by methods that do not importantly interfere with the economical allocation of productive resources. Maximum employment need not be obtained at the cost of reduced real income. The attempt to increase employment by raising barriers to international trade would mean just that. To insure this employment by protection would mean a corresponding contraction of employment in higher-wage American export industries. On general grounds, therefore, high-tariff protection of the synthetic-rubber industry should be condemned as tending to reduce rather than augment the over-all volume of employment.

Besides, the amount of employment opportunities involved in synthetic-rubber manufacture are trifling. As demonstrated above, a certain minimum of capacity should be maintained at any price if it is unable to assert itself against the competition of crude rubber. A considerable margin of the industry in existence at the end of World War II represents surplus capacity in any case. Since the operation of all facilities requires only 20,000 employees (p. 189), subsidization of, say, one-half of the industry would involve no more than 10,000 employees in an economy that some hope will furnish 60 million jobs.

Prior to the war, the supply of plantation rubber was subject to monopolistic control which did raise the price of rubber over what it would have been in the absence of organized restriction. While the monopoly power enjoyed by the parties to the IRRA was not outrageously exploited, as was the earlier Stevenson plan, it could have been so abused. A measure of anxiety among the potential victims is perfectly understandable. However, the future invulnerability of the United States to such potential danger does not rest on the country's independence of foreign rubber supplies. The situation at the end of World War II is very different from that at the beginning.

Possessing a huge synthetic-rubber industry and weighing the problem of protection or nonprotection, the United States will enjoy a formidable bargaining position. Without substantial exports to this country, the Malaysian rubber growers face a tremendous crisis of readjustment. Free entry of crude rubber into the United States could be made conditional on the absence of a producers' control over the supply of plantation rubber, or, if renewal of restriction were approved, the United States could secure a strong voice in the shaping of regulative policies. Moreover, the retention of a potent synthetic-rubber industry, capable of supplying about one-quarter of the country's requirements and of relatively rapid expansion, would insure the United States permanently against exploitive price policies on the part of a comprehensive Malaysian control organization.

Indeed, the very probability that synthetic-rubber consumption and production will gradually expand should make the producers of natural rubber wary of hastening the growth of their rival by furnishing it a strong price incentive. On the other hand, it seems equally fortunate that continuing and unhindered availability of crude rubber will serve as a useful check on possible monopolistic arrangements by United States synthetic-rubber manufacturers. This advantage should not be underrated.

Availability of synthetic rubbers will admittedly exert some stabilizing effect on rubber prices. As is true of many chemicals produced in a few highly capitalized plants, prices of synthetic rubbers can be expected to fluctuate much less than crude-rubber prices did before World War II. However, except in so far as the price of synthetics tends to place a ceiling on upward gyrations of crude-rubber prices, the latter are left to fluctuate as much as before. The beneficial effect of relatively stable synthetics prices will therefore be confined largely to the extent of their share in aggregate rubber consumption and, as mentioned above, the benefit involved will tend somewhat to increase this share. Yet, considering the national economy as a whole, to shoulder the cost of large-scale subsidization in order to benefit from stabler prices seems to exchange a small evil for a greater one. It is surely preferable to explore more economic means of damping excessive fluctuations of crude-rubber prices (pp. 240–45).

DISADVANTAGES OF PROTECTION

Subsidized synthetic-rubber production on a large scale is not only unnecessary and uneconomic in the light of the reasons advanced in support of protection. In addition, sweeping protectionist arrangements have adverse effects that cannot be ignored. Some of these disadvantages have already been mentioned. Thus, protection or subsidization in any form would exact heavy financial sacrifices from the American taxpayer or the ultimate consumers of rubber goods, no matter how concealed. Reduction of imports of crude rubber through protection would diminish the purchasing power of foreign countries that are large importers of American goods and would thereby harm American export trades.

There are still other drawbacks to large-scale subsidization. Protection is an inevitable breeder of domestic arrangements toward monopoly and monopolist profits. Protection also serves as an impediment to technological progress. The rate of obsolescence is notoriously heavy in new industries, and must be particularly so where an immense plant capacity was constructed within the shortest possible time. A considerable portion, if not most, of the synthetics plants to be protected or abandoned might be markedly obsolete on the basis of technological knowledge accumulated by 1950. Some are obsolete now, but subsidization will encourage manufacturers to go on using them. If they are abandoned, on the other hand, future re-expansion of the industry in peacetime would proceed in a more economical fashion.

Intense market competition between plantation and synthetic rubbers will also serve as a constant and powerful incentive toward rapid technical progress. On the other hand, by raising rubber prices, protection would seriously retard, if not thwart, the development of new bulk uses of rubber. Indeed, as an impediment to sharply expanding consumption, protection has its most vicious effect.

Finally, it seems appropriate to cite the ill effects large-scale subsidization of American synthetic-rubber manufacture would have on the plantation-rubber exporting countries. Not only would Great Britain's adjustment to her new position of a debtor country be still further aggravated. To the economies and plane of living of the Far Eastern rubber-growing areas, the radical diminution or complete cessation of American rubber imports would deliver a terrific blow. Politically and morally, it would be almost imperative for the Allies to discover and finance ways and means of replacing rubber as an important source of Malaysian livelihood.

INSURING THE SECURITY MINIMUM

The minimum capacity for producing synthetic rubbers that has been stipulated as a requirement of military security—about 250,000 tons for all types—may very likely be maintained without government assistance. Despite higher prices, specialty rubbers will find expanding markets for specialty uses, and, owing to their desirable properties, general-purpose rubbers of the Buna-S and Butyl type will likewise be consumed in considerable volume, even if crude rubber should be the cheaper material. If protection is needed at all, it will probably be for only a small margin of the minimum capacity involved, and the over-all subsidy needed is, therefore, likely to be small.

Such assistance could be effectively granted in any one of several ways.[10] It is important to select the method that will bring the desired result without involving large costs or offsetting disadvantages. An infant-industry tariff, providing for an import duty of about 3 or 4 cents a pound, might accomplish the desired balance. Yet such an arrangement would not only raise the price of all rubber to American consumers; it is also open to the serious objection that temporary duties of this kind have an apparently unavoidable tendency to be increased and become permanent. The result would be expensive rubber and expensive rubber articles in the long run. The alternative establishment of a system of import quotas, while still more effective restrictively, is even more objectionable on the same

[10] See the able discussion of this subject in U.S. Tariff Commission, *Rubber*, pp. 27–29.

grounds and, in view of a highly variable demand, would be very difficult to administer. With both methods the clumsiness of the protectionist device is out of proportion to the small margin of protection required.

A temporary advantage might be extended to the new industry by the condition under which government-owned plants are released to private ownership. Ordinarily, the purchase price is computed on the basis of construction costs minus depreciation. Yet the government might charge a lower price than would be arrived at by this method of calculation. To some extent that would be justified under any circumstance, since construction costs in many cases included exceptional expenditures due to faulty preparations of plans or to overtime payments to workers and bonus payments to contractors aimed at speeding up construction. Apart from such allowances, the government might negotiate a purchase price that would contain a clear subsidy of varying proportion, release without payment being the only limit to the size of the subsidy. The objection to this procedure is that it would be extremely difficult to adopt a plan of selective subsidization, that is, to grant it to the more efficient plants and deny it to the others.

However, recourse to a more direct and flexible form of subsidization may seem desirable. The report of the United States Tariff Commission mentions the possibilities of granting a direct subsidy of a given amount per pound of synthetic rubber produced or of guaranteeing a given price or profit per pound.[11] Administration of such a policy might prove clumsy. Especially, it would be difficult to avoid extension of an insufficient or excessive subsidy. Nevertheless, the guaranty of a minimum price seems less objectionable than protection by either tariff duties or import quotas. There should be a well-defined procedure, however, for periodically examining and revising the amount of the subsidy. It should be decreased or withdrawn as soon as the subsidized production of synthetic rubbers becomes substantially in excess of security requirements.

Another way would be to specify the use of artificial rubbers in the manufacture of equipment for the armed forces and

[11] *Ibid.*

other government agencies. Provided the specification of synthetic rubber in military equipment is confined to applications that increase equipment cost but do not affect its performance, this idea appears worth exploring. Such an arrangement might well furnish all the government assistance that is necessary, and competitive bidding for the contracts would tend to keep the subsidy from becoming excessive. It might also be considered whether synthetic rubbers for use in government equipment should be produced in government plants organized on the basis of arsenals.

Another way of insuring the maintenance of minimum production of American synthetic rubbers would be United States participation in an international rubber control scheme of the restrictive type. This idea will be further discussed in the final chapter (pp. 232–34). At this point the remark must suffice that such a solution would be liable to entail all the disadvantages resulting from the IRRA, particularly production patterned on an uneconomic and rigid pattern, relatively high rubber prices, and the possibilities of undue monopoly profits.

Some observers have urged that, for reasons of security, a certain plant capacity should be maintained in standby condition. Yet chemical plant facilities of the complex type in question deteriorate more rapidly when idle than when operating. Furthermore, they are likely to become quickly obsolete. The time to establish and maintain standby facilities is when international crises point to the danger or imminence of war. Maintenance of idle plants for long periods of time, perhaps twenty years, seems to be a policy of doubtful value.

PROTECTION OF DOMESTIC AND NEAR-BY SOURCES OF CRUDE RUBBER

The protection of near-by sources of crude rubber—guayule in the continental United States, tree rubber in Central and South America—has been widely urged as a measure of preparedness for future emergencies. The fostering of a rubber-plantation industry in Latin America is also advocated on the grounds of providing the countries concerned with an additional cash crop that would diversify and strengthen their economies.

Security considerations here are irrelevant because of the advent of the synthetic-rubber industry and the possibilities of stockpiling natural rubber. Reliance on these two sources of supply is less precarious than dependence upon Latin-American production and maritime shipping routes. If means are sought to buttress the Inter-American good-neighbor policy by diversifying the economies of Latin-American countries, surely cheaper and more effective ways can be found. As the location of a thriving plantation-rubber industry, South America does not favorably compare with Malaysia. The prevalence of a leaf fungus, the wide spread of malaria, the necessity of developing lengthy lines of inland transportation, and the scarcity of suitable labor are the chief handicaps.[12] To be sure, some of these obstacles might be overcome in the course of time, though not without great cost. But there is no likelihood that the transportation and labor problems can be satisfactorily solved in the foreseeable future. To withstand the competition of Malaysian rubber, a South American plantation industry would need heavy subsidies in one form or another.

Conditions are more favorable on some of the West Indian islands and, perhaps, in some of the "banana Republics" of Central America. Here transportation facilities are good, and high population densities indicate a potentially large labor supply. The cultivation of Hevea trees in small mixed plantings, interplanted with upland rice, root crops, bananas, coffee, castor beans, etc., may merit investigation. But the alternatives in mixed cropping are numerous. It is very doubtful whether Central American peasants would be willing, without subsidies, to produce plantation rubber at prices likely to prevail in the 1950's. In any event, the total output capacity involved would be small, probably under 50,000 tons a year.

"In order to establish a sound postwar industry in private hands," a Congressional Committee has proposed the subsidization of a certain amount of domestic guayule production (possibly 400,000 acres).[13] Under the most advanced methods of

---

[12] These points are elaborated at greater length in Knorr, *Rubber after the War*, pp. 39–44.

[13] H. Rep. 2098, 78th Cong., 2d Sess., *Study of Rubber in United States, Mexico, and Haiti* (Jan. 2, 1945), p. 21.

cultivation and processing known today, guayule rubber has no chance to compete with Hevea rubber or, probably, with some of the synthetics. To make it artificially competitive would require very large subsidies per unit of the product. Representative Poage proposes a guaranteed price of about 28 cents a pound, possibly twice the prospective price of Malaysian rubber or Buna-S. With maintenance of a synthetic-rubber industry and stockpiles of crude rubber, no rational argument, even one based on national security, commends such a policy.

CONCLUSION

Owing to certain superior qualities of its products and rapid strides made in reducing output costs, a large part of the American synthetic-rubber industry may, without any type of governmental assistance, survive the competition of crude rubber once the Malaysian industry has been rehabilitated. In the event that only a minor proportion should so survive in a free market, a moderate amount of selective protection is required for reasons of military security. For the sake of preserving healthy economic conditions, such protection should not be granted to more than one-fourth of the capacity built during World War II. In combination with a permanent stockpile of crude rubber, an industry of that magnitude should offer satisfactory security.

If protection is necessary, the method should be direct, flexible, and selective. Tariff barriers or import quotas should be ruled out for various reasons, but principally because they would increase the price of all rubber consumed in the United States. The guaranty of a variable minimum price per pound of synthetic rubber, and the use of artificial materials in the manufacture of military (and perhaps other government) equipment wherever compatible with satisfactory performance, seem to offer the least objectionable solutions. Aside from regulating the transition from war- to peacetime conditions, nothing further should be done to encourage a high-cost Latin-American plantation industry or the maintenance of guayule production. Neither is required by national security or other national interests.

CHAPTER XIII

PROBLEMS OF INTERNATIONAL REGULATION

According to the conclusions and tentative estimates advanced in chapter xi, the plantation-rubber industry will be confronted, after the war, with many of the same problems that it faced in the 1930's. After the transition period the existence of a great deal of surplus production capacity is indicated, although total rubber consumption is likely to be higher than before the war. Unless the industrially advanced countries manage to steady the course of the business cycle, violently fluctuating prices of rubber will likewise reappear on the post-transition scene. Indeed, from the standpoint of the crude-rubber grower, this problem may appear in a more unfavorable setting than before. The availability of synthetic materials may put a ceiling on upward price fluctuations while downward fluctuations are unchecked. As in the middle 1930's, the possibility of shelving or solving these problems by international agreement and control is already uppermost in the minds of representatives of the plantation industry.

THE PROBLEM OF SURPLUS OUTPUT CAPACITY

During a transition period every pound of crude rubber will be needed; no major marketing problem will exist, and prices, even if controlled, may be high in prewar terms, if not in terms of the abnormally high production cost of the rehabilitation period. Thereafter, probably by 1950, the consequences of surplus output capacity are likely to recommence troubling the rubber-plantation countries and, to a lesser degree, the synthetic-rubber industry.

At best, if synthetic materials should be incapable of competing with crude rubber for bulk uses or if no more than a small portion of the American synthetic industry were protected by government measures, and if world rubber consumption is expanding at least at the prewar rate, the surplus-capacity problem will be of lesser magnitude than before World War II. Excess production capacity might amount to as little as one-fifth of Malaysian capacity. At worst, if cheap synthetic rubbers—with or without subsidization—effectively rival the plantation product for bulk uses and only a slow secular increase in world consumption takes place, the problem will be far more formidable than in the 1930's. Malaysian capacity might be as much as double the world's requirements for natural rubber.

Neither of these extreme positions is likely to become reality. Production facilities will probably be redundant to the extent of one-third to one-half of Malaysian capacity. This assumption is predicated on the abandonment of at least half of the American synthetic-rubber plants, the absence of large and protected synthetic-rubber industries outside the Americas, and the relatively speedy economic recovery of Continental Europe. However, unless the American synthetic-rubber industry is fairly promptly converted to a reduced peacetime basis, excessive rubber stocks also may accumulate toward the end of the transition period.

While again faced with the dilemma of surplus output capacity, the post-transition situation of the rubber-plantation industry will differ both from its prewar position and from the position of the American synthetic-rubber industry. In terms of product quality, production costs, and world absorption capacity, the synthetic industry also will be confronted with surplus output capacity. The three conditions mentioned will determine the extent of redundancy. Like the plantation industry, the synthetic industry will be composed of units of greatly varying efficiency, with a considerable portion technically obsolete. Both industries are capable of marked increase in average productive efficiency; many observers assume, however, that improvement can be consummated more swiftly in the chemical plants than in the plantations.

It is the dependence of the crude-rubber grower upon export markets that makes his prospects fundamentally different from those of the synthetic-rubber manufacturer. Artificial rubbers of the special-purpose type are certain to be exported from the

United States. Yet, unless general-purpose synthetic materials can out-compete crude rubber in the free world market, the export market for American products of all types will be insignificant in relation to the domestic market. Although economically undesirable, a large American synthetic-rubber industry could be protected by relatively simple devices. The continued prosperity of the crude-rubber producing countries, on the contrary, is dependent on large export markets in general, and on considerable United States imports in particular. If surplus production capacity in the 1950's is large, the burden of adjustment will, for this reason, fall primarily on the plantation industry.[1] To be sure, depressed price levels as a result of excessive exports will also affect the markets for synthetic products, but a sufficient market for artificial rubbers could easily be secured by government intervention.

Encumbered with excess production capacity, the Malaysian plantation industry will face the permanent rival, only potential in the 1930's, of a synthetics industry. This factor will greatly limit the freedom of action formerly enjoyed by the industry and by countries producing natural rubber. Whatever remedies they may resort to for the purpose of relieving the price-depressing pressure of surplus output capacity, any policy and action tending to increase costs and prices will be sure to court eventual disaster. Only an industry revitalized by the removal of obsolete units and excessive fixed charges and progressive in the adoption of superior planting and processing techniques can hope for long-run prosperity by encouraging rubber consumption and successfully asserting itself against the rival synthetics industry.

This does not necessarily mean that the resurrection of the prewar IRRA is out of the question. Indeed, because of the propensity of business men and governments to solve immediate problems without considering long-run effects, a restrictive aggreement of that type may be felt both desirable and ex-

---

[1] Dependence on export markets was the chief weakness of the Chilean nitrate industry in its competition with synthetic nitrates. In the event of open competition between the two products, the products of the synthetic material successfully prevailed upon their governments to grant them tariff protection. Chile was unable to retaliate in kind. See Plummer, *International Combines in Modern Industry*, p. 108.

pedient to adopt. A restriction scheme could be set up to prevent the price of the plantation product from falling markedly
below the level at which the synthetic material begins actively
to compete. The potential expansion of synthetic-rubber production and consumption would act as an effective deterrent
to desires to raise rubber prices above that level. Economically,
the feasibility of such a control arrangement would depend on
the extent to which restriction added to ordinary production
costs. Redundant output capacity might form so large a proportion of the total and the average restriction rate required
might therefore be so severe that the plantation industry would
stand to gain little or nothing by such a plan.

Such a control project would, of course, be purely defensive
and open to the same objections that applied to the old IRRA
(chapter ix), except that the lessened degree of monopoly power
enjoyed by the agreement countries would not permit them to
pursue any desired policy of high prices. From the viewpoint
of the rubber-plantation countries, an additional drawback to
such control would lie in its discouragement of new bulk uses
based on cheap rubber, and in the encouragement given to the
rival synthetic-rubber industry. The smaller the spread between
the prices of crude and synthetic materials, the greater would
be this incentive. At the same time, the rubber-growing industry would remain burdened with high-cost and obsolete producing units and retain an internal organization obstructive to the
swift improvement of general productive efficiency.

The establishment of a restriction plan patterned on the former IRRA would be more feasible were the synthetic-rubber-
producing industries included in the agreement. H. Eric Miller,
chairman of a large British estate company, stated:

> Two alternatives lie ahead of us. Either we have to fight for our exist-
> ence in open competition with the newly established synthetic industry, or,
> the two industries, together with the manufacturers, will work out some
> mutual accommodation to enable the world to have the benefit of the best
> that our different raw materials are capable of giving.[2]

---

[2] *India-Rubber Journal*, Nov. 6, 1943, pp. 457–58. Similarly, T. H. Graham, chair-
man of the Malayan General Company, quoted in *Economist*, Nov. 21, 1942, p. 643; and
A. C. Matthew, chairman of the Rubber Growers Association, in "The Future of Crude
Rubber," *Great Britain and the East*, June 6, 1942, p. 12.

While opposing a restrictive control plan of the old type, the London *Economist* likewise suggested that the problem of excess capacity be solved by an international agreement containing a satisfactory formula for the sharing of the world market between natural and synthetic rubbers.[3] Promising a technically simple solution of the problem of protecting a substantial proportion of the synthetics industry, such an arrangement may be found acceptable by some groups in the United States (see p. 226).

From the viewpoint of protecting a certain portion of the American synthetic-rubber industry, an international arrangement of this type appears clearly undesirable. As a protective device, it would raise prices of all rubbers consumed in this country and would therefore be as obnoxious as protection by tariff duties or import quotas (see p. 224). Only in the event that, in a free market, synthetics should be capable of asserting themselves heavily for bulk uses should the United States consider an international marketing agreement. The purpose would be that of easing the burden of adjustment placed on the plantation industry. It should be temporary, and restrictions on the marketing of synthetic products should be gradually relaxed and finally removed. Such a co-operative policy might be defended on the ground that a large part of the plantation industry has become a war casualty in a common war effort.

From the viewpoint of the rubber-producing countries, inclusion of the synthetics-producing industry would render international restriction more practicable than would their exclusion. The general objections to any form of tight restriction scheme on an equalitarian basis hold good. The close price spread between crude rubber and synthetic materials of the general-purpose type likely to be maintained under such a scheme furthermore would almost certainly encourage the use of the artificial products. In that event the crude-rubber-producing countries could hardly prevent a gradual revision of national quotas in favor of the synthetic-rubber-producing countries.[4]

[3] *Economist*, July 31, 1943, p. 150.

[4] See again the illustrative history of agreements between the producers of natural and synthetic nitrate, in Plummer, *op. cit.*, pp. 103-9.

Like any scheme of the cost-raising, restrictive type, it would also fail to encourage extended consumption of cheap natural rubber in bulk uses.

The chances of long-run prosperity for the crude-rubber-producing countries depend upon successful competition with artificial products and on the utmost promotion of increased rubber consumption. In turn, both conditions depend upon cheap natural rubber. This is also in the general interest of an expansive world economy and in the special interest of consumers of rubber goods. Indeed, this coincidence of ultimate interest imparts sense to the unusual demand that commodity agreements be consumer-oriented, that the consumer rather than the producer be made the starting point of organization.[5]

The extent to which such orientation is practicable is unfortunately doubtful. To produce cheap rubber profitably, the plantation industry, like the synthetic-rubber industry, must be as progressive as possible in improving productive efficiency per man-hour of work and per unit of invested capital. Organized restriction for the sake of preserving obsolete and redundant capacity is absolutely incompatible with such progressiveness. The prime necessity for both plantation and synthetics industries is to eliminate this obstructive burden.

It has been suggested that, for the type of industry involved, fairly unrestricted competition or complete government dictation to all individual producers are the only effective alternatives toward this object.[6] Both alternatives are fraught with attendant evils. Indeed, government dictation pure and simple is inconsistent with the political systems of the major rubber-producing countries. However, this does not necessarily mean that governments are without influence. Since any elaborate control scheme for crude rubber is impracticable without government backing, governments could well make their support conditional on the acceptance of certain policies. Providing public compensation for war damages and assisting in the rehabilitation of reoccupied areas, governments have additional means of affecting the reorganization of the world's rubber

[5] "International Commodity Control," *Nature*, Nov. 8, 1941, p. 542.

[6] R. F. Martin, *International Raw Commodity Price Control* (New York, 1937), p. 14.

plantations. The only question is whether a government, pressed by influential interest-groups, would differ substantially from organized producers and investors in its concept of a desirable policy.

That the amputation of redundant and obsolete capacity by way of unbounded competition would involve severe hardships for the entire industry has been demonstrated above (pp. 169–70). Again it is necessary to point out, however, that the elimination of high-cost producers is an economical, not a wasteful, process. While imprudent investors would lose, the surviving portion of the industry would be left with a regenerated structure and with low output costs. The price-depressing effects of capacity reduction by attrition and the consequent suffering imposed on efficient producers, prudent investors, and labor, as well as on other trades and public finances in the producing countries, justifies the search for a better solution than unrestricted competition. The possibility that under "cut-throat" competition extremely low prices of crude rubber would give emphasis to the demands of synthetic-rubber manufacturers for protection only adds to that urgency.

It should be expected that any alternative to totalitarian planning or unchecked competition that reduces capacity along economic lines will be in the nature of a compromise. Most likely it will include some amount of public authority, as well as competition, and will probably achieve only roughly the object sought. The important thing is that the objective be approximated and that the measures yield a net social gain in the long run.

WAYS OF ADJUSTMENT

The following suggestions are offered as a contribution toward a program designed to satisfy the minimum requirements of an expanding and adaptive world economy and yet mitigate the pains of the necessary adjustments.

1. An exploratory rubber conference of the major rubber-producing and -consuming countries might be called as soon as the transition period is well under way. Besides dealing with the problems of transition itself, this conference should discuss

in a preliminary fashion the rubber problems of the future. There is a strong predisposition in the United States to postpone any such open discussion until after the transition period. This attitude is justified in so far as it springs from the realization of the unpredictable course of developments in the synthetic-rubber industry. The crude-rubber-producing countries, on the other hand, need to know what form United States policy is likely to take, because such knowledge may influence their own disposition to rehabilitate the plantation industry. To some extent, these countries have a right to be accommodated; and, even if discussion has to proceed on the basis of a variable set of assumptions as to the probable qualities and costs of synthetic rubbers, certain policy questions could probably be cleared and tentative commitments made.

High on the agenda of such a conference should be the formation of a permanent rubber commission composed of delegates from the nations represented, assisted by a competent staff of experts, and furnished with pertinent information by the producing countries. This commission should be requested to assemble and study all facts and data on the current qualities, production costs, and prices of various rubbers, as well as on the trends of world production and consumption. In the light of their findings and reasonable estimates based thereon, the commission should also be asked to prepare a report on the merits of various proposals for the solution of the surplus-capacity problem.

2. A second rubber conference with some approach to policy-making power should be convened before the transition period shows signs of coming to an end. All the essential facts relating to all types of rubber, their properties, costs, and prospective markets can be expected to be available at that time. Should it be clear that a general-purpose synthetic is likely to displace crude rubber, unassisted, in half or more of all bulk-use consumption, then the synthetic-rubber-manufacturing countries (especially the United States) might seriously consider measures to ease the adjustment difficulties of the crude-rubber-producing areas. In that event, the majority of the rubber plantations might well be regarded in the nature of a war casualty or war-

destroyed industry. Without the wartime scarcity of natural rubber, the advent of the synthetics industry would surely have been very slow; only, in this case, what was a blow to some Allies was an ultimate boon to another. On more general grounds, the United States may well see fit to collaborate with the United Kingdom and the Netherlands toward an economic reorganization of the depressed Malaysian rubber areas.

The most important measures to be taken might lie outside the field of rubber. But the plight of the plantation industry could be somewhat reduced by decisions of the United States and other countries to lay in strategic stockpiles of crude rubber. Furthermore, it might be worth considering whether the synthetic-rubber-producing countries should not pledge themselves to refrain from exporting, for a certain number of years, artificial rubbers of the general-purpose type.

Should the relative position of different rubbers be the reverse, with natural rubber likely to recapture most of the vast consumption field of bulk uses, then different problems would arise. The synthetic-rubber-producing countries might agree not to resort to all-out protection of their industries, and to protect, if necessary at all, only the capacity essential to national security. In turn, the crude-rubber-producing countries might pledge themselves not to resort to bounties or other means of augmenting the competitive advantage of their product. They also might agree to remove prospective surplus-output capacity and to invite the participation of major rubber-consuming countries if such removal should be regulated on an international basis.

The conference should also examine the possibilities of moderating excessive gyrations of rubber prices, a goal that is in the interest of both producing and consuming industries. (The nature of this problem and approaches to its solution are examined in another part of this chapter.) Finally, the conference should set up a permanent agency for the collection of data on the world rubber trade and absorption, and establish facilities for international consultation on all problems and policies of importance to the large rubber-producing and -consuming countries.

3. The actual amputation of surplus-output capacity is within the province of the producing countries themselves. Obstacles to the adoption of suitable remedies will be proportionate to the amount of capacity affected. If this should approximate half of the entire production facilities, the industries and countries concerned will face a formidable crisis, and extraordinary measures will be necessary to weather it in orderly fashion. In that event the entire economies of the areas involved will be drastically affected, and reorganization will need to be planned on the broadest possible basis. If redundant capacity is of lesser magnitude, correspondingly less radical solutions may suffice. In estimating the approximate extent of excess capacity, the planners must be aware of the diminished importance of reserve capacity. Before World War II, when the expansion of capacity required at least six years, a strong case could be made for the maintenance of a reserve. With the emergence of the synthetic-rubber industry, capable of expanding within less than one year, this necessity has ceased to constitute a major problem.

Capacity-reducing measures can be set in motion by the producing countries, both on a national and an international basis. On a national scale, attention might first be accorded to the selective rehabilitation of the liberated rubber plantations. Every pound of accessible latex will have to be tapped when the first plantation areas are reoccupied by the Allied nations. But when permanent rehabilitation measures are taken, the governments concerned should seriously consider means of retiring those plantations that, on account of low productivity, are sure to remain high-cost producing units. It is important, however, that the surviving portion of the industry be not burdened, in the form of fixed costs, with the compensation granted to the owners of retired properties. In drafting such plans, the authorities should take full cognizance of the fact that the new synthetic-rubber industry is likely to capture a large share in the future world rubber market. The rubber-plantation industry will therefore remain in a precarious position, and the chief plantation countries would do well to lessen their dependence on rubber exports by diversifying their agricultural production.

Next, the governments might consult with planters' associations to explore opportunities for merging smaller rubber companies and, in the process, retire other plantations of low productivity. Again, due care should be taken that the high-cost units eliminated do not leave a fatal legacy in the form of increased overhead costs for the surviving estate companies. Payment to the owners of abandoned plantations should therefore not be made in cash or debenture stock but in ordinary shares. This is the only economical way of eliminating inefficient producing units through amalgamations.[7]

Unless the task of capacity curtailment is of staggering proportion, a great many if not all of the redundant and obsolete estate plantations could be removed in these ways. In order to be effective it might well be advisable for the several producing countries to co-ordinate their respective policies by agreement. The treatment of native producers will undoubtedly prove a contentious matter. There can be no doubt that, from the standpoint of production costs, most obsolete plantations are owned by estate companies. The rubber companies, on the other hand, are well organized and capable of exerting strong pressure on government. It is hard to believe that they will not combat a radical retrenchment of the estate industry in favor of smallholders' production. Yet the governments concerned must realize that a marked shift in this direction is imperative if the rubber-producing industry is to be reorganized in a healthy fashion.

4. In the event that the foregoing policies do not insure the required degree of output contraction, or are made ineffectual by the opposition of vested interests, then perhaps the only defensible alternative to the immediate reinstitution of free competition is the establishment of a temporary restriction scheme on a strictly non-equalitarian basis. With certain modifications the basic administrative features and institutions of the former IRRA could be re-employed for the purpose. The adoption of sharply graduated and selective assessment rules would mark the chief departure from the previous policy, which based assessment largely on a historical production pattern (see pp. 113–14). The non-equalitarian assessment of estate quotas on an efficiency

[7] On this point see "Efficiency in Mergers," *Economist*, Nov. 25, 1944, p. 696.

basis could be carried out by dividing estates into perhaps four categories of productive efficiency. Deviation from optimum yields and optimum size, as well as other cost factors, might be taken into consideration in framing the formula.

Under such a control arrangement the high-cost producer would not only be prevented from reducing high unit costs by increasing output, as he is wont to do in a free market but selective quota allotment would in fact increase already high unit costs by curtailing output. The prohibition of trading in export rights would further increase the pressure on him. It is hard to see how such a system could fail to induce the necessary amount of disinvestment, while the efficient producers could produce profitably at relatively moderate prices. A restriction scheme of this type might accomplish the desired purpose within about four years. Unlike the old IRRA, its essence would not be defensive but aggressive and geared to change.

It will probably be objected that a non-equalitarian scheme is unacceptable to the estate industry. But the position of that industry may be so insecure, and the efficient producers so convinced that only extraordinary remedies can assure their survival, that acceptance is not impossible. The governments concerned could at least confront the industry with the choice of unrestricted competition or a plan that would eliminate rather than preserve obsolete capacity. If the arrangement is found acceptable, its administration could be improved over the provisions of the former IRRA by enhancing its flexibility in fixing export quotas. The principle of quarterly revisions might be retained. But there is no reason why changes must be in terms of 5 or 10 or 15 per cent. Alterations by 3 or 7 per cent are equally feasible. The matter of extending effective representation to the major importing countries should also be duly considered, although this problem has become less acute in consequence of the existence of the synthetic-rubber industry.

THE PROBLEM OF FLUCTUATING PRICES

In the past, wildly fluctuating rubber prices have been vexatious to producers and industrial consumers alike. They also have impeded the expansion of rubber consumption in certain uses. The former IRRA attempted without conspicuous success to confine these fluctuations to a moderate range. The availability of synthetic rubbers will not necessarily provide a fully satisfactory remedy. To be sure, like the prices of many other chemical products, synthetic-rubber prices will not be as volatile as those of crude rubber. Indeed, they will exert a steadying influence on the development of crude-rubber prices and, provided synthetic-rubber production and consumption bulk large in proportion to crude rubber, short-term fluctuations of the latter may be effectively dampened. However, it is quite possible that, over the medium and long term, crude-rubber prices may fluctuate independently and with considerable volatility. If the share of synthetic products in the rubber market should be relatively small, such extreme price instability is possible also over the short term.

The quest for a suitable remedy must start with the realization that crude-rubber prices share their propensity to fluctuate with many other industrial raw materials. Abrupt changes in the volume of industrial production are the common and most potent cause of this phenomenon. Provided the efforts of the leading industrial nations to stabilize industrial production by contracyclical measures are successful, no additional action may be required to confine the swings of crude-rubber prices. If these endeavors prove abortive, the search for specific remedies will acquire renewed impetus.

It is imperative that a price-stabilizing device be not designed with exclusive regard to its prime purpose. The requirements of an expansive and reasonably adaptive world economy demand that the net effect of the device shall not be unduly restrictive but shall permit moderate price adaptations to changed business conditions and the gradual operation of secular market trends. Except in major emergencies, direct price-fixing involves too much of a strait jacket. Control of production and export on the model of the IRRA brings evils overbalancing the social gain. The only expedient that, in theory, may accomplish some measure of price stability and yet satisfy the need for economic change is a properly managed buffer stock.

The function of a buffer stock is to confine price fluctuations within a certain range by drawing supplies from the market when falling prices reach the minimum of the desired range, and releasing supplies to the market when rising prices approach the maximum of that range.[8] The appropriate size of a buffer stock for crude rubber would have to be discovered experimentally by trial and error. Undoubtedly it would have to be large because of the extreme fluctuations in rubber consumption, the period of supply rigidity, and the tendency of industrial consumers to reduce their own inventories when the stock-holding function is partly assumed by someone else. Nevertheless, the cost of even a large stock should not be prohibitive. On the assumption that a buffer-stock loan could be floated at 3 per cent interest, the price of crude rubber would not be increased by more than 1 to 2 per cent, depending upon the volume of consumption. Profits arising from the difference between the stock's buying and selling prices and, if necessary, the receipts from a small tax on rubber exports could be used to pay the costs of management and storage and for the servicing of the loan.

A buffer-stock scheme represents a delicate control device. Successful moderation of price fluctuations in the long run requires certain favorable conditions, some of which can be manipulated while others are generated by forces beyond the control of the buffer-stock authorities. The most important of these conditions are listed in the following paragraphs, and are examined in the light of the prospective postwar position of the crude-rubber industry and market.

1. The absence of a considerable surplus capacity is almost essential to the satisfactory functioning of a buffer stock for crude rubber. With redundant capacity in existence and supply inelastic to price declines, a buffer stock would face the alternative of either accumulating huge stocks or of drastically lowering the basic price. The prospects of a buffer stock therefore depend upon the capacity adjustments discussed in the first part of this chapter. It could be set up while a temporary and non-equalitarian restriction plan is in operation (pp. 239–40). But to maintain indefinitely an equalitarian restriction plan of the pre-

---

[8] A buffer stock for crude rubber is proposed in P. L. Yates, *Commodity Control* (London, 1943), pp 127–28.

war type in order to make a buffer-stock scheme workable is to replace the evil of fluctuating prices by the probably greater evil of nonadaptive restriction. The marked unresponsiveness of supply to price change requires, even in the absence of surplus-output capacity, that the buffer-stock plan be not too ambitious in narrowing the permissible range of price changes.

2. The absence of violent and protracted depressions and booms is another condition favoring the long-run success of a buffer stock for crude rubber. Swings of the business cycle as violent as in 1929–32 might overstrain the resources of such a stock. This risk also could be lessened by not aiming at too narrow a range of permissible price fluctuations.

3. A buffer-stock scheme should perhaps retard, but not indefinitely arrest, powerful secular trends in a commodity market. This is a requirement of enduring success as well as of an expansive and adaptable world economy. Thus, if the secular trend is toward an increasing replacement of crude rubber by synthetic materials in world rubber consumption, the price of the plantation product will tend to decline. The buffer stock could attempt to make the decline orderly and gradual, but not to stem it in the long run. Effective provision for the judicious adjustment of the basic price is therefore essential to the satisfactory operation of a buffer stock.

4. Finally, the manner in which crude rubber held in the buffer stock would be disposed of in the event of abandonment of the scheme must be definitely determined in advance. Otherwise, the accumulated stock would act as a constant threat to the stability of the crude-rubber market and, in particular, would depress the price level of the commodity. If reserve stocks of crude rubber are held in one or several leading importing countries for reasons of military security, the buffer stock also must be protected, by international agreement, against sudden and disrupting releases from such stockpiles.

It may be concluded that the wider the price range fixed by the buffer stock, the less exacting are the requirements of favorable conditions for its smooth working. A stock operating with a relatively low floor and high ceiling could be expected to function even in the event of relatively wide fluctuations of the

business cycle. A suitable compromise between the desirability
of stable prices and the requisites of workability might be found
with permissible fluctuations of, perhaps, 15 or 20 per cent below and above the pivotal price, and with regular annual reviews of the latter. Additional flexibility could be gained,
conceivably, by the incorporation of a simple sliding-scale
system of releases and purchases. Limited operations involving
definite quantities could be authorized when the market price
deviates more than, say, 15 per cent from the basic price, operations on a larger scale to begin with a further deviation of 5
per cent.

Despite the automatic features involved, the administration
of such a buffer stock could not be freed of responsibility for
its satisfactory working. The fixing of the initial basic price is
of utmost importance, especially should subsequent revisions be
limited in range. Continued success will depend partly on the
review and revision of the pivotal price. No mechanical device,
such as a moving average, can be relied upon for sure guidance.
Vital decisions will thus be left to the discretion of the policy-
making committee. Ability to co-operate and to make reasonably accurate forecasts of market trends will be indispensable,
and the composition of the body should therefore be determined
with great care.

The questions of including major consuming countries in the
agreement and their representatives on the guiding committee
arise inevitably in any discussion of the buffer-stock device. Because of the effect of unstable prices on the position of industrial
consumers, importing countries have as much interest as producers in the purpose of a buffer stock. Their participation is
urged, moreover, since the operation of a powerful buffer stock
lends itself to price-rigging in favor of producers and to the
detriment of consumers.

Prior to World War II, these reasons would indeed have appeared convincing if not compelling. Whether they will be in
the 1950's will depend upon the competitive position of synthetic
rubbers vis-à-vis crude rubber. Should it be extremely weak
and unlikely to improve within a short period of time, the leading
rubber-importing countries should press for equal participation

in a buffer-stock arrangement. Should it be very strong, their inclusion would be superfluous. The issue becomes doubtful if the competitive position of synthetic rubbers is in between these two extremes. What happens to crude-rubber prices would in that event remain of interest to the consuming countries. Yet, with the influence of synthetic-rubber producers likely to exceed that of the ultimate rubber consumer, the interest might conceivably be in relatively high crude-rubber prices, whereas, for equally plausible reasons, the crude-rubber producing countries might embrace the opposite attitude. From the viewpoint of net social gains, the value of representing synthetic-rubber-producing countries on the buffer-stock committee might at least be questioned.

CONCLUSION

While their definite setting and true extent cannot now be foreseen, national and international rubber problems of great complexity and consequence are certain to arise in the late 1940's or the early 1950's. Sizable portions of whole industries, large investments, and the prosperity of several countries will be at stake. Good will and restraint of self-interest, expertise, and statesmanship will be needed to solve these problems in accordance with the requirements of an expanding world economy while localizing and easing the pains of adjustment.

Detailed plans and specific proposals offered now would be premature. Knowledge of the comparative state and prospects of the crude- and synthetic-rubber industries must be gathered. In the interest of orderly and yet speedy adjustment, it is essential that the emerging problems be dealt with as soon as their full character is revealed. Indeed, the fundamental nature of some can be anticipated now, and remedies can be investigated in principle.

As stated in the Preface, every solution should be designed in principle to further rather than to obstruct the raising of planes of living throughout the world. This means primarily that production must be concentrated in the most efficient (low-cost) production units, and that the springs of further progress in efficiency not be clogged. Any interference with this principle in the interest of other social objectives must be kept to a minimum.

Thus, protection of comparatively inefficient producing units for the sake of national security should not be resorted to as long as equally effective and socially less costly alternatives exist. Protection should go no further than is imperatively required, and should assume a form that is least obstructive of economic progress. It should also be relaxed and abandoned as soon as compatible with security requirements. If it is found desirable to exert a stabilizing influence on unduly fluctuating prices, a practicable method must be discovered that allows the price system to work for the economic organization of production. Finally, if painful but necessary amputations of output capacity are to be forced into an orderly pattern, readjustments along economic lines must remain the primary goal.

As long as the system of private capitalism prevails, losses to investors are not only an inevitable, but also a socially desirable prerequisite of its satisfactory functioning. Economic progress means change, and change means losses to some investors as well as profits to others. Whenever interference with the free market requires government tolerance or support, government must assume ultimate responsibility for seeing that the desire of business to reap profits and avoid losses does not lead to schemes whose net effect is detrimental to the general social good.

APPENDIX TABLES

TABLE I.—EXPORTS OF CRUDE RUBBER BY PRODUCING REGIONS, 1900–40*

(*Thousand tons*)†

Year	Wild rubber[a]	Plantation rubber[b]	Total	South-eastern Asia[c]	Oceania[d]	South America[e]	Central America[f]	Africa
1900	43.3	.8	44.1	.8	...	27.8		15.5
1901	44.8	.4	45.2	.4	...	31.0		13.8
1902	41.9	.2	42.1	.2	...	29.5		12.4
1903	48.6	.8	49.4	.8	...	32.2		16.4
1904	51.2	1.9	53.1	1.9	...	32.5		18.7
1905	53.6	2.5	56.1	2.5	...	35.0		18.6
1906	59.8	2.9	62.7	2.9	...	39.3		20.5
1907	66.0	7.8	73.8	7.8	...	47.1		18.9
1908	64.4	5.2	69.6	5.1	...	49.3		15.1
1909	72.6	5.6	78.2	5.6	...	54.0		18.6
1910	83.0	11.1	94.1	11.1	...	44.7	18.2	20.1
1911	76.5	17.5	94.0	17.5	.01	43.1	15.1	18.3
1912	81.0	33.3	114.3	32.3	.03	49.9	12.2	18.9
1913	66.5	53.6	120.1	53.6	.02	44.1	6.4	16.0
1914	48.2	74.6	122.8	74.5	.05	40.1	.8	7.3
1915	54.4	116.3	170.7	116.2	.12	43.6	2.7	8.1
1916	52.4	161.7	214.1	161.6	.14	39.7	2.3	10.4
1917	56.7	221.3	278.0	221.1	.22	44.1	2.2	10.4
1918	39.4	180.9	220.3	180.7	.24	29.4	2.9	7.1
1919	50.8	348.9	399.7	348.4	.35	42.2	1.7	7.0
1920	36.8	305.1	341.9	304.6	.37	29.0	1.5	6.4
1921	24.1	277.4	301.5	277.1	.29	20.4	.1	3.6
1922	23.9	379.3	403.2	379.2	.09	20.5	.4	3.0
1923	25.5	379.5	405.0	379.4	.13	18.6	1.3	5.6
1924	31.2	391.8	423.0	391.3	.45	24.4	1.4	5.4
1925	40.4	488.2	528.6	487.3	.72	28.8	4.0	7.8
1926	40.8	583.1	623.9	581.9	1.00	26.5	4.7	9.8
1927	45.0	565.1	610.1	563.6	1.31	31.4	5.1	8.7
1928	32.4	623.6	656.0	622.0	1.33	22.0	3.1	7.4
1929	29.1	839.4	868.5	838.3	.90	21.8	1.2	6.3

* Data for 1900–09 from P. W. Barker, *Rubber Statistics 1900–1937* (U.S. Dept. Comm., Bur. Foreign and Domestic Comm., Trade Promotion Series 181, 1938), p. 5; for 1910–40 from Sir Andrew McFadyean (ed.), *The History of Rubber Regulation 1934–1943* (London, 1944), pp. 226–30. The two sources are in approximate agreement for the years 1910–20.

† In this and following tables, "tons" refers to long tons of 2,240 pounds.

[a] South America, Central America, and Africa ex Liberia. This division is approximately accurate.

[b] Total minus wild rubber.

[c] Territories participating since 1934 in International Rubber Agreement

[d] Including Philippines and Portuguese Timor.

[e] Including Trinidad.

[f] Including Mexico.

247

TABLE I—*Concluded*

Year	Wild rubber[a]	Planta-tion rubber[b]	Total	South-eastern Asia[c]	Oceania[d]	South America[e]	Central America[f]	Africa
1930	20.7	804.7	825.4	803.3	1.26	14.8	1.1	4.9
1931	15.7	785.4	801.1	784.4	.88	12.3	...	3.5
1932	8.5	701.3	709.8	700.5	.82	6.5	...	2.0
1933	12.2	839.3	851.5	838.1	1.24	9.9	...	2.3
1934	13.1	1,019.4	1,032.5	1,017.8	1.48	9.4	.4	3.4
1935	18.5	811.7	830.2	809.4	1.52	12.6	.5	6.2
1936	24.6	841.7	866.3	838.5	1.61	16.5	1.3	8.4
1937	30.4	1,135.8	1,166.2	1,131.7	1.77	17.6	3.6	11.5
1938	28.3	843.2	871.5	838.4	1.92	16.3	2.9	12.0
1939	29.5	960.2	989.7	952.7	2.11	17.2	3.0	14.7
1940	34.9	1,360.1	1,395.0	1,350.2	2.70	21.3	4.7	16.1

TABLE II.—EXPORTS OF CRUDE RUBBER FROM PRINCIPAL
PRODUCING COUNTRIES, 1922–41*

(*Thousand tons*)

Year	Total	Ma-laya[a]	Nether-lands Indies	Cey-lon	India	Burma	Bor-neo[b]	Thai-land	French Indo-China	Others
1922	403.2	212.4	102.5	46.7	4.9		7.5	.7	4.5	24.0
1923	405.0	181.7	137.1	37.4	3.8	2.7	9.9	1.7	5.1	25.6
1924	423.0	176.0	150.5	37.0	4.5	3.2	11.3	3.0	5.8	31.7
1925	528.6	210.9	193.6	45.6	6.3	3.8	13.8	5.4	7.9	41.3
1926	623.9	277.0	207.9	58.9	6.5	3.3	15.5	4.0	8.8	42.0
1927	610.1	232.4	231.5	55.8	7.0	4.4	17.5	5.5	9.5	46.5
1928	656.0	294.4	228.3	57.3	7.2	3.6	16.8	4.8	9.6	34.0
1929	868.5	455.5	255.2	80.3	7.9	5.5	18.7	5.1	10.1	30.2
1930	825.4	442.7	240.9	75.6	6.8	5.2	17.4	4.3	10.3	22.2
1931	801.1	422.0	257.2	62.3	5.4	4.5	16.7	4.5	11.8	16.7
1932	709.8	405.7	211.1	49.3	1.1	3.0	12.3	3.6	14.4	9.3
1933	851.5	445.1	281.2	63.8	1.4	3.8	18.4	7.4	16.9	13.5
1934[e]	1,032.5	480.5	379.7	79.1	6.0	6.3	28.9	17.7	19.6	14.7
1935[e]	830.2	369.9	287.2	54.2	8.1	4.9	28.0	28.3	28.7	20.9
1936[e]	866.3	358.8	310.6	50.1	8.6	5.8	29.2	34.6	40.8	27.8
1937[e]	1,166.3	492.8	433.6	70.0	10.0	7.2	39.1	35.6	43.4	34.6
1938[e]	871.6	345.3	300.9	49.3	8.0	6.7	27.3	41.6	59.2	33.3
1939[e]	989.7	361.6	369.9	61.6	9.7	6.6	36.4	41.8	65.2	36.9
1940[e]	1,395.0	540.9	537.5	88.4	13.0	9.8	52.2	43.9	64.4	44.9
1941[e]	*1,500.0*	*575.0*	636.0	102.4	4.1	8.8	*55.0*	*45.0*	*50.0*	23.7

* Data from McFadyean, *op. cit.*, pp. 226–29. Figures in italics are International Rubber Regulation Committee (IRRC) estimates in whole or in part.

[a] Including Brunei and Labuan.

[b] Including North Borneo and Sarawak, excluding Dutch Borneo, Brunei and Labuan.

[e] From 1934, the figures for regulated territories (those officially named) represent net exports under the scheme.

TABLE III.—IMPORTS OF CRUDE RUBBER, 1922–41*

(Thousand tons)

Year	Total	United States	United Kingdom	Industrial Europe*a*	Other Europe	USSR	British Dominions*b*	Japan	Others
1922.......	399.8	296.4	11.7	59.4	1.5	2.5	11.8	15.9	.6
1923.......	413.6	301.7	12.7	63.1	1.8	3.0	15.0	15.4	.9
1924.......	421.2	319.1	11.6*c*	70.3	2.6	2.3	17.6	19.6	1.3
1925.......	525.1	385.6	4.9	89.0	2.5	7.1	23.4	11.1	1.4
1926.......	622.0	400.0	84.9	78.5	3.3	6.5	29.3	18.1	1.4
1927.......	640.2	403.5	59.8	101.2	4.9	12.7	36.2	20.5	1.5
1928.......	610.5	407.6	4.4	107.3	8.1	15.1	39.8	25.6	2.5
1929.......	915.8	528.6	122.8	152.3	10.2	12.6	51.6	34.3	3.4
1930.......	835.5	457.4	120.0	160.5	10.6	16.1	34.4	32.7	3.7
1931.......	809.5	476.2	85.2	126.4	8.5	27.8	33.3	43.5	8.6
1932.......	710.6	393.7	43.6	132.2	10.9	30.0	33.1	56.0	11.1
1933.......	800.8	398.3	73.4	168.8	14.3	30.8	34.1	66.8	14.3
1934.......	962.6	439.2	156.9	169.8	20.5	47.3	40.1	69.9	18.9
1935.......	932.3	455.8	126.8	177.3	21.5	37.6	38.7	57.6	17.0
1936.......	832.3	475.6	7.4*c*	180.7	22.1	31.0	46.6	61.7	22.0
1937.......	1,120.4	592.5	91.0	231.0	24.3	30.5	61.9	62.2	27.0
1938.......	928.4	406.3	132.0	226.9	25.4	26.8	43.6	46.3	21.1
1939.......	937.7	486.3	69.2	197.6	22.6	30.0	58.3	42.4	31.3
1940.......	1,300.0	811.6	....	....	4.5	....	81.5	....	29.1
1941.......	1,450.0	....	....	....	....	....	....	....	....

* Data from McFadyean, *op. cit.*, pp. 232–35. Figures in italics are IRRC estimates in whole or in part.

a Austria, Belgium, Czechoslovakia, Denmark, France, Germany, Italy, Netherlands, Norway, Sweden, Switzerland.

b Canada, Australia, New Zealand, Union of South Africa.

c Imports minus re-exports.

TABLE IV.—ABSORPTION OF CRUDE RUBBER, 1922–40*

(Thousand tons)

Year	Total	United States	United Kingdom*a*	Rest of world*b*	Year	Total	United States	United Kingdom*a*	Rest of world*b*
1922.....	403.5	301.5	10.3	91.7	1932.....	688.6	336.7	78.6	273.3
1923.....	445.5	319.4	27.0	99.1	1933.....	820.9	412.4	79.5	329.0
1924.....	464.3	328.8	21.9	113.6	1934.....	919.1	462.5	90.1	366.5
1925.....	553.2	388.5	30.1	134.6	1935.....	936.3	491.5	95.0	349.8
1926.....	542.9	366.2	39.7	137.0	1936.....	1,038.4	575.0	99.2	364.2
1927.....	594.7	373.0	44.8	176.9	1937.....	1,095.1	543.6	114.6	436.9
1928.....	684.1	437.0	48.5	198.6	1938.....	933.9	437.0	106.9	390.0
1929.....	803.8	467.4	72.0	264.4	1939.....	1,096.8	592.0	122.7	382.1
1930.....	708.8	376.0	74.8	258.0	1940.....	1,100.0	648.5	...	...
1931.....	679.9	355.2	76.6	248.1					

* Data from McFadyean, *op. cit.*, p. 236. Figures in italics are IRRC estimates in whole or in part.

a Through 1933 net imports corrected for changes in warehouse stocks. From 1934 100 per cent absorption estimated on the basis of returns received by the IRRC from the majority of limited Kingdom importers.   *b* Aggregates of net imports.

TABLE V.—WORLD STOCKS OF CRUDE RUBBER, DECEMBER 31, 1913–40*

(Thousand tons)

Year	Grand total^a	Total in five positions	United States, trade	United Kingdom London, Liverpool	United Kingdom Manufacturers	Afloat	Under customs control	Para, Manaos	Singapore, Penang	Inside regulated areas^b
1913..	...	...	...	6.0	...	...	...	...	...	...
1914..	...	...	...	7.3	...	...	...	...	...	...
1915..	...	...	....	7.4	...	...	...	...	...	...
1916..	...	...	...	11.3	...	...	...	...	...	...
1917..	...	...	...	17.2	...	...	...	...	...	...
1918..	...	...	...	16.0	...	...	...	...	...	...
1919..	...	...	54.3	23.2	...	37.0	...	...	...	...
1920..	...	...	97.8	55.7	...	37.0	...	...	...	...
1921..	...	...	99.8	79.7	...	32.0	...	...	...	...
1922..	...	...	94.7	81.1	...	45.0	...	...	...	...
1923..	...	232.9	76.8	66.8	...	50.0	...	3.0	36.3	...
1924..	...	164.6	56.1	32.4	...	53.0	...	2.5	20.6	...
1925..	...	148.4	51.2	6.3	...	65.0	...	2.5	23.4	...
1926..	...	234.0	72.5	51.3	...	77.0	...	3.0	30.2	...
1927..	...	263.6	99.3	66.3	...	67.0	...	3.5	27.5	...
1928..	...	247.4	65.5	22.6	...	118.0	...	4.4	36.9	...
1929..	...	332.3	122.1	73.3	...	96.0	...	3.7	37.2	...
1930..	...	453.3	201.0	118.6	...	87.0	...	5.1	41.6	...
1931..	...	589.3	322.0	127.1	...	85.0	...	5.6	49.6	...
1932..	...	589.2	379.0	92.7	...	81.0	...	5.6	30.9	...
1933..	...	616.4	365.0	86.5	...	117.0	...	3.0	44.9	...
1934..	725.9	681.3	355.0	134.9	43.2	126.0	1.3	3.3	62.1	65.7
1935..	644.9	595.3	312.0	164.3	44.7	86.0	5.0	4.7	28.3	77.8
1936..	464.2	434.0	223.0	78.5	24.4	103.0	5.9	2.5	27.0	75.0
1937..	531.9	501.6	262.0	57.8	22.1	135.0	8.2	1.8	44.8	113.8
1938..	465.1	436.8	231.5	86.9	18.6	90.0	9.7	1.3	27.1	143.8
1939..	359.2	325.2	125.8^c	28.2	24.3	152.0	8.2	5.3	15.3	131.7
1940..	668.1	470.4	288.9^d	20.3	76.0^e	245.0	9.0	2.2	26.8	...

* Data from McFadyean, *op. cit.*, pp. 237–38. Dots (..) indicate lack of data.
^a Outside regulated areas.
^b Excluding Siam. Not included in grand total.
^c Including 1,400 tons barter stocks.
^d Including 72,700 tons barter stocks and 40,100 tons other government reserves.
^e Including 40,500 tons government stocks.

TABLE VI.—PRICES OF CRUDE RUBBER PER POUND, ANNUALLY 1922–41*

Year	London High	London Low	London Range	London Average	New York High	New York Low	New York Range	New York Average
1922	1s. 3d.	0s. 7d.	0s. 8d.	0s. 9d.	28.4	13.6	14.8	17.3
1923	1 7	1 1	5	1 3	37.1	24.8	12.4	29.6
1924	1 8	9	10	1 2	39.6	18.4	21.2	26.1
1925	4 8	1 4	3 3	2 11	123.0	34.2	88.8	72.5
1926	4 0	1 6	2 4	1 12	91.0	36.8	54.2	49.4
1927	1 8	1 4	5	1 6	42.2	33.0	9.2	37.8
1928	1 8	8	1 0	11	41.2	16.8	24.5	22.3
1929	1 1	8	6	10	26.9	15.5	11.4	20.5
1930	8	4	5	6	16.4	7.4	9.0	10.2
1931	4	2	2	3	8.5	4.3	4.3	6.1
1932	3	2	2	2	4.8	2.6	2.1	3.4
1933	4	2	2	3	9.8	2.9	6.9	5.9
1934ᵃ	7	4	3	5	15.1	8.8	6.4	11.0
1934ᵇ	8	6	2	7	15.9	11.8	4.1	13.9
1934ᶜ	8	4	3	6	15.9	8.8	7.1	12.9
1935	7	5	2	6	13.6	10.4	3.3	12.3
1936	11	6	5	8	23.0	13.5	9.5	16.4
1937	1 2	7	7	10	26.9	14.0	12.9	19.4
1938	9	5	3	7	17.1	10.2	6.9	14.6
1939ᵈ	9	8	1	8	16.9	14.9	1.9	16.1
1939ᵉ	1 0	9	3	11	24.0	18.0	6.0	20.2
1939ᶜ	1 0	8	4	9	24.0	14.9	9.1	17.5
1940	1 2	11	3	1 0	23.9	18.1	5.8	19.9
1941	1 3	1 0	3	1 2	24.8	19.0	5.8	22.1

* London prices (in shillings and pence) for Standard Quality Ribbed Smoked Sheet, from McFadyean, *op. cit.*, p. 239. New York prices (in U.S. cents) for Plantation Ribbed Smoked Sheets, from publications of the U.S. Department of Commerce as far as available. In 1941 the Rubber Reserve Company's selling price to the trade was fixed at 22½ cents per pound for No. 1-X Ribbed Smoked Sheets on August 6, and this fixed price has been included for the last five months in calculating the average for the year.

ᵃ Pre-regulation.   ᵇ Regulation.   ᶜ Total.   ᵈ Prewar.   ᵉ War.

Table VII.—Basic Quotas of Agreement Countries, 1934–43*

(Thousand tons)

Country	1934ᵃ	1935	1936	1937	1938	1939	1940	1941	1942	1943
Total	996.5	1,118.5	1,254.0	1,298.5	1,335.2	1,519.0	1,541.6	1,554.7	1,563.0	1,569.0
British Malaya..	504.0	538.0	569.0	589.0	602.0	632.0	642.5	648.0	651.0	651.5
Netherlands Indies	352.0	400.0	500.0	520.0	540.0	631.5	640.0	645.5	650.0	651.0
Ceylon	77.5	79.0	80.0	81.0	82.5	106.0	107.5	109.0	109.5	110.0
India	6.8	12.5	12.5	12.5	13.0	17.5	17.7	17.7	17.7	17.7
Burma	5.2	8.0	8.5	9.0	9.2	13.5	13.8	13.8	13.8	13.8
State of North Borneo	12.0	13.0	14.0	15.5	16.5	21.0	21.0	21.0	21.0	21.0
Sarawak	24.0	28.0	30.0	31.5	32.0	43.0	43.8	44.0	44.0	44.0
Thailand	15.0	40.0	40.0	40.0	40.0	54.5	55.3	55.7	56.0	60.0

* Data from *Statistical Bulletin* (International Rubber Regulation Committee, London), October 1941, VII, 1.

ᵃ Annual basis. Since the agreement went into effect June 1, the actual quotas were 7/12 of the stated amounts.

Table VIII.—Export Quotas under Regulation: Percentages of Basic Quotas, 1934–41*

Year	First quarter	Second quarter	Third quarter	Fourth quarter	Annual average Jan.–Dec.	Annual average July–Juneᵃ
1934..............	100ᵇ	90ᶜ	80ᵈ	70ᵉ	87 1/7	78 3/4
1935..............	75	70	65	60	67 1/2	61 1/4
1936..............	60	60	65	65	62 1/2	71 1/4
1937..............	75	80	90	90	83 3/4	77 1/2
1938..............	70	60	45	45	55	47 1/2
1939..............	50	50	60	75	58 3/4	73 3/4
1940..............	80	80	85	90	83 3/4	93 3/4
1941..............	100	100	100	120	105	....

* Data from *Statistical Bulletin* (International Rubber Regulation Committee, London), October 1941, VII, 1.

ᵃ Twelve months beginning July of the year indicated.   ᵇ June–July.   ᶜ August–September.   ᵈ October–November.   ᵉ December.

TABLE IX.—EXCESS (+) OR DEFICIT (−) OF ACTUAL COMPARED WITH
AUTHORIZED EXPORTS OF CRUDE RUBBER, 1934–41*

(Thousand tons)

Year	Grand total	British Malaya	Nether-lands Indies	Ceylon	India	Burma	Borneo[a]	Thai-land
1934[b]....	+ 11.9	+ 12.2	− 1.5	+ .02	+ .18	− .19	+ 1.17	...[c]
1935.....	− 10.8	+ 5.4	−18.7	− .89	+ .48	+ .31	+ .89	+ 1.67
1936.....	+ 2.9	+ 2.3	+ 1.9[d]	−1.02	− .34	− .20	− .80	+ 1.10
1937.....	+ 4.5	+ 2.8	+ 3.8	−3.24	+ .12	+ .12	− .58	+ 1.54
1938.....	− 22.3	− 11.4	− .2	−7.14	− .77	−1.52	− 1.20	− .07
1939.....	− 8.4	− 1.7	+ 1.0	−6.44	− .21	− .21	− .12	− .83
1940.....	− 3.1[c]	− 4.4	− .5	−4.82	+ 1.63	+1.52[e]	+ 1.95	+ 1.55
1941[f]....	*+202.0*	*+100.0*	*+41.3*	*+7.28*	*+16.02*	*+6.76*	*+15.00*	*+15.00*

* Data from McFadyean, *op. cit.*, p. 231. Figures in italics are IRRC estimates in whole or in part.

[a] North Borneo and Sarawak.

[b] Figures refer only to the last seven months as regulation went into effect June 1, 1934.

[c] The agreement was not ratified until 1935 in Thailand, therefore no data for 1934.

[d] The IRRC decided that there would be no deduction from the Netherlands Indies "Permissible Exportable Amount" for 1936 on account of the carryover at the end of 1935.

[e] Under Article 5(2) of the International Agreement exporting territories were permitted to carry forward only 10 per cent of their "Permissible Exportable Amount" in any year, therefore India was authorized to carry forward only 1,487 tons to 1941 and Burma only 1,152 tons, although their actual carryovers were 1,629 and 1,525, respectively.

[f] The large carryovers in some countries in 1941, especially Malaya and Netherlands Indies, were partly owing to the interruption of transport due to war against Japan; in the case of India it was mainly due to her increasing domestic consumption.

TABLE X.—UNITED STATES PERCENTAGES OF CRUDE-RUBBER ABSORPTION IN GROUPS OF PRODUCTS IN TONS OF CRUDE RUBBER, EXPRESSED AS PERCENTAGES OF TOTAL ABSORPTION, 1931–40*

TIRES, TUBES, AND RELATED PRODUCTS

| Year | Total | Mainly for cars and trucks | | Other pneumatic tires and tubes | | Solid and cushion tires | | Sundries and repair materials |
		Pneumatic casings[a]	Pneumatic tubes[b]	Bicycles	Airplanes	For highway transport	All other	
1931	81.7	66.7	12.6	.3	0	.9	.1	1.1
1932	80.7	67.2	11.2	.4	0	.7	.1	1.1
1933	77.9	65.3	10.3	.5	0	.5	.1	1.2
1934	78.8	65.5	10.4	.5	0	.3	.1	1.9
1935	77.3	64.7	9.8	.5	0	.3	.1	1.9
1936	77.0	64.8	9.6	.8	0	.1	.2	1.5
1937	75.3	63.1	9.5	.7	0	.1	.2	1.2
1938	77.0	64.0	9.9	.6	0	0	0	2.5
1939	76.8	64.2	9.4	.7	0	0	0	2.4
1940	76.1	64.1[c]	8.9	.6	.3	0	0	2.2
Average 1938–40	76.6	64.1	9.4	.6	.1	.1	.1	2.4

OTHER RUBBER PRODUCTS

Year	Total	Mechanical rubber goods	Insulated wire compounds	Boots and shoes	Heels and soles	Sub-total of major products[d]	Druggists	Stationers
1931	18.3	5.6	1.2	3.5	2.8	13.1	.5	.4
1932	19.3	5.2	.8	4.3	3.6	13.9	.6	.4
1933	22.1	7.0	.8	4.9	4.1	16.8	.5	.4
1934	21.2	7.9	.8	4.4	2.9	16.0	.7	.4
1935	22.7	9.2	1.1	4.3	2.4	17.0	.8	.4
1936	23.0	9.8	1.4	4.7	1.9	16.8	.7	.5
1937	24.7	10.7	1.6	4.6	2.2	19.1	.9	.5
1938	22.9	8.5	1.6	4.0	3.1	17.2	.8	.5
1939	23.2	9.3	1.3	3.6	3.0	17.2	.9	.5
1940	23.9	9.6	1.8	3.3	2.5	17.1	.8	.5
Average 1938–40	23.3	9.1	1.6	3.7	2.8	17.2	.9	.5

* Data originally published in quarterly statistical bulletins of the Rubber Manufacturers Association of America, here taken from *Statistical Bulletin* (International Rubber Regulation Committee, London), December 1937, III, 17; and (for 1935–40) from *ibid.*, October 1941, VII, 20.

These are based on data for the approximate following percentage of the United States rubber industry:

| 1931....92 | 1933....90 | 1935....86 | 1937....80.5 | 1939......73.4 |
| 1932....87 | 1934....93 | 1936....79 | 1938....73.6 | 1940......71.4 |

These percentages do not apply equally to all groups.

[a] Excluding bicycle and airplane tire casings, but in 1931–33 including a small number of motorcycle inner tubes.   [b] Excluding bicycle and airplane inner tubes.

[c] Including farm tractor tires and tubes 2.3 and motorcycle tires and tubes .06, for which separate data are not earlier available.   [d] Total of four preceding columns.

TABLE X—*Concluded*

OTHER RUBBER PRODUCTS

Year	Bathing apparel	Rubber clothing	Automobile fabrics	Other rubberized fabrics	Hard rubber goods	Rubber flooring	Sporting goods	Sponge rubber*	Miscellaneous
1931.....	.3	.3	.2	.8	.3	.3	.7	...	1.4
1932.....	.4	.3	.1	.9	.3	.3	.5	...	1.6
1933.....	.3	.2	.2	1.1	.3	.2	.4	...	1.7
1934.....	.3	.2	.3	1.0	.5	.2	.4	.4	.8
1935.....	.2	.2	.2	1.0	.5	.2	.5	.9	.8
1936.....	.2	.1	.1	.9	.5	.2	.5	.6	.7
1937.....	.2	.1	.1	.9	.6	.3	.4	.9	.7
1938.....	.2	.1	.1	1.1	.5	.3	.5	.8	.7
1939.....	.1	.1	.1	1.0	.6	.3	.5	1.1	.8
1940.....	.1	.1	.1	.9	.8	.3	.5	2.1	.5
Average 1938–40..	.1	.1	.1	1.0	.6	.3	.5	1.3	.7

* In 1931–33 included with Miscellaneous.

ANNOTATED BIBLIOGRAPHY

The following bibliography is selective. Its purpose is to refer the reader to the principal literature that remains essential to a proper understanding of the world rubber economy and its problems. In order to save space, specific references to periodical literature have been kept to a minimum.

ARMSTRONG, GEORGE S., AND COMPANY, INC. *The Rubber Industry. An Engineering Interpretation of the Economic and Financial Aspects of American Industry IV.* New York, 1942
  A good technical account of synthetic rubbers and their manufacture.

BARKER, P. W. *Rubber: History, Production, and Manufacture.* U.S. Dept. Comm., Bur. Foreign and Domestic Comm., Trade Promotion Series 209. Washington, 1940
  A good source of factual information.

———. *Rubber Statistics, 1900–1937: Production, Absorption, Stocks and Prices.* U.S. Dept. Comm., Bur. Foreign and Domestic Comm., Trade Promotion Series 181. Washington, 1938
  A valuable collection of statistical data on the subjects covered.

BARUCH COMMITTEE. *Report, see* UNITED STATES CONGRESS. HOUSE

CARLSMITH, L. E. *The Economic Characteristic of Rubber Tire Production.* New York, 1934
  A good analysis of the factors influencing crude-rubber absorption in the manufacture of tires and shoes.

Economist. London, weekly
  The occasional articles and comments of this journal on rubber problems and policies are eminently reasonable and forthright.

FISHER, H. L. *Rubber and Its Uses.* Brooklyn, 1941
  Written by a rubber chemist, this book presents useful summaries of the processes of rubber-goods manufacture and the production of synthetic rubbers.

GEHLSEN, C. A. *World Rubber Production and Trade, Economic and Technical 'Aspects, 1935–1939.* International Institute of Agriculture, Studies of the Principal Agricultural Products on the World Market 7. Rome, 1940
  The bulk of this monograph is devoted to technical and scientific aspects of crude-rubber production. There is a chapter on the early history of synthetic rubbers. The machinery of the IRRA is outlined in considerable detail, but there is only a fragmentary attempt at economic appraisal.

GENERAL MOTORS CORPORATION. *The Dynamics of Automobile Demand.* New York, 1939
  A collection of papers written by A. T. Court, S. M. DuBrul, S. L. Horner, C. F. Roos, and Victor von Szeliski, giving an excellent examination of the factors governing the demand for automobile usage in the United States.

257

GEORGE, HEINZ. *Kautschuk.* Leipzig, 1938

An admirable analysis of the world rubber market up to 1937. The chapter on the nature of the demand for rubber is particularly valuable. The section on the IRRA is brief and less penetrating than the remainder of the book.

GRIST, D. H. *An Outline of Malayan Agriculture.* Straits Settlements and Federated Malay States, Dept. Agr., Malayan Planting Manual 2. Kuala Lumpur, 1936

Chapter ix ("Rubber") presents a descriptive account of Hevea breeding and rubber cultivation.

HOLT, E. G. *Pre-war Costs of Production for Plantation Rubber.* In United States War Production Board, Office of Rubber Director. *Special Report . . . . on the Synthetic Rubber Program: Plant Investment and Production Costs.* Washington, Aug. 31, 1944. Appendix A, pp. 13–26

An admirable analysis.

India Rubber World. New York, monthly

In the absence of a satisfactory book on the manufacture and the properties of synthetic rubbers, this trade journal and the *Rubber Age* (New York) are invaluable sources of technical and scientific information.

INTERNATIONAL LABOUR OFFICE. *Intergovernmental Commodity Control Agreements.* Montreal, 1943

The section on rubber (pp. 104–31) presents the full text of the IRRA of 1934 and 1938, as well as amending protocols.

KNORR, K. E. *Rubber after the War.* Food Research Institute, War-Peace Pamphlets 4. Stanford University, Calif., February 1944

A discussion of postwar rubber problems in the light of the newly-established synthetics industry in the United States.

LEWIS, HARRISON. *Rubber Regulation and the Malayan Plantation Industry.* Rev. by E. G. Holt. U.S. Dept. Comm., Bur. Foreign and Domestic Comm., Trade Promotion Series 159. Washington, 1935

Written by a former vice-consul at Singapore, this pamphlet is an invaluable collection of pertinent facts on crude-rubber production, with special reference to British Malaya. The section on the IRRA is restricted to a description of the basic regulation features.

MCFADYEAN, SIR ANDREW, ed. *The History of Rubber Regulation, 1934–1943.* London, 1944

An official history of the IRRA, prepared for the former International Rubber Regulation Committee by members of its staff, presenting many facts on control problems previously unknown to outsiders. It is also an apologia, and its interpretative sections must be read with caution. The special problems of the native rubber-growing industry are largely ignored. There is a valuable appendix containing pertinent documents and statistics.

Malayan Agricultural Journal. Straits Settlements and Federated Malay States, Dept. Agr. Kuala Lumpur, monthly

A journal which, up to the end of 1941, published periodical reports on the state of the Malayan rubber-planting industry.

NAUNTON, W. J. S. *Synthetic Rubber.* London, 1937

A scholarly treatise written before the establishment of large-scale synthetic-rubber industries.

RAE, GEORGE. "Statistics of the Rubber Industry," *Journal of the Royal Statistical Society* (London), 1938, Vol. CI, Pt. II, pp. 317–65

An excellent economic analysis of the economics of rubber plantations and the world rubber market, with a valuable collection of statistical data. The IRRA is described, but, except for a few general remarks, no appraisal is given.

ROWE, J. W. F. *Rubber. Studies in the Artificial Control of Raw Material Supplies 2.* London and Cambridge Econ. Serv. Special Memorandum 34. London, 1931

A superb economic analysis of the rubber-growing industry up to 1929, and of the Stevenson plan.

———. *Markets and Men: A Study of Artificial Control Schemes in Some Primary Industries.* New York, 1936

Chapter vi ("Control Schemes in Rubber") gives a popularly written but, on the whole, conscientious survey of the problems of the plantation-rubber industry. The case for restriction is discussed with greater thoroughness than the case against it. Chapters viii–xi are a valuable contribution to the literature on the general problems of international commodity control.

Rubber Age. London, weekly

A trade journal supplying information on all problems of the rubber world as viewed from Great Britain.

Rubber Age. New York, monthly, see under *India Rubber World*

RUBBER MANUFACTURERS ASSOCIATION. *Crude Rubber.* New York, May 10, 1943

A compilation of facts on crude-rubber production, consumption, and trade.

Rubber News Letter. U.S. Dept. Comm., Bur. Foreign and Domestic Comm., Leather and Rubber Division (mimeographed). Washington, biweekly

Issued until the end of 1939, this periodical is a valuable source of information on crude-rubber production, consumption, and trade. In addition to reports from Malaysia and official comments, there are reprints of pertinent items that appeared in foreign journals and reports.

Statistical Bulletin. International Rubber Regulation Committee. London, monthly

An official source of rubber statistics.

UNITED STATES CONGRESS. HOUSE. *The Rubber Situation. Message from the President* .... 77th Cong., 2d Sess., H. Doc. 836. Washington, 1942

The famous Baruch Committee report, written by B. M. Baruch, J. B. Conant, and K. T. Compton.

———. HOUSE. COMMITTEE ON AGRICULTURE. *Study of Rubber in United States, Mexico, and Haiti.* 78th Cong., 2d Sess., H. Rept. 2098. Washington, 1945

An able report on the wartime development of guayule cultivation in the United States and in Mexico.

———. HOUSE. Subcommittee of the Committee on Interstate and Foreign Commerce. *Petroleum Investigation (Gasoline and Rubber).* Hearings,

77th Cong., 2d Sess., on H. Res. 290 . . . . and H. Res. 15, H. Res. 118, and H. Res. 383. Washington, 1943

An interesting collection of facts and opinions on the early development of the United States synthetic-rubber program.

UNITED STATES CONGRESS. SENATE. Special Committee Investigating the National Defense Program. *Investigation of the National Defense Program. Additional Report* . . . . 77th Cong., 2d Sess., S. Rept. 480, Pt. 7. Washington, 1942

A well-balanced report by the Truman Committee on the United States rubber position after Pearl Harbor.

———. SENATE. Subcommittee of the Committee on Agriculture and Forestry. *Utilization of Farm Crops. Industrial Alcohol and Synthetic Rubber.* Hearings, 77th Cong., 2d Sess., on S. 224, and 78th Cong., 1st and 2d Sess., on S. 224 . . . . and S. Res. 80. 8 pts., Washington, 1942–44

Voluminous hearings focusing on the problem of making butadiene from grain alcohol rather than from petroleum fractions. It contains a great deal of miscellaneous information on the history of the United States synthetic-rubber program.

UNITED STATES TARIFF COMMISSION. *Rubber.* War Changes in Industry Series Report 6. Washington, September 1944

A good, though not exhaustive, discussion of postwar problems of public policy that will arise in the United States on account of its new synthetic-rubber industry. The question of postwar international agreements is given little attention.

UNITED STATES WAR PRODUCTION BOARD. OFFICE OF THE RUBBER DIRECTOR. *Progress Reports 1–6.* Washington, Nov. 30, 1942—July 25, 1944.

An invaluable source of information on the rubber position of the United States during World War II. The reports on the synthetic-rubber industry are particularly useful. So are the three reports listed next below.

———. OFFICE OF THE RUBBER DIRECTOR. *Special Report* . . . . *Recommending Termination of Special Powers.* Washington, July 25, 1944

———. OFFICE OF THE RUBBER DIRECTOR. *Special Report* . . . . *on the Synthetic Rubber Program: Plant Investment and Production Costs.* Washington, Aug. 31, 1944

———. RUBBER BUREAU. *1944 Year End Report.* Washington, Feb. 1, 1945

WHITTLESEY, C. R. *Governmental Control of Crude Rubber.* Princeton, 1931

An exhaustive and admirable study of the all-round economic effects of the Stevenson plan. This is the American counterpart to Rowe's study.

WILK, KURT. "International Administrative Regulation: The Case of Rubber," *American Political Science Review,* April 1942, XXXVI, 323–37

A brief discussion of the administrative features of the IRRA, with an extensive bibliography.

YATES, P. L. *Commodity Control.* London, 1943

Chapter vi ("Rubber") gives a brief summary of the problems of the Malaysian rubber-producing industry and proposes the establishment of a buffer stock after the war. Chapter xi ("Lessons") examines in general merits and methods of the buffer-stock device.

INDEX

Absorption, rubber, 46; in tires and tubes, 47; in other uses, 47; *see also* Consumption

Acreage, rubber, *see* Area

Advisory Panel, under IRRA, 116, 119, 127, 128, 129–30, 133, 134–35, 136, 149, 150–51, 165, 173–75

Africa, rubber production in, 5, 9; rubber exports, 38; *see also* Liberia

Agency system, 24–25, 157, 210

Agreements, rubber, *see* Control; International Rubber Regulation Agreement; Restriction

Agriculture, U.S. Department of, 183

Amazon basin, 9, 11, 12, 60, 90

Area under plantation rubber, 100; in principal producing countries, 20–21, 23; operated by estate companies, 20, 23; operated by native producers, 20, 23

Army and Navy Munitions Board, U.S., 184

Artificial rubbers, *see* Synthetic rubbers

Automobiles: consumption of rubber in, 71, 202–03; demand for, 74–79; production, 50–52; usage, 55–57, 74–77; *see also* Tires and tubes

Baldwin, Stanley, 100

Barter agreement, Anglo-American, 135–36

Baruch Committee report, 178, 184–85

Batavia, 41

Belawan, 41, 44

Bicycles, 9, 56

Borneo: area under rubber, 20–21; exports, 38–39

Brazil, 10, 82, 89–90, 99

British Celanese, Ltd., 177

British Malaya: area under rubber, 20–21; exports, 38; production costs, 160; rubber regulation in, 119–20

British North Borneo Company, 111

Bud-grafting, 17–21, 28, 36

Buffer stock, rubber: and price stabilization, 171; postwar schemes, 241–45; prewar proposals, 150–52; problems of, 152, 242–45

Buna-N, *see* Perbunan

Buna-S, 176, 177, 183–84, 190; characteristics, 191–92; competition with crude rubber, 191–92, 208–12, 224; manufacture, 186–87; price, 198, 208, 209, 211; production, 189; production costs, 193, 196–98

Burgess, P. J., 151

Burma: area under rubber, 20–21; exports, 38–39

Business cycle: effect on automobile market, 74–77; effect on rubber market, 79–80, 91, 101–05, 130, 241, 243–44; effect on rubber-goods market, 74–79; effect on rubber stocks, 84; *see also* Demand for rubber

Butadiene, 186, 190; manufacture, 187; production, 188–89; production costs, 196–97

Butyl, 188; characteristics, 191; competition with crude rubber, 191–92, 208–12, 224; manufacture, 187; price, 195, 208, 209, 211; production, 189; production costs, 193, 195

Campbell, Sir John, 116

Canada, 14, 56; rubber imports, 40; synthetic-rubber industry, 184, 206, 207

Capital, *see* Investments

Ceylon: area under rubber, 20–21; exports, 38–39; production costs, 160; production in World War II, 180

Churchill, Winston, 94, 95–96

Clone, rubber, 17–18, 20

Collyer, J. L., 195, 215

Colombo, 41, 44

Commerce, U.S. Department of, 130, 135

Congress, U.S., 182

Consumers, rubber: and control, 163–66; and representation in control, 116, 119, 133, 173–75; *see also* Consumption

Consumption, crude-rubber: in principal importing countries, 40–41; in the United States, 41–43, 46–57; per capita, 55, 201; postwar, 5, 199–205; trends in, 47–57; variability of, 58–59, 71–81; *see also* Absorption; Demand